More Praise for *The Promise of Mediation*

"In recent years, we have witnessed the erosion of the core values of mediation in favor of service to the forces of professionalism and legalism. The first edition of *The Promise of Mediation* served as a stunning reminder of the potential of mediation to empower individuals and communities in conflict. I credit Bush and Folger with reminding the field of its core values. Since the first edition, they have worked tirelessly to support the development of a practice congruent with these values. I believe that their efforts have produced a new model of mediation, one that provides a unique role for the mediator—especially the community 'citizen mediator.' When we use the transformative model, we're offering a form of help that no one else in society is offering to our fellow citizens."

> —Thomas Wahlrab, member, board of directors,
> National Association for Community Mediation,
> and coordinator, Dayton (Ohio) Mediation Center

"Being human is what human beings do. Yet our approaches to conflict analysis and resolution often dehumanize conflicts, by marginalizing emotions and avoiding discussion of painful histories. In this book, Bush and Folger help us re-imagine mediation within a relational framework where emotions and painful histories are essential features of the conflict transformation process. This framework not only focuses on the connection between people, but also favors reflection on the parties' experiences, as human beings. And by implication, mediators, as human beings, are encouraged to trust the parties in terms of their ability to move through the problems. Conflict is thus reframed as a contribution to the development of interaction, rather than a feature of life that needs 'management.' While this book contributes to our understanding of a model of mediation, it also humanizes conflict, and in the process, celebrates what it means to be a human being."

> —Sara Cobb, director, Institute for Conflict Analysis and
> Resolution, George Mason University

The Promise of Mediation

Robert A. Baruch Bush
Joseph P. Folger

The Promise of Mediation

· ·

The Transformative Approach
to Conflict

Revised Edition

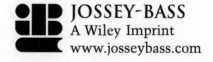

JOSSEY-BASS
A Wiley Imprint
www.josseybass.com

Published by Jossey-Bass
A Wiley Imprint
989 Market Street, San Francisco, CA 94103–1741   www.josseybass.com

Jossey-Bass books and products are available through most bookstores. To contact Jossey-Bass directly call our Customer Care Department within the U.S. at 800–956–7739, outside the U.S. at 317–572–3986, or fax 317–572–4002.

Jossey-Bass also publishes its books in a variety of electronic formats. Some content that appears in print may not be available in electronic books.

Library of Congress Cataloging-in-Publication Data

Bush, Robert A. Baruch.
   The promise of mediation : the transformative approach to conflict /
Robert A. Baruch Bush, Joseph P. Folger.— Rev. ed.
      p.   cm.
   Includes bibliographical references (p.   ) and index.
   ISBN 0-7879-7483-8 (alk. paper)
   1. Mediation.   2. Conflict management.   3. Conflict (Psychology)   4. Social conflict.   5.
Social interaction.   6. Interpersonal conflict.   I. Folger, Joseph P., date-
II. Title.
   HM1126.B87 2005
   303.6'9—dc22   2004009427

Printed in the United States of America
REVISED EDITION
HB Printing   10 9 8 7 6 5 4

Contents

To the fellows, associates, and supporters of
the Institute for the Study of Conflict Transformation,
whose many contributions helped make this volume possible.
And to the many mediation practitioners, program directors,
scholars, and commentators whose courageous acceptance of and
support for the transformative model over the past decade
have increasingly made the promise of mediation a reality.

Acknowledgments

. . . .

Since the publication of the first edition of *The Promise of Mediation,* we have had the good fortune of working closely with many talented and dedicated people, who have contributed enormously to the development of the transformative model of practice. In many important and central ways, this second edition is the result of their contributions to theory building, research, training design, implementation, and program development.

Much of this work was launched by two foundations that provided generous financial support to the development of transformative practice soon after the first edition of this book was written. We want to thank the Hewlett Foundation's Conflict Resolution Program, under the administration of Steve Toben, and the Surdna Foundation's Effective Citizenry Program, under Robert Sherman, for this pivotal support. The initial projects that were funded by these organizations created a network of people, who have contributed powerfully to developing transformative theory and linking it to mediation practice. We are also deeply grateful to Cindy Hallberlin for the opportunity she provided to use the transformative model in the REDRESS Mediation Program that she launched at the U.S. Postal Service. This program provided an invaluable opportunity to develop and implement transformative mediation in one of the largest workplace organizations in the United States.

We want to extend special thanks to Dorothy Della Noce and Sally Pope for their work with us since the beginning of these projects. They have made enormous contributions through a range of endeavors that they have initiated and led over the past ten years. We are especially indebted to them for the astute work they have done on numerous articles and publications, especially the two pieces that they coauthored with us that became the basis for Chapters Two and Six of this book. Their vision also contributed to the cofounding of the Institute for the Study of Conflict Transformation, a nonprofit organization dedicated to creating resources that support transformative conflict intervention.

We deeply appreciate the board, management team, and associates of the Institute for their work and contributions to the development of transformative practice. We owe special thanks to Judy Saul and Jim Antes for their contributions to the Training Design Consultation Project and the Practice Enrichment Initiative as well as their influential contributions as members of the Institute's board, its management team, and its research task force. We are indebted to Andrew Thomas, Judge William Thomas, Steve Toben, and Cindy Hallberlin for their vision and direction as board members of the Institute.

We are also very grateful for the work of the Institute's associates, many of whom have been instrumental in implementing transformative practice in their own programs and organizations and have been involved with us in a range of important projects since *The Promise of Mediation* was first published. These associates are Winnie Backlund, Patricia Bass, Deb Bopsie, Roger Brach, Melissa Broderick, Paul Charbonneau, Maria Cuzzo, Julie Denny, Kenneth Fox, Barbara Foxman, Deborah Gaber, William Galloway, Patricia Gonsalves, Elayne Greenberg, Cherise Hairston, Martin Harris, Donna Turner Hudson, Steve Jacobsen, Kristen Johnson, Neil Kaufman, Lou Ann Lucke, Leslyn McBean, Jody Miller, Peter Miller, Suzanne Motheral, Janet Mueller, Paula Pace, Kristine Paranica, Louise Phipps Senft, Dan Simon, Kent Swinburne, Thomas Wahlrab, Sara Jane Wellock, and Michelle Zaremba. We also want to thank Jennifer Jorgensen for her skill and dedication in handling the administration of the Institute and building a network among its associates.

The Institute's work has been generously supported, for the past four years, by grants from the Hewlett Foundation's Conflict Resolution Program, and we express our profound thanks to the foundation and to program officers Steve Toben and Terry Amsler for their confidence in the importance of the Institute's contributions to the field.

We want to acknowledge and thank leaders in the mediation field who have welcomed discussion and implementation of the transformative model—in particular, James Alfini, Heidi and Guy Burgess, Warren Cunningham, Louis Gieszel, Michael Lang, Lela Love, Sharon Press, Len Riskin, Jean Sternlight, Joseph Stulberg, Paula Trout, Mark Umbreit, Dan Weitz, and Rachel Wohl. We also want to thank the many university programs that have sponsored courses, major presentations, or symposia on transformative practice, including Hofstra University Law School, Hamline University, the Straus Institute for Dispute Resolution at Pepperdine University, the University of Maryland Law School, Southern Methodist University, South Texas College of Law, University of Texas, Texas A&M University, University of Florida, Dayton Law School, Aalborg University, Auckland University, and Latrobe University.

Special thanks go to the administration of Hofstra Law School, for offering early and continuing logistical support for the projects mentioned previously and for the Institute for the Study of Conflict Transformation.

We feel an extra measure of gratitude for the many mediation programs that have adopted and implemented the transformative model, including, among others, the U.S. Postal Service REDRESS Program, as mentioned previously; the Community Dispute Resolution Center (Ithaca, New York); the Dayton (Ohio) Mediation Center; the Montgomery County (Pennsylvania) Mediation Center; the University of North Dakota (Grand Forks) Conflict Resolution Center;

the Greenwich (United Kingdom) Mediation Centre; the Dutchess County (New York) Mediation Center; the Baltimore (Maryland) Mediation Center. The work done by both professionals and volunteers in programs like these has been instrumental in establishing the transformative model as a viable approach to practice. We also give our special thanks to those who, together with Cindy Hallberlin, have contributed to the development and implementation of the U.S. Postal Service REDRESS Mediation Program, including Anthony Vegliante, Mary Elcano, Karen Intrater, Traci Gann, Kim Brown, Kevin Hagan, Geoff Drucker, Lisa Sharp, Andrew Colsky, Pat Richter, Pat Boylan, Trisch Bass, Laree Martin, Richard Reyes, and their many wonderful colleagues. In addition, we are indebted to Lisa Bingham for her work in conducting and publishing extensive research on the REDRESS program in all stages of its development and implementation.

Our continued appreciation goes to our students at Temple and Hofstra Universities, whose day-to-day participation in many discussions and assignments continue to stimulate and shape our thinking. Our interactions with students have contributed in many ways to the development of ideas in this book.

We also want to thank our families for their support over the years. Their generosity has given us ample, guilt-free time to devote to this work, and their confidence in our enterprise has encouraged us at every step. Special thanks to Shulamis Bush for editorial help.

Finally, we want to express our appreciation to the professional staff at Jossey-Bass, especially Alan Rinzler and Seth Schwartz, for their careful editorial guidance in the development of this new and revised edition. And we will always be grateful to those who supported the publication of the first edition, particularly Cedric Crocker at Jossey-Bass, the late Jeff Rubin at Tufts University, and Linda Putnam at Texas A&M University.

The Institute for the Study of Conflict Transformation, mentioned here and in Chapter Four, is an excellent source of further resources on the transformative model of conflict practice, including other publications on transformative mediation as well as the mediation videotape on which Chapters Four and Five are based (and we thank the actors who played the parties in the videotape: Julia Denny, Bernice Joland, and Elizabeth Van Dyke). The Institute can be accessed on the Web at www.transformativemediation.org.

Robert A. Baruch Bush
Brooklyn, New York

Joseph P. Folger
Collingswood, New Jersey

The Promise of Mediation

Introduction

Ten years ago, we wrote *The Promise of Mediation* to call our colleagues' attention to a disturbing state of affairs in the mediation field. In our view, the potential that mediation offered to foster and support positive human interaction within conflict was being squandered. Instead mediation was being used to shore up institutional processes that operate to control, contain, and settle conflict, because of a prevailing view that conflict interaction is a fundamentally negative social force. We argued for an alternative approach to mediation, now known as *transformative mediation*, basing our argument on a theory of the larger political and social values implicit in different conflict intervention approaches.

Part of the reason for linking our model to certain underlying values was our conviction that those values—referred to in the first edition as constituting a *relational worldview*—are the soundest basis for constructing social institutions. However, the emphasis on underlying values was also part of the wake-up call that we intended our book to carry: we wanted to suggest that mediation practice in general is not "value-free" but is based on ideological or value premises, no matter what model is being used. Indeed, in the Foreword to the first edition, series editor and Harvard scholar Jeff Rubin noted, "The fact that Bush and Folger are so frankly ideological and value driven in their analysis will also disturb those readers who wish for a value-neutral appraisal of the mediation industry." Rubin foresaw that—in large part due to its explicitly value-based approach—*The Promise of Mediation* would garner both ardent support and strong criticism. And he was right on both counts. Many have found the book's clarification of value premises helpful in giving them a more stable place to stand: a value center that they sensed but could not easily find on the then-existing map of the field. It helped people align their practices with the implicit values, the core ideology, that ultimately made practice meaningful and coherent. But others found the book's message unsettling, because it challenged the presumption of value neutrality that allowed them to practice without articulating any core premises to explain and justify their enterprise.

In both of these kinds of response, appreciative and critical, the first edition of our book has fulfilled the purpose we had in mind. That purpose, stated most generally, was to wake up the field from its inattention to the link between core values and practices and to shift it toward a greater attention to those values, especially *relational values*, and the practices they engender. We believe that this shift has begun to take place. There is greater and more critical attention today to the value implications of particular forms of mediation practice, and there is greater acknowledgment that there are indeed distinct "models" of practice being used. We see the disagreement that has unfolded about these various models as a healthy sign, a sign that the field is moving through its awkward adolescence. Equally important to us, there is greater acceptance that the transformative model of mediation is not only appealing and coherent at the value level but also workable and sustainable at the level of actual practice. Transformative mediation has become a well-defined choice, as the ideological foundations of this model have been more fully articulated, and as the nature of transformative training and practice has been developed. Our experience with implementing transformative mediation in numerous organizational, governmental, and private practice arenas has strengthened our sense of the appropriateness and viability of this model of practice in all contexts where mediation is practiced.

In keeping with the shifts we see in the field, our intentions in this new and revised edition are different than they were ten years ago. Our goals in this book are to explain why this form of practice is important and needed, to illustrate how mediators actually work within this framework, to clarify the impact that this practice has on parties' conflict interaction, and to suggest how it can be implemented in the present institutional context of mediation practice. We describe the ways in which the field has shifted—in discourse, conceptualization, and practice—toward recognizing both the value dimensions of mediation and the viability of alternative models of practice, and the transformative model in particular. At the same time, we address the fact that there is still resistance to transformative values and practices, stemming most of all from the pressures and demands of institutional users and stakeholders in certain arenas with historical importance to the field. And we propose ways of understanding and dealing with these sources of resistance.

Chapter One offers some further context for discussion of the transformative model, by describing several different views of the mediation process that are often heard in the field, and situating the transformative model among those views.

Chapter Two sets forth a full picture of the premises, goals, and benefits of the transformative model of mediation, grounded in theory and research on human conflict and accompanied by concrete illustrations. The definition of mediation as supporting *conflict transformation* is explained, as is the nature of the mediator's role. This chapter also clarifies certain ambiguities in our articulation of the values and practices of the transformative model in the first edition that led to difficulty for some in grasping the aims and methods of the model. In particular, we clarify our use of the term *moral growth* and its relation to the transformative model and the process of changing conflict interaction. We also make a clearer distinction between the private and public benefits of transformative mediation and focus more on the benefits of the model to disputing parties themselves.

This chapter draws in part from a chapter coauthored by Baruch Bush and Sally Pope for another volume (Bush and Pope, 2004).

Chapter Three documents how the transformative model has influenced the field and has gained a solid foothold within it in the decade since the publication of the first edition of *The Promise of Mediation*. First, the chapter shows that the concerns we raised in the first edition, about the field's undue emphasis on the goal of settlement, have come to be shared much more widely. Second, the chapter describes how the rhetoric of "good practice" has shifted to give more attention to values and practices similar to those of the transformative model. Finally, the chapter documents the growth in the explicit use of the transformative model in many organizations and contexts, as well as the substantial advances in the "technology" of transformative practice that have been achieved by trainers and practitioners using the model.

Chapters Four and Five present, in two parts, an entirely new case study to illustrate the use of the transformative model. The case—a difficult contract dispute between a homeowner in an upscale development and the development's homeowner association—is taken from a videotaped mediation simulation, based on a real case but using professional actors as parties. The case is presented in full, in script form, with commentary by the authors that includes considerable material on the essential skills of transformative mediation practice. The videotape itself is available from the Institute for the Study of Conflict Transformation, mentioned previously in the Acknowledgments.

Chapter Six offers a review of some of the most common misconceptions about the transformative model of mediation, as well as clarifications that address and correct these misconceptions.

Finally, Chapter Seven addresses, at a deeper ideological level, the reasons why many in the mediation field are increasingly moving away from certain forms of prevailing practice that are viewed as troublesome and toward transformative practice. We show how understanding this shift rests on a clear view of the values and worldviews on which fundamentally different forms of practice are built.

In summary, these are the main benefits that readers can expect to get from this new and revised edition of *The Promise of Mediation:*

- A broad picture of how the field has shifted in the last decade and how that shift has resulted in more acceptance of the transformative model

- A significantly clearer articulation of the values, theory, and practices of the transformative model, including the clarification of ambiguities that may have caused difficulty in accurately understanding the model

- A rich new case study, based on a videotaped mediation session, that offers a vivid picture of the model in practice and a substantial amount of new information about how to be an effective practitioner

- A vision for the future that shows how the model can coexist with other approaches to mediation, as well as where the market for transformative mediation specifically is emerging and developing

1

The Mediation Field

An Overview and Four Stories

Roughly thirty-five years ago, in a variety of places around the United States, many groups and individuals became interested in a process of dispute resolution called *mediation*. Although mediation had long been used in labor disputes, the new surge of interest extended to many other contexts, including community, family, and interpersonal conflict. The use of mediation has grown over the last three decades or so. Prior to 1965, mediation outside the labor relations arena was practically unheard of. Then, in the late 1960s, attention was focused on mediation from two very different directions: civic leaders and justice system officials saw in mediation a potential for responding to urban conflict and its flash points; and community organizations and legal reformers saw in mediation a potential for building community resources alongside the formal justice system. Though the motives and approaches were quite different, the combined effect was to make the idea of mediation of neighborhood or community disputes a widely accepted and legitimate concept.

In practical terms, this meant the expansion of the community mediation field from a few isolated programs in 1970 to nearly two hundred by the early 1980s and to more than double that number today. Moreover, as a result of its acceptance in this field, mediation was used in an increasingly broad range of nonlabor disputes: divorce, environmental, housing, institutional (including prisons, schools, and hospitals), small-claims, personal injury and insurance, and general business disputes, as well as claims involving governmental agencies (Singer, 1990). In recent years, this trend has continued. Private businesses and even lawyers are finding mediation attractive, spurring the start-up and expansion of for-profit mediation services. The use of volunteer and professional mediators has been institutionalized in many court programs, so much so that courts often cannot imagine how caseloads could be handled without the use of these mediation programs. In many instances, the increasing reliance on mediation within the courts has been due to the courts' proclivity to require mediation, not only in divorce and small-claims cases but in civil litigation generally.

Across the mediation field, mediation is generally understood as an informal process in which a neutral third party with no power to impose a resolution helps the disputing parties try to reach a mutually acceptable settlement. This common formulation captures some of the major features of the process, especially its informality and consensuality. It also reflects the view that the most significant effect of the process is the production of a voluntary settlement of the dispute. Settlement is often seen as the primary or even sole value of mediation in institutional settings like the courts, where disposition of cases is the main motivation for using mediation.

There is nevertheless an extraordinary divergence of opinion about how to understand the growth of the mediation field and how to characterize the mediation enterprise itself. This divergence is so marked that there is no one accepted account of how the mediation field evolved or what it represents. Instead the literature of the field reveals several very different accounts or "stories," told by different authors and stressing different dimensions of the mediation process and its private and public benefits. Thus mediation is portrayed by some as a tool to reduce court congestion and provide "higher-quality" justice in individual cases, by others as a vehicle for organizing people and communities to obtain fairer treatment, and by still others as a covert means of social control and oppression. And some (including us) picture mediation as a way to foster a qualitative transformation of human interaction. Indeed these are the four main accounts that run through the literature on mediation. We call them, respectively, the Satisfaction Story of the field, the Social Justice Story, the Oppression Story, and the Transformation Story.

Four Stories of the Mediation Process

The fact that there are four distinct and divergent stories of the mediation field suggests two important points. On one level, it suggests that the field is not monolithic but pluralistic—that there are in fact different approaches to mediation practice, with varied impacts. The stories represent these different approaches. On a deeper level, the existence of divergent stories suggests that although everyone sees mediation as a means for achieving important private and public goals, people differ over what goals are most important. So the stories also represent and support different goals, some of which are seen by some people as more important than others for the process to fulfill.

Recounting the different stories of the field is therefore a good way both to illustrate the diversity of mediation practice and to identify the value choices implicit in varying approaches to practice. The following summary of the four stories presents each one as it might be told by its authors and adherents.

The Satisfaction Story

According to this story, "The mediation process is a powerful tool for satisfying human needs and reducing suffering for parties to individual disputes. Because of its flexibility, informality, and consensuality, mediation can open up the full dimensions of the problem facing the parties. Not limited by legal categories or rules, it can help reframe a contentious dispute as a mutual problem. In addition, because of mediators' skills in dealing with power imbalances, mediation can reduce strategic maneuvering and overreaching. As a result of these different features, mediation can facilitate collaborative, integrative problem solving rather than adversarial, distributive bargaining. It can thereby produce creative, 'win-win' outcomes that reach beyond formal rights to solve problems and satisfy parties' needs in a particular situation or, alternatively, remedy parties' difficulties. The mediation field has employed these capabilities of the process to produce superior quality solutions for private disputants in cases of all kinds—that is, solutions that best satisfy the parties' needs and remedy their difficulties.

"Furthermore, in comparison with more formal or adversarial processes, mediation is characterized by an informality and mutuality that can reduce both the economic and emotional costs of dispute settlement. The use of mediation has thus produced great *private* savings for disputants, in economic and psychic terms. In addition, by providing mediation in many cases that would otherwise have gone to court, the mediation field has also saved *public* expense. It has freed up the courts for other disputants who need them, easing the problem of delayed access to justice. In sum, the use of mediation has led to more efficient use of limited private *and* public dispute resolution resources, which in turn means greater overall satisfaction for individual 'consumers' of the justice system.

"This holds true for all the various contexts in which mediation has been used. Child custody mediation, for example, has produced better-quality results for both children and parents than litigated rulings. Small-claims mediation has resulted in higher party satisfaction with both process and outcome, and higher rates of compliance than litigation. Environmental and public policy mediation have produced creative and highly praised resolutions, while avoiding the years of delay and enormous expense that court action would have entailed. Moreover mediation in these areas has reduced court caseloads and backlogs, facilitating speedier disposition of those cases that cannot be resolved without trial in court. In these and other kinds of disputes, mediation has produced more satisfaction for disputing parties than could have been provided otherwise."

· · · · · · · ·

The Satisfaction Story is widely told by a number of authors. Many are themselves mediators, either publicly employed or private practitioners or "entrepreneurs" (Williams, 1997; Hoffman, 1999; Moore, 2003). Some are academics. Some who are both practitioners and scholars have been very influential in supporting this story of the movement (Stemple, 1997; Golann, 1996; Susskind and Field, 1996; Menkel-Meadow, 1995; Mnookin and Ross, 1995; Fisher and Brown, 1989; Susskind and Cruikshank, 1987; Folberg and Taylor, 1984; Fisher and Ury, 1981). Also quite influential are the many judges and other justice system officials who tell this story, including former Chief Justice Warren Burger (1982) and many other judicial leaders (see Galanter, 1985).

The next two interpretations of the mediation field, the Social Justice Story and the Transformation Story, differ somewhat from the Satisfaction Story. The Satisfaction Story claims to depict what has generally occurred in the use of mediation thus far, whereas the other two describe something that has admittedly occurred only in part thus far. In effect, these are "minority" stories of the field, but each is still seen by its adherents as representing mediation's most important potential.

The Social Justice Story

According to this story, "Mediation offers an effective means of organizing individuals around common interests and thereby building stronger community ties and structures. This is important because unaffiliated individuals are especially subject to exploitation in this society and because more effective community organization can limit such exploitation and create more social justice. Mediation can support community organization in several ways.

Because of its capacity for reframing issues and focusing on common interests, mediation can help individuals who think they are adversaries perceive a larger context in which they face a common enemy. As a result, mediation can strengthen the weak by helping establish alliances among them.

"In addition, mediation reduces dependency on distant agencies and encourages self-help, including the formation of effective grassroots community structures. Finally, mediation treats legal rules as only one of a variety of bases by which to frame issues and evaluate possible solutions to disputes. Mediation can therefore give groups more leverage to argue for their interests than they might have in formal legal processes. The mediation field has used these capacities of the process, to some extent at least, to facilitate the organization of relatively powerless individuals into communities of interest. As a result, those common interests have been pursued more successfully, helping ensure greater social justice, and the individuals involved have gained a new sense of participation in civic life.

"This picture applies to many, if not all, of the contexts in which mediation is used. Interpersonal neighborhood mediation has encouraged co-tenants or block residents, for example, to realize their common adversaries, such as landlords and city agencies, and to take joint action to pursue their common interests. Environmental mediation has facilitated the assertion of novel (and not strictly legal) claims by groups that have succeeded in redressing imbalances of power favoring land developers. Even mediation of consumer disputes has helped strengthen consumers' confidence in their ability to get complaints addressed, which has led to other forms of consumer self-help and has increased consumer power. In short, mediation has helped organize individuals and strengthen communities of interest in many different contexts—and could be used more widely for this purpose."

• • • • • • •

The Social Justice Story of the mediation field has been told for a long time, though by a relatively small number of authors, usually people with ties to the tradition of grassroots community organizing. Examples include Paul Wahrhaftig (1982), an early figure in community mediation, and Ray Shonholtz (1984, 1987), founder of the Community Boards Program, long known for its organizing orientation. More recently, Carl Moore (1994) and Margaret Herrman (1993) have echoed this account. Although the numbers of its adherents are few, this story has been told consistently from the earliest stages of the field.

The third story, the Transformation Story, focuses on some of the same features of the mediation process as the first two. However, it characterizes them, and especially their consequences, in distinct and quite different terms than the other stories.

The Transformation Story

According to this story, "The unique *promise of mediation* lies in its capacity to transform the quality of conflict interaction itself, so that conflicts can actually strengthen both the parties themselves and the society they are part of. Because of its informality and consensuality, mediation can allow parties to define problems and goals in their own terms, thus validating the importance of those problems and goals in the parties' lives. Further, mediation can support the parties' exercise of self-determination in deciding how, or even whether, to settle a dispute, and it can help the parties mobilize their own resources to address problems and achieve their goals. The mediation field has (at least to some extent) employed these aspects of the process to help disputing parties activate their inherent capacity for deliberation and decision making in adverse circumstances. Participants in mediation have, as a result, gained a greater sense of strength of self, including self-respect, self-reliance, and self-confidence. This has been called the *empowerment* dimension of the mediation process.

"In addition, the private, nonjudgmental character of mediation can provide disputants a nonthreatening opportunity to explain and humanize themselves to one another. In this setting, and with mediators who are skilled at enhancing interpersonal communication, parties often discover that they can feel and express some degree of understanding and concern for one another despite their disagreement. The field has (again, to some extent) used this dimension of the process to help individuals activate their inherent capacity for understanding the problems of others. Mediation has thus engendered, even between parties who start out as fierce adversaries, acknowledgment and concern for each other as fellow human beings. This has been called the *recognition* dimension of the mediation process.

"Although empowerment and recognition have been given only partial attention in the mediation field thus far, a consistent and wider emphasis on these dimensions would contribute to the transformation of conflict interaction from a negative and destructive social force into a positive and constructive social force—helping individuals to interact with more confidence in themselves and empathy for each other, and helping to transform society as a whole from a truce between enemies into a network of allies.

"This picture captures the potential of mediation in all types of disputes, not just certain areas in which human relationships are considered important (implying that elsewhere they are not). Consumer mediation can strengthen the confidence of and evoke recognition between merchants and consumers, transforming the character of commercial transactions and institutions. Divorce mediation can strengthen and evoke recognition between men and women, changing the character of male-female interaction generally. Personal injury mediation can strengthen and evoke recognition between insurance assessors and accident victims, transforming the character of compensation processes. In every area, mediation could, with sufficient energy and commitment, help transform the quality of social interaction and, ultimately, social institutions."

♦ ♦ ♦ ♦ ♦ ♦ ♦

The Transformation Story of the mediation process was not widely told in the published literature of the field prior to the publication of the first edition of this book. The few who expounded it included practitioners such as Albie Davis (1989) and academics such as Leonard Riskin and Carrie Menkel-Meadow (in some of their work, see Riskin, 1982, 1984; Menkel-Meadow, 1991; see also Dukes, 1993), as well as the authors of this volume (see Folger and Bush, 1994; and Bush, 1989–1990). Nevertheless, beyond the world of the printed word, this story was given voice in informal discussions among both academics and mediation practitioners. It was, as it were, the underground story of the movement, often the motivating force behind practitioners' involvement. The publication of *The Promise of Mediation* gave greater voice to this story and attracted numerous authors to articulate the story more fully (Burns, 2001; Della Noce, 1999; Pope, 1996; Jorgensen, 2000; Beal and Saul, 2001; Moen and others, 2001; Jorgensen and others, 2001; Bush and Pope, 2002).

Here, then, are three very different accounts of the mediation enterprise. Each of them expresses two different kinds of messages about the field. On one level, each story is a *description*, purporting to recount what the mediation field has actually done and what its actual character is today (in whole or in part). On another level, each story is a *prescription*, suggesting what the field *should* do to fulfill what the story's authors see as the most important private and public goals or values that mediation can help achieve.

The final story of the field differs from all the others. The first three all see positive effects or potentials in the process, although each sees them differently. The fourth, by contrast, sees only negative effects or potentials. It presents not a prescription for the field but a warning against it. We call it the Oppression Story.

The Oppression Story

According to this story, "Even if the field began with the best of intentions, mediation has turned out to be a dangerous instrument for increasing the power of the state over the individual and the power of the strong over the weak. Because of the informality and consensuality of the process, it can be used as an inexpensive and expedient adjunct to formal legal processes, seeming to increase access to justice but actually operating to extend the control of the state into previously private domains of social conduct. Once having entered those domains, and given its lack of both procedural and substantive rules, mediation enlarges the discretion and power of state-sponsored decision makers, and it can magnify power imbalances and open the door to coercion and manipulation by the stronger party. Meanwhile the posture of 'neutrality' excuses the mediator from preventing this. As a result, in comparison with formal legal processes, mediation has often produced outcomes that are unjust—that is, disproportionately and unjustifiably favorable to the state and to stronger parties. Moreover, because of its privacy and informality, mediation gives mediators broad strategic power to control the discussion, giving free rein to mediators' biases. These biases can affect the framing and selection of issues, consideration and ranking of settlement options, and many other elements that influence outcomes. Again, as a result, mediation has often produced unjust outcomes.

"Finally, because mediation handles disputes without reference to other, similar cases and without reference to the public interest, it results in the disaggregation and privatization of class and public interest problems. That is, the use of mediation has helped the strong 'divide and conquer.' Weaker parties are unable to make common cause and the public interest is ignored and undermined. In sum, the overall impact of the field has been to extend the state's control of individuals' lives; to neutralize social justice gains achieved by the civil rights, women's, and consumers' movements, among others; and to reinforce the status quo and the privileged position of those who benefit from it.

"This oppressive picture is found in all of the field's uses of mediation. Divorce mediation removes safeguards and exposes women to coercive and manipulative 'bargaining' that results in unjust property and custody agreements. Landlord-tenant mediation allows landlords to escape their obligations to provide minimally decent housing, which results in substandard living conditions and unjust removals for tenants. Employment discrimination mediation manipulates victims into accepting buy-offs and permits structural racism and sexism to continue unabated in businesses and institutions. Even in commercial disputes between businesses, mediation allows the parties to strike deals behind closed doors that disadvantage consumers and others in ways that will never even come to light. In every area, mediation has been used to consolidate the power of the strong and increase the exploitation and oppression of the weak."

. . . .

The Oppression Story is clearly a different kind of story than the other three. Rather than offering a description of and prescription *for* the mediation field, it sounds a warning *against* it. This story is almost as widely told as the Satisfaction Story, but by very different authors. They include numerous critics of the mediation field, such as early and influential figures Richard Abel (1982) and Christine Harrington (1985). Minority critics of the process, like Richard Delgado (1985), and feminist critics, like Trina Grillo (1991) and others (Bryan, 1992; Fineman, 1988), also tell the Oppression Story. In general, many—although not all—writers and thinkers concerned with equality tend to interpret the mediation field through the Oppression Story and to see it as a serious threat to disadvantaged groups (see Menkel-Meadow, 1991; Fiss, 1984; Tomasic, 1982; Nader, 1979).

Now that all the stories have been presented, a clarification of one crucial term is in order. Some authors have used the term *transformation* to mean the *restructuring of social institutions* in a way that redistributes power and eliminates class privilege (see Harrington and Merry, 1988; and Dukes, 1993). It should be clear that as we use the term here—in the Transformation Story and throughout the book—transformation does *not* mean institutional restructuring in this sense but rather *a change in the quality of conflict interaction*. When the term is used to mean institutional restructuring, it does not carry any necessary implication of qualitatively different social interaction, but rather connotes a reallocation of material benefits and burdens among individuals and groups. We see this aim as encompassed within the concept of social justice or fairness, and in the framework presented here this kind of societal restructuring is the concern of the Social Justice and Oppression Stories, not the Transformation Story. Transformation, in the sense used here, connotes change in the quality of social interaction, in and beyond conflict, although this kind of change will very likely lead to changes in social institutions as well.

Implications of the Stories: What Is and What Should Be

Although all four accounts of the mediation field are in circulation, they are rarely laid out side by side as presented here. A few observers have noted the existence of multiple accounts of the field, although they have not identified the whole range described here (for instance, Harrington and Merry, 1988). Far more commonly, however, only one of the four stories is told by a given author or speaker who believes it to be the "true" story of the field. One account describes mediation as creative problem solving, which produces settlements that satisfy needs and reduce suffering on all sides of conflicts. Another sees mediation as helping to organize and build coalitions among individuals, so as to generate greater bargaining power for the "have-nots." A third pictures mediation as working to support empowerment and recognition and thus changing the quality of conflict interaction so as to increase human strength and understanding even within the crucible of human conflict. The fourth sees mediation as enhancing state control and applying pressure and manipulation in ways that cause greater unfairness to the already disadvantaged.

Placing all four stories side by side reveals some important points. First, it supports the view that the mediation field is diverse and pluralistic. Not all mediators follow the practices described by any one story of the process. Rather, there are different approaches to mediation practice, with different and varied impacts, and the different stories depict these different approaches. Therefore, at a factual level, none of the stories is "the true story" of the field; rather, each is probably a valid account of the practices of some number of mediators working in the field today.

At the same time, setting out all the stories together, and then looking at what we know about current mediation practice in general, makes it clear that the stories are not all equally reflective of the actual state of the field today. For example, a growing body of research tells us that despite diversity among mediators a dominant pattern of practice has emerged, and this dominant approach to mediation practice focuses on getting settlements (see Henlser, 2001; Welsh, 2001a; Kolb and Associates, 1994; Folger and Bush, 1994; Greatbatch and Dingwall, 1994; Alfini, 1991; Silbey and Merry, 1986). It gives little attention to coalition building or to transforming conflict interaction through empowerment and recognition. In short, the different stories of the field are not equally accurate as reports of the overall state of mediation practice and its impacts at present.

Although views differ, people in the mediation field itself generally see the Satisfaction Story as the most convincing report of the current state of the field. Supportive outsiders share this view, although critics tend to see the Oppression Story as more reflective of the current reality of practice. And almost everyone would agree that neither the Social Justice nor the Transformation Story reflects the "what is" of the mediation field today, although this situation has been changing in the decade since the first edition of this book was published (Folger and Bush, 2001a).

As noted earlier, however, a second insight that emerges from recounting the four stories is that there are different views of what private and public benefits mediation practice should aim to supply. In this light, each of the four stories presents a different view of not only *what is* but also *what should be* the character of mediation practice. Regardless of which story we accept as a report of the field's present character, the future depends on which story we believe in as a prescription for what mediation should be providing, for both private parties and society. If the Satisfaction Story reflects the bulk of what is actually going on today and the Transformation Story reflects a minority voice in the field, the question remains: Does this correspond to our view of how things should be? The answer depends on how we feel about each story's premises regarding what are the most important private and public benefits (or harms) of the mediation process.

Those premises should be evident from the stories themselves. The Satisfaction Story's premise is that the most important private benefit of mediation is maximizing the satisfaction of individuals' needs or, conversely, minimizing their suffering—producing the greatest satisfaction, or the least harm, for the individuals on both (or all) sides of a conflict. This story stresses mediation's capacity to reframe conflicts as mutual problems and to find optimal solutions to those problems, because this is how the ultimate benefit is produced: needs are met and harm is avoided. In addition, the important public benefit of mediation is an increase in systemic efficiency, as mediation relieves pressures on more formal, legal institutions like courts.

Both the Social Justice and Oppression Stories are driven by another, although related, premise: the most important concern is promoting equality between individuals or, conversely, reducing inequality. This premise is still indirectly concerned with meeting needs and avoiding suffering; but the emphasis here is that needs should not be met, nor suffering alleviated, unequally, and especially that structures that permit such inequality should be altered. These two stories take opposite views of the mediation field from one another, but only because they make different assessments of mediation's impact on equality. The Social Justice Story stresses mediation's capacity to organize individuals around common interests and concludes that the resulting coalitions produce the benefit of increasing equality. The Oppression Story stresses mediation's capacity to manipulate and exert pressure covertly and warns that such manipulation and pressure will work against the disadvantaged and risk making inequality worse.

Finally, the Transformation Story's premise is that the most important benefit of mediation is the transformation of the parties' conflict itself from a negative and destructive interaction to a positive and constructive one—which represents both a private benefit to them and a public benefit to society, as discussed in the following section. This story stresses mediation's capacity for fostering empowerment and recognition, because when these occur in conflict, the quality of the interaction is transformed from destructive to constructive.

Whatever our view of where mediation practice stands today, our view of what its future direction should be depends on which of the premises regarding mediation's private and public benefits we find most convincing. Let us assume that the present reality of mediation practice, and its impacts, are most accurately described by the Satisfaction Story. If so, and if we agree with the premise that satisfying needs and alleviating suffering should be considered the most important benefit of the process, continuing in the present direction makes good sense. If instead we adopt the premise that preventing inequality is the most important factor, we might argue for less attention in mediation practice to settlement and more to coalition building and safeguarding weaker parties against pressured settlement. In either case, we would not care much whether mediation was able to transform conflict interaction and probably would not even be aware of this when it occurred. Only the premise that conflict transformation is the most important benefit would lead us to argue for less attention to settlement *and* protection and more focus on conflict transformation.

Implicit in this discussion is the assumption that in mediation, as in any other social process, it is difficult if not impossible to produce all the different benefits together (Bush, 1984). In practice, producing one benefit inevitably means forgoing the others to some degree, whether because of direct conflicts between the steps necessary to achieve them or simply because of limited resources. Consequently, setting our own direction as mediators, as well as setting policies that govern the field's future direction, requires a view of which of the different benefits promised by the different stories we believe is most important, both to private users of mediation and to society as a whole. Just as the stories cannot be combined into a single description of the field, they cannot be combined into a single prescription either. Rather, the stories present us with choices regarding what mediation's future should be. To explain our own choice to work within the transformative model of mediation, we offer an initial overview of why we think conflict transformation matters; then, in Chapter Two, we explain the theory of this model of mediation.

The Value of Conflict Transformation: An Initial View

The mediation process contains within it a unique potential for transforming conflict interaction and, as a result, changing the mindset of people who are involved in the process. This transformative potential stems from mediation's capacity to generate two important dynamic effects: empowerment and recognition. In simplest terms, *empowerment* means the restoration to individuals of a sense of their value and strength and their own capacity to make decisions and handle life's problems. *Recognition* means the evocation in individuals of acknowledgment, understanding, or empathy for the situation and the views of the other. When both of these processes are held central in the practice of mediation, parties are helped to trans-

form their conflict interaction—from destructive to constructive—
and to experience the personal effects of such transformation.

Discovering the Potential for Empowerment and Recognition

When the use of mediation first expanded to new arenas of practice, few fully grasped either the special capacity of mediation for
fostering empowerment and recognition or the immense importance
of the phenomenon of conflict transformation. Nevertheless many
had strong intuitions on both counts. So even though the emphasis was on mediation's capacity to help resolve disputes and effec-
tuate settlements, there was an awareness that mediation had other
important though somewhat less tangible impacts. It was as though
a researcher had discovered a substance, very useful for one purpose,
that she realized was capable of other valuable effects; but she had
not yet determined what those other effects were or how they could
be generated.

Gradually, practitioners and scholars have gained a clearer picture of the valuable effects and benefits of mediation. Increasingly,
attention is being paid to the special capacities of the process to
transform conflict interaction by supporting empowerment and
recognition. Some have even come to realize that working with
empowerment and recognition usually results in reaching settlements that the parties build, whereas focusing on settlement usually results in ignoring empowerment and recognition. So even
though these different dimensions of mediation are not necessarily
inconsistent, the relative emphasis given to them makes a crucial
difference in what happens during a mediation session and what
comes to be defined as valuable or needed.

Many in the mediation field have begun to grasp how important
it is to focus on empowerment and recognition, and why. The
broader significance of these phenomena is becoming clearer as dispute resolution scholars see that mediation's transformative dimensions are connected to an emerging, new vision of self and society,
one based on *relational connection* and understanding rather than on

individual autonomy alone. Scholars and thinkers in many fields have begun to articulate and advocate a major shift in *moral* and *social vision*—from an *individualistic* to a *relational and interactive conception*. They argue that although the individualist ethic of modern Western culture was a great advance over the preceding social order, it is now possible and necessary to go still further and to achieve a full integration of individual freedom and social conscience, in a relational social order enacted through new forms of social processes and institutions.

Mediation, with its capacity for transforming conflict interaction, represents an opportunity to express this new *relational vision* in concrete form. Indeed this potential is what drew many to it in the first place. Mediation was appealing not because resolution or settlement was good in itself and conflict bad, but because of the way in which mediation allowed disputing parties to understand themselves and relate to one another through and within conflict interaction. In short, many have come to feel that empowerment and recognition— the transformative dimensions of mediation—are important in themselves as expressions of a much broader shift to a new social and moral vision. So, like the researcher who finally grasped the fuller workings and importance of her mysterious discovery, some in the mediation field have developed an appreciation for the workings and importance of mediation as a transformative process.

Since the initial writing of this book, an increasing number of people within the mediation field and in related areas of conflict practice have spoken of and supported the value of a *transformative vision* of mediation practice. Important public and private discussions and debates have occurred among theorists and practitioners about why transformative practice matters and how it differs from other approaches to mediation. These discussions have gone on at international conferences and at national and regional meetings of practitioners, as well as during mediation training sessions and within mediation centers across the country. These discussions have been useful because they have allowed many in the field to become clearer about the benefits they believe mediation can provide, in both the short and the long term, and for both private parties and society as a whole.

In addition, funders in the conflict field have given substantial support over the past ten years to developing methods of training and assessment for transformative practice. As a result of this support, the technology of transformative work has advanced significantly since 1994. The development of practice tools has helped to clarify how empowerment and recognition can be achieved in the interaction among disputing parties during mediation sessions. This support for training has also helped to spark interest in how the core principles of the transformative framework can be carried into other third-party practice arenas. Perhaps most important, the past decade has seen an increasing number of institutional stakeholders—administrators, program managers, and organizational consultants—clarify for themselves and for their organizations why this vision of practice matters. As a result, these institutional stakeholders have designed and implemented programs that strive to enact the transformative model of mediation practice. All of these developments are clear signs that the transformative potential of mediation is receiving increasing attention and support in mediation theory, policy, and practice.

But in a larger sense, this is not simply a book about mediation. This is a book about a process that has the potential to express a new vision of social interaction. The future of mediation is a matter of general and serious concern, because it implicates the future of an emerging relational vision of social life as a whole. If the vision cannot be expressed in a concrete context such as mediation, it remains mere theory. Just as that vision suggests a possible integration of individual freedom and social conscience, mediation offers a potential means to integrate the concern for rights and justice and the concern for caring and connection. In short, mediation presents a powerful opportunity to express and realize a particular vision of human life. To help capture this opportunity and to bring that vision into reality are the larger purposes of this book.

Those in the mediation field who sense that this vision of human interaction can be realized in mediation have seen powerful glimpses of it in their practice. Cases unfold in ways that illustrate how the quality of parties' interaction is changed during mediation sessions as they achieve greater clarity about themselves and their concerns, and as they gain greater understanding of each other. Although mediation sessions in which these shifts occur are often emotional and sometimes painful, the change in the conflict interaction is valued highly by the parties—independent of whether agreement is possible on any particular set of issues being discussed. Often, by the end of such sessions, asking parties to commit to specific points of agreement may seem unnecessary or superfluous because something of greater value has occurred: the interaction between the parties has changed in ways that eclipse any particular problem or dispute. This change is valued by parties not only because it alleviates the consequences of destructive escalation in their current conflict but also because it has a positive impact on them as individuals.

I'll Never, *Ever,* Train *You!*

One case recently mediated in the U.S. Postal Service REDRESS Mediation Program illustrates in a general way the value that transformative mediation offers to parties in conflict. The REDRESS program is an internal mediation program that addresses claims of employment discrimination within this governmental agency. Other employers, public and private, are adopting similar programs. The REDRESS program, in particular, has adopted transformative mediation as its preferred model of practice. Employees who file claims of discrimination of any kind may choose to mediate their claims prior to a formal, internal investigation. Although attendance in mediation is mandatory for managers who have been named, the managers are under no obligation to make any concessions or take any corrective actions as they participate in the process. They can raise and address any issues related to employee conduct and behavior and respond as they wish to the charges of discrimination. At the conclusion of mediation, employees who have filed charges can maintain or withdraw their claims of discrimination. If they maintain their charges, they can take their issues to the next step in the administrative process.

Mark, a letter carrier in his early thirties with ten or so years of experience, had filed a claim of discrimination against the postal service. His claim specifically targeted the actions of his immediate supervisor, Louis, and Gwen, the manager to whom Louis reported. Louis and Gwen were of the same age, fifteen or twenty years older than Mark.

After some introductory remarks by the mediator, Mark chose to speak. Addressing the mediator, he described himself as having a history of activism within the postal service; he said he had advocated for himself and other letter carriers over the years when demands on carriers' productivity had exceeded what could be fairly expected of them; he spoke of having a better knowledge than other employees of the postal guidelines that govern managerial prerogative and set standards of performance for carriers, as well as the labor contract between the postal service and the carriers' union. He said that he had always acted as a source of information for other carriers regarding the boundary between their rights and management's expectations of them.

After ten or fifteen minutes of speaking in this vein, Mark paused; Louis and Gwen, sensing that Mark had more to say, did not speak. When Mark resumed speaking, he shifted his focus away from the mediator, but still not directly toward Louis or Gwen. Now, there was an introspective quality to his demeanor, as if he were in conversation with himself. He said that he had come to feel that he wanted to be doing more with himself than driving a mail truck and delivering mail. For some months, he had been toying with the possibility of trying to become a supervisor. But although the idea of broadening his experience and taking on more responsibility was attractive, he wasn't sure he really wanted to take this step because he felt uneasy with the prospect of exercising authority over employees, especially those with whom he had a personal history. He said he had not applied for formal training as a supervisor because being accepted as a trainee would, in a sense, commit him to becoming a boss. He knew that managers and supervisors could, if they chose to, undertake to informally train employees. Informal training, Mark felt, would allow him to experiment with a shift in his circumstances without demanding that he ultimately choose to change.

Here, Mark directed his gaze directly at Louis and continued. He said that it had been difficult for him to approach Louis with the idea of training because Louis had always "had it in for" Mark. Louis was brusque in issuing Mark instructions; he was intolerant and dismissive of input or suggestions from Mark. In fact, Mark felt that for years it had been impossible to have a two-way conversation with Louis. Mark's worst expectations about Louis were confirmed a month or so before the mediation, when he did ask Louis about the possibility of an informal training.

For the first time, rather than making reference to Louis, Mark addressed himself to Louis directly, "When I asked you about training, you told me, 'I will never, ever, under any circumstances train you to do anything.'"

Despite the fact that Mark's long narrative had taken over thirty minutes, both Louis and Gwen maintained attentive postures throughout—sometimes looking directly at Mark, sometimes gazing downward in a thoughtful way. They displayed no sign of impatience or restlessness.

After giving a summary of Mark's narrative and confirming with him that he had voiced all he wished to at that moment, the mediator turned to Louis and Gwen and invited them to speak. *"You've been listening, following along with what Mark has been saying. Are there points either of you want to make?"*

Louis chose to begin by responding to Mark's accusation about the refusal to train him. *"I should probably never say 'never.' But of all the people under me, you have been about the last I would want to train. Although I have no complaints about you doing your job—you're good at that—you've made a career of opposing everything I try to do. When I reassign or change [delivery] routes, you've had objections. When I make any change in how the mail is cased [sorted], you've opposed it. When I do anything to make our operation more efficient or try to raise morale, you've been loud in objecting to it. Your attitude, which you've shared with everybody, is that there is a war between management and employees. We're the enemy, and it's been your job to do everything you can to resist us."*

Louis had become visibly angry; his speech grew sharper and more intense as he continued to unfold a history of what he viewed as obstructive, antagonistic behavior on Mark's part. It seemed that in describing those instances of resistance by Mark, he was revisiting the moments in which they had occurred. He continued on in that vein for several more minutes before reaching a conclusion.

"As I said, you're good at your job. You're smart, you adjust to what comes up in doing your route, you get through it on time, and you're here when you're supposed to be here. You don't make mistakes. When you're just doing your job, you're an asset. (Here, Louis raised his voice and leaned forward, toward Mark.) But what makes you think I would want to extend myself to someone who has spent years trying to make everything I do harder by being a 'jailhouse lawyer'? What makes you think I've seen you as having potential when everything you do has made me think you just don't get it?"

After the long pause that followed, Gwen said, "'Getting it' means taking what we do here seriously and wanting to do more." After a further pause, the mediator summarized all that Gwen and Louis had said, taking care to reflect the force with which Louis had at times conveyed his response to Mark.

In the aftermath of the mediator's summary, Mark addressed Louis, "Well, I've been thinking of doing more. That's why I came to you."

Louis appeared thoughtful, as if weighing Mark's words. He said, "I'm not sure you understand what 'more' really means."

Now, Louis, and sometimes Gwen, delineated what, from experience, they felt the role of being a manager in the postal service demanded. As they spoke at length, Mark leaned back in his chair in a stance of listening. More than once, he said, "I think I could do that." In response to this, Louis said, "Well, you'd have to do more," and he went on to further depict the posture he felt being an effective manager required.

Gwen told of her own trajectory: how she had determined that she wanted to try to become a supervisor; how hungry she had been to acquire a knowledge of postal operations; how she had, of her own initiative, sought out and read the manuals that described those various complex operations.

Louis said that undertaking to become a supervisor shouldn't be easy. Mark said that he would like to try. Louis said, "I want you to apply for formal training. Don't worry about being accepted. Nobody is the first time. But putting together the information and completing the form really takes time and it's really hard. I want to see you do that. I'll even help you if you want me to." Louis paused for a moment, then continued, "If you do that, I'll start training you within three months." Mark agreed that he would apply for formal training.

The mediator stated the understanding that the three had reached and then asked if they wanted to keep their agreement an informal one or if they preferred to capture it in writing,

in contractual form. Gwen and Louis said it was up to Mark.
Mark leaned back in his chair, folded his arms, and looked
downward. After some moments had passed, he made eye
contact with Louis and said, "I'll just drop the complaint."
Gwen said, "You did the right thing," and she and Louis each
extended their hand across the table.

Louis then said, his voice full of emotion, "It will be a priv-
ilege to train you." He laughed and went on, "And fun too,
because I'm going to watch you start to see the world the way
I do."

Following the Transformative Route Through a Conflict

This mediation "closed" a discrimination case that arose in the U.S.
Postal Service. It ended a conflict that had surfaced as a charge of
discrimination by an employee against his manager. From a purely
case management point of view, the case "settled"—it did not escalate into a formal administrative hearing or a court battle. But in
another sense, the closure of this case was a minor part of what this
mediation accomplished. What happened during the mediation was
a powerful shift in interaction that could be felt by the parties and
was supported by the mediator as the session unfolded. The interaction between the employee and his managers shifted from
being closed, defensive, and self-absorbed to being more open, trusting, and acknowledging. This shift, although at times difficult and
challenging for the parties, allowed for an exchange of perceptions,
feelings, and desires as they clarified what was important to them
and as they gained a more accurate understanding of each other's
perspectives.

Mark, Louis, and Gwen were all able to clarify for themselves
and to each other their own views about what transpired between
them and how they saw the roles and responsibilities of management. Mark indicated that he saw himself as an advocate for employees, protecting them from undue pressure or infringement by
management. He clarified how he viewed these actions—actions

he knew Louis and Gwen saw as objectionable to some degree. He suggested that in stepping beyond his letter carrier role he was demonstrating that he had the capability to accept greater responsibility. Mark also expressed his desire to move up in the organization and explained his fears about how a possible promotion might affect his relationships with his coworkers. He clarified that his request for informal training was linked to his concerns about preserving these relationships. He felt that signing up for formal training would make his fellow employees aware of his intentions and thereby jeopardize his coworker relationships. This was of particular concern to Mark because he had no assurance that taking the formal training would definitely lead to a management position. Mark's ability to clarify these views for himself and to Louis and Gwen throughout this session contributed significantly to opening up and changing the escalating conflict interaction that had led to Mark's formal charge of discrimination.

Louis and Gwen also contributed to the shift in conflict interaction as they articulated their concerns about Mark's behavior and indicated their views about what effective management entails. They were able to explain why they saw Mark's efforts to support employees as obstructionist and unsupportive of the organization. For them, Mark's moves to protect employees were seen as blocks to needed change and development within the postal service. Louis also explicitly acknowledged the quality of Mark's competent performance in his current role as a letter carrier, and both Louis and Gwen clarified what "doing more" as a manager meant to them. They were, in a way, giving Mark concrete and useful information about how he could reach his goal of becoming a manager. They were also revealing to Mark how they saw themselves and their work, and what it meant to them—something they assumed he had never understood before.

Expressing these important and revealing views opened and deepened the discussion. Although the change in interaction created discomfort and heated argument, it allowed for the exchange of important information that was not openly and clearly discussed in their prior workplace interactions. All of the parties became clearer about their own views through the open expression of them, and all found a voice to express their sentiments to each other in a direct and revealing way.

The expression of each person's views was accompanied by increasing acknowledgment of each other. The willingness to listen and take in what each was saying conveyed an intention to hear and think about the other's point of view. In the face of the personally challenging comments that were being made, this willingness to hear the other's views was significant in reshaping the interaction. Beyond being attentive to each other, the parties expressed an understanding of each other's experiences and views. Louis acknowledged the quality of Mark's letter carrier work and noted his efforts to extend himself further, while still clarifying that he held a very different sense of how aspiring managers should act. Louis also acknowledged Mark's concern about taking the risk of formal training and tried to allay his fears about accepting this option as a route to a managerial position. Sensing that Mark felt unsure about his abilities to succeed at the training, he offered to help Mark start this training process and assured him that most people don't make the cut in their initial attempt. All of these comments showed understanding and concern for what Mark was thinking and feeling.

Similarly, Mark was willing to consider Louis and Gwen's views on what is entailed in preparing for and enacting the management role. Mark indicated a willingness and ability to do what these managers were suggesting—including the option of applying for formal training. The support that Mark received from Louis and Gwen as this session unfolded made him less concerned about losing the close relationships he had built with his current coworkers. The connection Mark was developing with his managers in mediation helped him to want to take the risk of applying for the formal training. He now was developing personal support that mattered as much as the camaraderie he had with his coworkers.

Although this conflict came to mediation as a charge of discrimination, the discussion that occurred as the interaction unfolded soon turned to a wide range of important issues that had more to do with clarifying and understanding expectations and professional objectives than it did with charges of inequitable treatment or favoritism. The shift in interaction that occurred in this session brought forth the parties' capacities to articulate their own views and to stand up for themselves as an employee or as managers. The ability to clearly and coherently explain themselves laid the groundwork for them to step beyond their own defensive and self-absorbed postures and to make the decisions they wanted to make. For Mark, it meant being able to try out the managerial training role. For Louis and Gwen, it meant supporting Mark in his efforts to be successful in that attempt.

All of these people knew, at some level, that during this session they had made choices—about revealing their desires and about acknowledging each other's views—that had powerful reparative effects on their working relationship. They were aware that they themselves had made statements and decisions that profoundly changed their interaction—interaction that easily could have continued to escalate. Failure to change their interaction in this way through this mediation could have led to continued frustration for Mark, a waste of his potential managerial talent, continued strained and threatening communication, and perhaps an increasingly tense work environment for the entire unit in which these employees worked. But instead, as a result of this experience of their own power to redirect events, they left the session with a firmer connection with each other and a greater awareness of their own potential resources—resources they could draw from when confronted with other workplace conflicts.

The Value of Conflict Transformation

Mediators who focus on the transformative potential of mediation often experience sessions much like this one. They see the turns that this conflict took not as serendipitous events but as the result of a focus on opportunities for empowerment and recognition that arise as conflict interaction unfolds. What this case suggests (and others like it, not only in the workplace but in many other contexts) is that an approach to practice is possible that realizes the transformative potential of the mediation process. But taking this approach requires a sustained focus on mediation's capacity to support conflict transformation. Transformative mediators concentrate on empowering parties to define issues and decide settlement terms for themselves, and on helping parties to better understand one another's perspectives. In keeping this focus, transformative mediators help parties recognize and exploit the opportunities for balancing strength of self and connection to others. When people can talk through difficult issues—making clear choices with greater understanding of those with whom they differ or disagree—they learn how to live in a world where difference is inevitable. They move outside themselves in attempting to understand and connect with others while remaining true to their own decisions and choices.

The strongest reason for believing that the Transformation Story should guide mediation practice is the story's underlying premise: that the benefit of conflict transformation—that is, changing the quality of conflict interaction—is more valuable than the other benefits that mediation can be used to produce, even though those other benefits are themselves important. The workplace mediation just described was intended to illustrate concretely why this view makes sense. At a more general level, it makes sense to see conflict transformation as the most important benefit of mediation both because of the character of the benefit itself and because of mediation's special capacity to achieve it.

Conflict transformation has a unique character compared with the benefits promised by the other stories of the mediation process, both private and public. Obtaining satisfying and fair outcomes is undoubtedly important to parties in conflict, as is minimizing the economic and emotional cost of doing so. However, the importance of these benefits rests on the assumption that people are separate beings who are affected by but not essentially connected to each other, so that meeting needs can be accomplished without necessarily changing the quality of the interaction itself. By contrast, the importance of conflict transformation rests on the assumption that people are, by their essential nature, both separate and connected beings, who are distressed whenever negative interaction between them continues, even if their separate needs get satisfied.

Some thinkers, including communitarian scholars, describe this quality as the inherent social nature of human beings. Others, including feminist and *dialogic* moral philosophers, describe it as the inherent moral nature of human beings—with the term *moral* connoting sensitivity to the claims of both self and other. Both kinds of thinkers are using different terms to describe the same quality of human nature. They and others, who follow what is generally known today as a *relational account of human nature and society*, recognize this dual consciousness, of simultaneous separateness and connection, as inherent in human beings. As will be discussed in Chapter Two, there is considerable evidence that the desire to change negative interaction is a primary motivator for parties in dealing with conflict, precisely because of this dual quality of human nature. In this light, the benefit of conflict transformation responds to the parties' inherent sense of *social* or *moral connection*, a basic part of their nature as human beings that is not addressed by the other benefits of mediation. Conflict transformation is therefore a different kind of benefit than those of the other stories of mediation.

Regarding public benefits, there is also a qualitative difference between the benefit of conflict transformation and the benefits of the Satisfaction and Social Justice stories. In a society where private needs are met and unfairness is prevented when conflicts occur, it is logical to assume that public benefits like increased productivity, freedom, equality, and order will follow. However, the attainment of those public benefits is likely to be short-lived if negative conflict interaction itself is not addressed—because then conflict will probably recur or even worsen, undermining the public benefits supposedly achieved. To put it differently, satisfying needs and reducing suffering and unfairness can make people temporarily better off, but solved problems are quickly replaced by new ones and justice done is quickly undone. Therefore people are made better off in one instance only to be made worse off in the one that follows, because nothing has changed fundamentally in the way people interact with each other, especially when conflict arises. But when parties are helped to change the quality of conflict interaction itself, so that when conflict arises people are more able to respond with self-confidence and empathy, it is possible to imagine fuller and fairer satisfaction of needs becoming a permanent condition. In this respect, the goal of transformation is unique because it carries the other goals along in its train.

Not only is the benefit of conflict transformation uniquely important, it is also a benefit that the mediation process is uniquely capable of achieving. This is an additional reason to see transformation as the primary benefit that mediation can offer to private parties and to the society. Other dispute resolution processes, like adjudication or arbitration, can probably do as good a job as mediation, or even better, in satisfying needs and ensuring fairness. But by the very nature of their operation, those other processes are far less capable than mediation (if at all) of fostering in disputing parties greater confidence and understanding, and thus producing conflict transformation. Mediation's capacity for doing so, by generating empowerment and recognition, is unique among third-party processes (Bush, 1989). Adjudication and arbitration both disempower disputants in differing degrees, by taking control of outcome out of the parties' hands and by necessitating reliance on professional representatives. As for fostering recognition, at best these processes ignore it; at worst, they destroy even the possibility of recognition, by allowing or encouraging varying degrees of adversariness. In short, even if the benefits of satisfaction and fairness are important, there are other and perhaps better means to obtain them; but if conflict transformation is important, only one dispute resolution process is likely to produce it: mediation. It therefore makes sense to see transformation as the most important benefit of mediation, because this valued end is one that mediation alone can achieve.

Many people in the field share this view of mediation's ultimate value, though they may not label it as a transformative view. This was exemplified by a conversation we had at a workshop with a colleague, a veteran mediator and program administrator. "What is so impressive about mediation," she said, "is that it assumes people are competent—that they have the capacity to handle their own problems." And, we added, it also assumes they have the capacity to give consideration to others. People can work things out for themselves, and they can extend themselves to each other. They also have the desire at some level to do both of these. "And even though they may not do these things automatically," our colleague pointed out, "if you create the right environment and give them some support, which is what mediation can uniquely do, people often will rise to the occasion and fulfill all these potentials. And when this happens, the conflict interaction changes and ultimately that changes the whole social environment." At another workshop, one of the participants put it even more simply: "It's obvious why this makes sense," he said. "Clear, confident, connected people don't hurt themselves or each other."

Whether or not the label was used, the point is clear: conflict transformation matters, and mediation is unique among third-party processes in its capacity to be transformative. It is this transformative power that makes mediation so important and worthwhile, not simply its usefulness in satisfying needs. This is the message the Transformation Story conveys: not that satisfaction and suffering, justice and injustice, are unimportant—but that conflict transformation, and the resulting achievement of the inherent human potential for social and moral connection, are even more important.

And mediation has a unique capacity for producing this benefit, for engendering conflict transformation.

This abbreviated account of why conflict transformation matters, both to disputing parties and to society as a whole, sets the stage for the following chapter, which offers a thorough introduction to the theory and practice of mediation as a conflict transformation process.

2

. . . .

A Transformative View
of Conflict and Mediation

A mediator is someone who intervenes to help when people are in the middle of conflict. Therefore anyone interested in serving as a mediator needs to reflect on two basic and related questions. The first one is this: What kind of help do these parties want and need from me? The second is this: What indeed is this phenomenon of conflict—with which I am supposedly going to help these parties—all about? A mediator who starts to intervene without clear and coherent answers to these questions could easily do a disservice to the parties, and to him- or herself. However, the answers are by no means obvious.

Why Mediate?
Four Theories of Conflict and Intervention

Consider the case of Jim and Susan, the adult children of Walter Ellis, who founded their family business. This case, which we will use throughout this chapter to illustrate our discussion of the transformative theory of conflict and mediation, is based on a real case mediated by one of our colleagues (though we have altered details to preserve confidentiality):

> *Jim and Susan share equally in the profits of the business and are due to inherit it when Walter, now quite ill, passes away.*

Jim, forty-eight, has worked at his father's side in the company since graduating college, taking on more and more of the management as Walter aged. Susan, forty, a homemaker and mother whose children are now in college, has had only a minor role in the business, helping to deal with employee grievances, and is now shouldering most of the responsibility for dealing with Walter's decline from a terminal illness. Still joined in both family and business, they are now deeply divided about the roles each should play in the two areas. Jim wants Susan (and her husband) to stay out of his way in the company. He feels that he has full right of management based on his years of hard work. And he also believes the business would suffer badly if Susan or her husband were to be given any significant role. Susan wants a much larger role in the company for herself and her husband. She feels that with her children grown, she has an equal right to share not only profits but control. And she also needs to find a place for her husband in the family business, because he was downsized from his company and can't find another job. Finally, she thinks that Jim owes both her and their father the obligation to spend more time with Walter in the hospice before he passes away. Jim and Susan are weighing their options about how to handle the conflict between them over all of this—including mediation.

Why does a person involved in a conflict, like Jim or Susan, come to a mediator? Clearly, the person is seeking help in dealing with the conflict—but what kind of help? In fact, people involved in conflict seek different kinds of help, from different kinds of intervenors. Some seek help in consolidating their power in order to dominate the other side (or resist domination)—typically provided by organizers or advocates. Some seek help in constructing principled arguments that will convince some outside authority of the rightness of their claims—typically provided by lawyers or legal advocates. Some seek help in searching for a solution that meets the seemingly conflicting needs of all sides—typically provided by counselors or planners.

The kind of help that people want depends on many factors, but at the most basic level it depends on how they themselves answer the second question mentioned previously: What indeed is this phenomenon of conflict all about? To put it another way, the kind of help I seek depends on what being involved in conflict means to *me*—what *I* find most significant and affecting, positively or negatively, about this experience. If I feel that the most significant aspect of conflict is that it may affect my power over others (or theirs over me), I want help in consolidating power. If I feel that the most significant aspect is that it may threaten my rights, I want help in vindicating those rights. If I feel that the most significant aspect is that it may result in my needs being unmet, I want help in finding a way to make sure my needs are met.

In essence, this describes what might be called three *theories of conflict*, three different views of what human conflict is about—all of which are indeed found in the literature of the conflict field: *power theory* (Abel, 1982), *rights theory* (Fiss, 1984) and *needs theory* (Menkel-Meadow, 1984). Arguably, people's behavior reflects all three theories; that is, they see conflict in all three ways, depending on their specific situation. This is probably why they seek help from different kinds of intervenors at different times—sometimes from organizers, sometimes from lawyers, and sometimes from planners. However, from the perspective of the *intervenor* reflecting on what kind of help the client wants, one theory alone is generally the primary basis for answering that question: lawyers assume clients want help in vindicating rights, organizers assume clients want help in asserting power, and planners assume clients want help in solving problems to meet needs. In effect, these assumptions really represent *two* levels of theory, the second one being the intervenor's theory *about* the client's theory of conflict. To put it more precisely, the intervenor has a *theory of client expectations*, which is itself based on certain assumptions about the client's own theory of conflict.

Ultimately, the intervenor's view of client expectations is what sets the intervenor's own views of his or her role in the intervention, obligations to the client, and methodology of practice.

We have associated each of the three theories of conflict with a different kind of intervenor—none of them mediators. However, because of the multifaceted character of the mediation field, as described in Chapter One, there are also mediators whose assumptions about client expectations reflect each of these three different theories of conflict—that is, some mediators assume clients are seeking protection from domination; some assume clients are seeking outcomes that come close to vindicating their rights; and some assume clients are seeking resolutions that meet their underlying needs and interests. Depending on which assumption the mediator makes about client expectations, the mediator's sense of role, obligations, and best practices will differ accordingly. The language of the mediation field has actually developed to reflect this diversity of views about the services that mediators can and should offer to clients (Riskin, 1996; Guthrie, 2001; D'Alo, 2003). Recent literature therefore recognizes that potential mediation users can retain *evaluative mediators*, who will steer them toward outcomes in substantial conformity with legal rights. Or they can retain *facilitative mediators*, who will work to generate a settlement that meets the needs of all sides. Or they can retain *activist mediators*, who will ensure that parties (and even outsiders) are protected against domination and unfairness in the process.

It was against this background that we first articulated the *transformative theory* of conflict and mediation, in the previous edition of this book. The transformative theory, like each of the others, starts with a unique set of answers to the questions with which this chapter began, leading to a different view of the mediator's role, obligations to clients, and practice methods. Before examining these specifics, however, it is important to acknowledge that we do not (and could not) claim that only the transformative theory is valid and the others are not. We therefore do not dismiss the other theories, a subject we return to in Chapter Seven. Rather, it is our purpose here to fully articulate the transformative theory itself and to explain why it represents a view of conflict and mediation that is not only valid but highly appealing, both because of the social scientific evidence that supports it and because of the values it reflects.

There is one final introductory point: Even though each of the different theories of conflict and mediation may be valid—including the transformative theory—we do not believe that they can be combined or integrated, at either the theoretical or practical levels. In effect, each of these theories represents a coherent viewpoint that guides one's view of both the meaning of conflict and the value of intervention. It is difficult, indeed impossible, to pilot a ship without a set course with a fixed point of orientation. One who tried to do so would risk getting lost or running aground. The same is true of any human undertaking. Many different courses may be chosen, with different orientations. But choice is ultimately necessary. We believe that most mediators ultimately choose a mode of practice that stems from one—and only one—of the underlying theories of conflict discussed here. We do not argue that only one of these theories or modes of practice is valid. But we do argue that only one can be coherently practiced at a time. The support for this proposition has been set forth elsewhere and can be examined. However, to fully understand and appreciate what follows in this volume, it is best to encounter the principles and practices of the transformative approach on their own terms. Doing so will give a sense of the coherence of the approach, even for those who remain skeptical about it.

The Transformative Theory of Conflict

The transformative theory of conflict starts by offering its own answer to the foundational question of what conflict means to the people involved. According to transformative theory, what people find most significant about conflict is not that it frustrates their satisfaction of some right, interest, or pursuit, no matter how important, but that it leads and even forces them to behave toward themselves and others in ways that they find uncomfortable and even repellent. More specifically, it alienates them from their sense of their own strength and their sense of connection to others, thereby disrupting and undermining the interaction between them as human beings. This crisis of deterioration in human interaction is what parties find most affecting, significant—and disturbing—about the experience of conflict.

Negative Conflict Interaction: A Case in Point

The transformative theory starts from the premise that interactional crisis is what conflict means to people. And help in overcoming that crisis is a major part of what parties want from a mediator. According to this view, what would transformative theory expect people like Jim and Susan to say about the family business conflict mentioned earlier in this chapter, if they were asked questions such as these: "What affects you most about this conflict you're involved in? What's the impact that seems to strike you hardest?" Here is a suggestion of how they might respond (and their voices echo what we regularly hear when parties talk about their personal experience of conflict, though these two may be more articulate than many):

> **Susan:** *From the very beginning, it was very hard to just suddenly feel so frustrated and helpless. You know, Dad is at the heart of this. So to have Jim tell me that Dad never wanted me to play a major role in the business, didn't think I was capable of it, when I knew that simply wasn't true at all. To have him tell me I don't know how my own father sees me! And tell me that, anyway, I just wasn't up to the work, that I should just satisfy myself with taking care of Dad. That made me so angry . . . but it also made me doubt myself. I was outraged, but I was also shaken. I mean, should I insist on pushing myself into the business more? Did I really know my abilities? And anyway, what could I do against this kind*

of solid resistance that Jim was putting forth? That feeling of helplessness and uncertainty was really hard for me.

Plus, I have to say, it was hard to find myself so full of anger and venom for Jim, the older brother I had admired for so long. How hard he had worked to make things work in that business, to build it up and make it a support for both our families, even when things had been very tough. But you know what? I couldn't see that anymore. All I could see was him closing his mind and his heart to both Dad and me. Locking himself up in his precious office and shutting the family out, scarcely even showing up at the hospice to see Dad or take some of the load off me. And for what? Power? Ego? Just to keep himself "in charge"? I didn't like myself—I don't like myself—for seeing him this way. But I just couldn't help it. The helplessness and the hostility. That's what was so hard. And the more this has gone on, the worse that has gotten.

Jim: *What's been hardest? Well, first of all, when Susan started showing up at the office and sounding off, handing out orders to the staff, that really threw me. After all the twenty-four-hour days and seven-day weeks I've poured into this business, especially since Dad's been out of the picture! Sure, there are problems with the staff, and sometimes Sue's been a help. But only when Dad or I asked her to help. I thought we both understood that there's got to be only one authority in the place, or else everything gets screwed up. She can't just march in and start taking over. Now, all of a sudden, she's telling me I've got major problems with two of my key people. I just didn't know how to respond to that. Don't I know my own managers? Wouldn't I know if something was out of whack? I thought so, but then I wasn't absolutely sure. And then she went and shuffled both employees' responsibilities without even checking with me! I was stunned . . . confused, I didn't know what to do!*

> *The other hard part is the unbelievable bad feeling that welled up toward Susan and her family. Her husband was always needling her about how she should "take more of a hand" in the business and "be more assertive" with me. I've always believed in keeping the peace, not letting anything split up the family. I thought I was pretty good at overlooking things and refusing to be negative. But I started to see Sue, and her husband, as selfish, greedy, ingrates, and worse. At one point, I thought to myself, the real reason she's down here at the office making trouble is that she just doesn't want to be bothered with Dad anymore. For her, he's as good as gone, and she wants to make sure that when he's really gone, she and her husband are positioned to muscle their way in and push me out of what I've worked my whole life for. I felt ashamed for attributing these kinds of motives to Sue. But I couldn't help it. The worst thing about this conflict is that it's brought out the worst in me. All my insecurities. All my mean-spiritedness. All my . . . small-ness. At some point, I thought, I'd be willing to give in just to end this nastiness. But by that time, it seemed that giving in wouldn't help. The air was just poisoned.*

Insights from the fields of communication, cognitive psychology, and social psychology, among others, all support this view of what conflict means to people (Folger and Poole, 1984; Folger and others, 2001; Bush and Pope, 2002; Beck, 1999; Rubin and others, 1994; Goleman, 1995). For example, in one study that asked people to describe their experience of conflict in metaphors, almost all of the negative metaphors reflected two primary states: powerlessness and alienation from the other person (McCorkle and Mills, 1992). Similarly, trainers who ask people to draw pictures that express their experiences of conflict report similar results (Charbonneau, 2001). Still other studies, examining what people value most in processes for handling conflict, find a strong preference for processes that maximize party decision making and interparty communication, because these features counteract and remedy the negative experiences of weakness and alienation that parties find so distressing (Lind and Tyler, 1988; Bush, 1996). In general, research like this suggests that conflict as a social phenomenon is not only, or primarily, about rights, interests, or power. Although it implicates all of those things, conflict is also, and most importantly, about peoples' interaction with one another as human beings. The evidence confirms the premise of the transformative theory, as reflected in the voices of Jim and Susan: what affects and concerns people most about conflict is precisely the crisis in human interaction that it engenders.

The Picture of Negative Conflict Interaction— and the Evidence Behind It

Figure 2.1 represents this view of the phenomenon of conflict as transformative theory understands it. Conflict, along with whatever else it does, affects people's experience of both self and other. First, conflict generates, for almost anyone it touches, a sense of their own *weakness* and incapacity. That is what Jim and Susan both mention first. For each of them, conflict brings a sense of relative weakness, compared with their preconflict state, in their experience of self-efficacy: a sense of lost control over their situation, accompanied by confusion, doubt, uncertainty, and indecisiveness. This overall sense of weakening is something that occurs as a very natural human response to conflict; almost no one is immune to it, regardless of his or her initial "power position." At the very same time, conflict generates a sense of *self-absorption:* compared with before, each party becomes more focused on self alone—more protective of self and more suspicious, hostile, closed, and impervious to the perspective of the other person. In sum, no matter how strong people are, conflict propels them into relative weakness. No matter how considerate of others people are, conflict propels them into self-absorption and self-centeredness.

Support for this account of the human experience of conflict comes from work in the fields of cognitive and social psychology, and neurophysiology, among others. For example, Aaron Beck

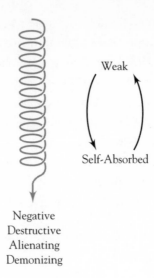

Weak

Self-Absorbed

Negative
Destructive
Alienating
Demonizing

Figure 2.1. The Negative Conflict Spiral.

(1999) describes extensive work documenting how people who are confronted with challenge or threat, as is common in conflict, experience a sense of their own powerlessness, diminishment, disregard, and victimization, leading to a sense of hostility, suspicion, and anger toward the other party. Daniel Goleman (1995), in his pathbreaking work on *emotional intelligence*, describes research showing how the neurophysiological response of the brain itself to conflict leads to the phenomena described by Beck. None of this occurs because human beings are "defective" in any way. It is rather because conflict has the power to affect our experience of ourselves and others, in virtually every context in which it occurs.

Indeed there is more to the picture, as Susan's and Jim's comments imply. As the cycling arrows in Figure 2.1 suggest, the experiences of weakness and self-absorption do not occur independently. Rather, they reinforce each other in a feedback loop: the weaker I feel myself becoming, the more hostile and closed I am toward you; and the more hostile I am toward you, the more you react to me in kind, the weaker I feel, the more hostile and closed I become, and so on. This vicious circle of *disempowerment* and *demonization* is exactly what scholars mean when they talk about *conflict escalation*. The transformative theory looks at it more as *interactional degeneration*. Before a conflict begins, whatever the context, parties are engaged in some form of decent, perhaps even loving, human interaction. Then the conflict arises, and propelled by the vicious circle of disempowerment and demonization, what started as a decent interaction spirals down into an interaction that is negative, destructive, alienating, and demonizing, on all sides.

That is what the spiraling line descending at the left of Figure 2.1 is meant to represent. The interaction in question does not end when conflict begins, but it degenerates to a point of mutual alienation and demonization. That is the conflict escalation or degeneration spiral. When nations get caught up in that spiral, the outcome is what we've seen all too often in the last decades—war, or even worse than war, if that's possible. For organizations, communities, or families who get caught up in the conflict spiral, the result is the negative transformation of a shared enterprise into an adversarial battle. The negative conflict spiral pictured by transformative theory is also documented by research studies on conflict. Beck (1999), for example, closely examines this kind of vicious cycle, describing how it ultimately can lead to mutual hatred and violence, at both the interpersonal and intergroup levels. Jeffrey Rubin and his colleagues in the field of social psychology describe the central role of fear, blame, and anger in producing conflict escalation (Rubin and others, 1994). International conflict theorists also recognize how escalation is the flip side of interactional degeneration into weakness and self-absorption (Northrup, 1989).

What Parties Want from a Mediator: Help in Reversing the Negative Spiral

Taking the transformative view of what conflict entails and means to parties, one is led to a different assumption, compared with other theories of conflict, about what parties want, need, and expect from a mediator. If what bothers parties most about conflict is the inter-actional degeneration itself, then what they will most want from an intervenor is help in reversing the downward spiral and restoring constructive interaction. Parties may not express this in so many words when they first come to a mediator. More commonly, they explain that what they want is not just agreement but "closure," to get past their bitter conflict experience and "move on" with their lives. However, it should be clear that in order to help parties achieve closure and move on, the mediator's intervention must directly address the interactional crisis itself.

The reason for this conclusion is straightforward: if the negative conflict cycle is not reversed, if parties don't regenerate some sense of their own strength and some degree of understanding of the other, it is unlikely that they can move on and be at peace with themselves, much less each other. In effect, without a change in the conflict interaction between them, parties are left disabled, even if an agreement on concrete issues is reached. The parties' confidence in their own competence to handle life's challenges remains weak-ened, and their ability to trust others remains compromised. The result can be permanent damage to the parties' ability to function, whether in the family, the workplace, the boardroom, or the com-munity (Folger and others, 2001). Recognition of this possibility and its ramifications for the workplace was the main reason for the U.S. Postal Service's decision to employ the transformative model exclusively in their REDRESS program for mediating workplace conflicts (Bush, 2001; Hallberlin, 2001). Moving *on*, in short, nec-essarily means moving *out* of the negative conflict interaction itself, and parties intuitively know this and want help in doing it.

From the perspective of transformative theory, reversing the downward spiral is the primary value that mediation offers to par-ties in conflict. That value goes beyond the dimension of helping parties reach agreement on disputed issues. With or without the achievement of agreement, the help parties most want, in all types of conflict, involves helping them end the vicious circle of disempowerment, disconnection, and demonization—alienation from both self and other. Because without ending or changing that cycle, the parties cannot move beyond the negative interaction that has entrapped them and cannot escape its crippling effects.

This is transformative theory's answer to the question posed previously: What kind of help do people want from a mediator? As transformative theory sees it, with solid support from research on conflict, parties who come to mediators are looking for—and valuing—more than an efficient way to reach agreements on specific issues. They are looking for a way to change and transform their destructive conflict interaction into a more positive one, to the greatest degree possible, so that they can move on with their lives constructively, whether together or apart. In fact, just as research supports the transformative view of conflict in general, it supports this view of what parties want from mediators. For example, extensive research on workplace mediation at the U.S. Postal Service shows that parties view interactional transformation as one of the most important reasons for using mediation (Bingham, 1997; Antes and others, 2001). The transformative model of mediation is intended to provide this benefit.

The Theory of Mediation as Conflict Transformation

Clarifying the transformative theory of mediation, and especially its view of the mediator's role, requires further discussion of the model of conflict interaction introduced in the previous section. However, to anticipate the endpoint of that discussion, transformative mediation can best be understood as a process of *conflict transformation*—that is, changing the quality of conflict interaction. In the transformative mediation process, parties can recapture their sense of competence and connection, reverse the negative conflict cycle, reestablish a constructive (or at least neutral) interaction, and move forward on a positive footing, with the mediator's help.

Party Capacity for Conflict Transformation: Human Nature and Capacity

To explain this view of mediation, we first return to the concept of interactional degeneration in conflict. How does mediation help parties in conflict reverse the negative conflict spiral? Out of what resource is that kind of transformation generated, and what is the mediator's role in doing so? The first part of the theoretical answer to this question points not to the mediator at all, but to the parties themselves. The critical resource in conflict transformation is the parties' own basic humanity—their essential strength, decency, and compassion, as human beings. As discussed earlier, the transformative theory of conflict recognizes that conflict tends to escalate as interaction degenerates, because of the susceptibility we have as human beings to experience weakness and self-absorption in the face of sudden challenge.

However, the theory also posits, based on what many call a *relational theory* of human nature, that human beings have inherent capacities for *strength* (agency or autonomy) and *responsiveness* (connection or understanding) and an inherent *social* or *moral impulse* that activates these capacities when people are challenged by negative conflict, working to counteract the tendencies to weakness and self-absorption (Della Noce, 1999). The transformative theory asserts that when these capacities are activated, the conflict spiral can reverse and interaction can regenerate, even without the presence of a mediator as intervenor. In fact, the same research that documents the negative conflict cycle also documents the power of the human capacities for strength and understanding to operate in the face of challenge and conflict, and ultimately to transform conflict interaction (Beck, 1999; Goleman, 1995; Kohn, 1990).

Figure 2.2 expands the picture presented earlier and illustrates this positive potential of conflict interaction. It is true, as we have seen with hundreds of parties in all of the different contexts that we've worked in, that people in conflict tend to find themselves falling into the negative cycle of weakness and self-absorption. But it is equally true that people do not necessarily remain caught in that cycle. Conflict is not static. It is an emergent, dynamic phenomenon, in which parties can—and do—move and shift in remarkable ways, even when no third party is involved. They move out of weakness, becoming calmer, clearer, more confident, more articulate, and more decisive—in general, *shifting from weakness to strength*. They move away from self-absorption, becoming more attentive, open, trusting, and understanding of the other party—in general, *shifting from self-centeredness to responsiveness* to other. Just as studies document conflict's negative impacts and the downward conflict spiral, they also document the dynamics of these positive shifts and the upward, regenerative spiral they engender (Beck, 1999).

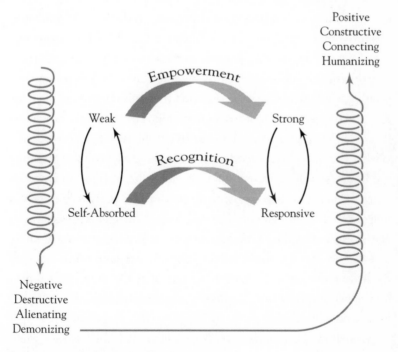

Figure 2.2. Changing Conflict Interaction.

The arrows moving from left to right in Figure 2.2 represent these shifts: the movements parties make from weakness to strength and from self-absorption to understanding of one another. In transformative theory, these dynamic shifts are called *empowerment* and *recognition* (Bush, 1989; Bush, 1989–1990). Moreover, as the figure suggests, there is also a reinforcing feedback effect on this side of the picture. The stronger I become, the more open I am to you. The more open I am to you, the stronger you feel, the more open you become to me, and the stronger I feel. Indeed the more open I become to you, the stronger I feel in myself, simply because I'm more open; that is, openness not only requires but creates a sense of strength, of magnanimity. So there is also a circling between strength and responsiveness once they begin to emerge. But this is not a vicious circle, it is a "virtuous circle"—a virtuous circle of conflict transformation.

Why conflict transformation? Because as the parties make empowerment and recognition shifts, and as those shifts gradually reinforce in a virtuous circle, the interaction as a whole begins to transform and regenerate. It changes back from a negative, destructive, alienating, and demonizing interaction to one that becomes positive, constructive, connecting, and humanizing, even while conflict and disagreement are still continuing. This reversal of the conflict cycle from negative and destructive to positive and constructive is what the spiral line ascending at the right of Figure 2.2 represents.

The keys to this transformation of conflict interaction are the empowerment and recognition shifts that the parties themselves make. No matter how small and seemingly insignificant, as these shifts continue and accumulate, they can transform the entire interaction. Is it hard for those shifts to occur? It most certainly is, especially for parties who have been overcome by the sense of weakness and self-absorption that conflict first brings. It's hard, but it's eminently possible.

Consider the case reported on National Public Radio some weeks after the September 11 tragedy in 2001, during a program of listener comments about how their lives had changed since the events of that day. One woman recounted how she'd been involved in an auto accident in Colorado. Her car was hit from behind by another driver—who didn't have any insurance. She said that if the accident had happened before September 11, she "would have gone after the man, taken legal action," and then continued:

> Much to my personal amazement . . . I found myself thinking instead about this middle-aged man. Obviously in some financial need, old car, had to let his insurance lapse. I followed the probable impact my signatures [on the legal complaint] would have on his life. He becomes a frequent recipient of steady threatening phone calls, probably winding up in court and getting his wages garnished.
>
> It didn't take me long to believe that if I made the expedient choice, I would become a terrorist. I kid you not. Americans are already stressed out, in need and in fear. Was I going to dump another load of terror, fear of the future, stress, and financial hardship on this guy? Was I really? I just couldn't do it.

The woman reported that the man promised to pay for the damage to her car, if he could do it in small increments over several weeks, and she said that this was what he'd been doing. Then she concluded:

> Maybe we both just got lucky. I suspect we're both surprised at who each other turned out to be. But I bet we're not the only Americans amazed at what we're finding within others and within ourselves these days [National Public Radio, Nov. 9, 2001].

The empowerment and recognition shifts are clearly visible in this woman's brief story, and the transformative impact is clear. As she says, it is amazing; yet this kind of conflict transformation almost certainly occurs between parties to conflict on a regular basis, when the capacities for strength and connection "kick in" and reverse the negative conflict spiral. It's important to note that, as illustrated by this case of two strangers involved in a car accident, the potential and value of conflict transformation is by no means limited to cases where the parties have some kind of preexisting and ongoing relationship. The reason is simple, as the case also illustrates: the negative conflict cycle is almost always a part of the parties' human experience of any conflict and almost always something that they want to change. The transformative model of mediation simply supports and builds on the parties' inherent human capacities for doing so, and the positive potential they hold for conflict transformation, no matter what type of case is involved.

A resident in an apartment building had slipped on icy stairs and broken his ankle during a tough spell of Michigan's winter weather. Several tenants in the building, including the one who suffered the injury, had previously notified the landlord about a crack in the gutter that ran directly above the staircase leading into the apartment. Every time the temperature hovered just above freezing, the gutter would leak. The water in the gutter would drip onto the stairs and then freeze overnight as the temperature dropped, making it treacherous for the tenants who left the building early in the morning. The landlord had never responded to any of the requests to fix this dangerous situation. Because the tenant thought the landlord was negligent and because he suffered through ankle surgery and eight weeks in a cast, he sued the landlord for lost wages and personal suffering.

As the case approached a hearing, depositions were taken from both sides. When the tenant was being deposed, the landlord's attorney asked at one point to look at the injury. The tenant's ankle had been, at this point, out of the cast for several weeks. When the attorney for the landlord looked at the swollen and black-and-blue ankle, he was somewhat startled and without thinking blurted out, "Is that swelling ever going to go down?" On hearing himself, the attorney immediately changed his startled expression, looked away from the ankle, and asked a different question. It seemed that the attorney wanted to acknowledge the suffering that the tenant experienced, but his formal role would not allow it. Although the legal process itself deters the transformation of the conflict through empowerment and recognition, the human impulse to respond this way often shines through even in the most adversarial forums of conflict.

Party Motivation for Conflict Transformation: The Relational View of Human Nature

Before going further, it is important to clarify some key premises that are implicit in the transformative theory's concept of conflict transformation. Thus far, we have emphasized that substantial evidence supports both the view that what people dislike most about conflict are its impacts of disempowerment and disconnection, as well as the view that people have the capacities to reverse the cycle that produces them. However, even if this evidence is accepted, two important questions remain: *Why* are people so deeply affected and touched by these impacts? And why, as a result, do they care so much about reversing the negative conflict spiral? Answering these "why" questions means going beyond the realm of practice and research, to the realm of belief or ideology.

Thinkers in different fields offer insights that shed light on these why questions—and all of their insights are grounded in the idea that there is a basic human nature or identity, common to all people, the core of which is a dual sense of both individual autonomy and social connection (Della Noce, 1999). Put differently, as a matter of basic human consciousness, every person senses that he or she is a separate, autonomous agent, authoring his or her own life, and at the same time senses that he or she is an inherently social being, connected to other people in an essential and not just instrumental fashion. Moreover, in this relational view, awareness of both individual agency and social connection is not just a peripheral characteristic—it is the very essence of human consciousness, the core of our identity as human beings. Each part of this duality—individuality and connectedness—is equally important to our fundamental sense of human identity, and we struggle constantly to give each its place and balance or "relate" them—hence the term *relational*—in all of our affairs.

This relational view of human nature is expressed in many fields today, in different terms. In social psychology, the study of human happiness and well-being finds that they are the results of having an integrated, relational sense of autonomy and social connection, more than any other factor (Bettencourt and Sheldon, 2001; Lind and Tyler, 1988). In political science, sociology, and law, communitarian theory asserts the importance of fostering both individual freedom and social responsibility, linking this to a belief in the relational nature of human identity (Sandel, 1982; Etzioni, 1996; Glendon, 1991). In moral philosophy, postmodern and feminist thinkers reject views of moral consciousness as stemming from *either* autonomy or connection, adopting instead a dialogic conception in which the fully developed *moral sense* attends equally to both, to the claims of self and other in dialogic relation, however difficult this may be (Gilligan, 1982, 1988; Handler, 1988; Koehn, 1998). The overall *relational worldview* implied by these different disciplinary views is discussed in Chapter Seven. The references here are offered as indicators that the relational view of human identity finds broad support today, in many fields.

We return to the previously asked questions: Why are people so affected and disturbed by the disempowerment and disconnection of the negative conflict cycle, and why does reversing that cycle matter to them so much? The answers flow from the relational conception of human identity as just summarized. If a person's core sense of identity is linked to a sense of both autonomy and connection, and if both of those are compromised at the very same time, it makes perfect sense that this will be a profoundly disturbing experience. In effect, the core sense of identity that undergirds the person's life—strong self connected to other—is thrown into question by conflict. This is why the weakness and alienation produced in negative conflict is so repellent to parties in conflict—it violates their very identity, their sense of who they are as human beings. To remain in such a condition is as painful to people as being imprisoned and forced to live in inhuman conditions.

This also explains why people who find themselves in negative conflict interaction look for ways to change and reverse the interactional degeneration, with or without a third party's assistance: because to remain in that negative interaction is to remain cut off from their basic human identity. This is the motivation for conflict transformation, although in a negative sense—people want to get out of the essentially inhuman experience of negative conflict interaction. However, the motivation for changing conflict action can also be seen from the positive angle. That is, we can assume that people retain some sense of their core humanity, even when embroiled in negative conflict interaction. Therefore the impulse to reassert their humanity, in terms of both strength of self and connection to other, can also be seen as the motivator for their efforts to change the conflict interaction. This was referred to in Chapter One as the social or moral connection inherent in human nature. Whichever adjective is used, the meaning is the same: it is the impulse to reassert one's core human identity, in a situation where it has been compromised.

Some years ago, a citizen called our Center and asked
whether we could help her talk to her neighbor. We told her
we would be glad to set up a mediation. She replied that no,
she didn't want to mediate, she wanted to talk directly to her
neighbor. It seems that she had been in a mediation before
and was not allowed to talk directly to the other party. More
recently, a party wrote, after a mediation at our Center, "I'm
proud to have let everything off my chest. . . . You don't have
to talk through lawyers. You talk for yourself" [Wahlrab, 2004].

The point of this discussion was to explain clearly why it makes
sense to say that parties' motivation to change negative conflict
interaction is both real and powerful. This view of party *motivation*
is a fundamental element of the transformative theory. An equally
fundamental element of the theory is the view that parties have the
capacity to change negative interaction, as argued above. Without
both of these elements, the transformative theory of mediation
would make little sense: if parties don't have the desire or motivation to change conflict interaction, it would be pointless to offer
them the means to do so; and even if they do have that desire, it
would be pointless to proceed if they did not also have the capacity to do so. The most important premises of the transformative theory are that parties have both the desire and the capacity for conflict
transformation. Helping to support this desire and capacity is the
"value-added" that the mediator brings to the table.

The Role of the Mediator in Conflict Transformation:
A Case in Point

For a more concrete sense of what the mediator's help can mean
to parties in conflict, consider what Susan and Jim might say about
the impact of participating in a mediation of their family business
conflict—with a transformative mediator:

Susan: It's odd to say this, but I have to say that in a way the mediation helped me start to take myself back. I mean, come back to the way I know I am. Even though I was still fighting with Jim about Dad and the business. For one thing, the mediator's invitations to me to talk, and her attentiveness, created a space for me to do just that—talk it out. Even if I wasn't always making sense or wasn't very clear, she'd listen, and she would repeat and go over what I said. It was like she was holding up a mirror, an audiovisual mirror, to let myself see and hear what I was saying. It was almost like talking with myself. And doing that helped me actually listen to my own thoughts, and as I did that I started to realize what I was trying to say and understand it better for myself. Then I could say it more clearly. So I began to get clearer, calmer, less desperate, and less frustrated. I mean, overall I'd say I began to get stronger right there in that room during the conversation. That was terrific!

When that happened, it began to be a different situation, because then I was experiencing the whole thing differently. More calmly. More confidently. So I could see the situation differently in some ways. And I could even listen differently to Jim. I could see him again without that cloud of anger and ill will. That in itself—that I could see him that way again— was really a tremendous relief, and it made an enormous difference in our ability to keep talking to each other. To go back to talking to each other about our disagreements in a constructive way.

Jim: As I said before, the really bitter part of the conflict was that it brought out the worst in me. My doubts in my judgment and understanding. Even worse, my need and my willingness to blame and demonize Susan, the very person I have to go on working and living with, to keep Dad's legacy to us intact. You know, you can't divorce your own sister. In the mediation, I don't know how, but I began to reconnect with, *how should I say it, the angels of my better nature. It's not just that I became more confident and clear about what I was thinking and saying. I did, but I also managed to take off those dark glasses. I began to see Susan again for who she really is (even if I totally disagree with her), a great sis and a loving daughter who is totally devoted to Dad and who cares about the business he built for us.*

I also realized, like I said, that Susan and I are connected in this life, whatever happens. But you can't stay connected to someone you don't trust and you don't respect—and you hate. It was so easy to lose that trust. It was happening so fast, and I couldn't seem to do anything about it. The mediation allowed me to realize that's what was happening and to choose not to let it happen, not to let it continue. Whether or not we agreed about what was the best course for the business, or for Dad. Once we turned that corner back to being ourselves, me and Susan, and being in control of ourselves, I knew that we'd eventually figure out how to do the right thing, whatever it was.

In sum, as Jim and Susan describe it, the nature of the mediation process in their case was one of interactional change (or transformation). That is, both of them changed the way they experienced and interacted with both self and other, in the midst of their continuing conflict. To put it differently, mediation supported them in a process of changing the quality of their conflict interaction and—most important—in reversing its negative and destructive spiral.

Mediators provide important help and support for the small but critical shifts by each party, from weakness to strength and from self-absorption to understanding. As suggested in Jim and Susan's comments, and as illustrated in depth in the case study in Chapters Four and Five, they do this by using their skills both to highlight the opportunities for shifts that surface in the parties' own conversation and to support the parties' efforts to utilize them. Figure 2.2 describes the potential effects of the mediation process on conflict interaction and the transformation and regeneration of the human interaction between the parties, even as the conflict continues to unfold. The figure as a whole reflects Susan's and Jim's descriptions of their experience of both the original spiral into destructive conflict and the regeneration of positive interaction through the mediation process.

In this picture, the mediator stands, as it were, at the bottom of the figure, offering specific forms of support that help the parties make empowerment and recognition shifts, when and as they choose, and thereby change the quality of their conflict interaction. This is perhaps the central claim of the transformative theory—that mediators' interventions can help parties transform their conflict interaction. And like the other elements of the theory, there is research to support it (Antes, Folger, and Della Noce, 2001; Moen and others, 2001).

Mediation as Conflict Transformation: Definitions and Guiding Principles

The previous discussion brings us to the definition of mediation itself, and the mediator's role, in the transformative model. Both of these definitions differ markedly from the normal definitions found in training materials and practice literature—in which mediation is usually defined as a process in which a neutral third party helps the parties to reach a mutually acceptable resolution of some or all of the issues in dispute, and the mediator's role is defined as establishing ground rules, defining issues, establishing an agenda, generating options, and ultimately persuading the parties to accept terms of agreement (Stulberg, 1981; Alfini and others, 2001; Moore, 2003; Folberg and Taylor, 1984).

By contrast, in the transformative model

• Mediation is defined as a process in which a third party works with parties in conflict to help them change the quality of their conflict interaction from negative and destructive to positive and constructive, as they explore and discuss issues and possibilities for resolution.

- The mediator's role is to help the parties make positive interactional shifts (empowerment and recognition shifts) by supporting the exercise of their capacities for strength and responsiveness, through their deliberation, decision making, communication, perspective taking, and other party activities.

- The mediator's primary goals are (1) to support empowerment shifts, by supporting—but never supplanting—each party's deliberation and decision making, at every point in the session where choices arise (regarding either process or outcome) and (2) to support recognition shifts, by encouraging and supporting—but never forcing—each party's freely chosen efforts to achieve new understandings of the other's perspective.

Specific practices tied to these definitions and goals are discussed in connection with the case study in Chapters Four and Five. How-

---

Separating content and process is, in practice, impossible. The distinction between content and process is not at all like the relationship between setting the table and preparing the food. It is more like the relationship between how food is prepared and the way it ultimately tastes. Choices about frying, baking or micro-waving have a direct impact on the texture and taste of the food. Similarly, process and content are intertwined—the choices made about process have a direct and inevitable influence on the way conflict unfolds. . . . The decisions a mediator might make about process at the beginning of a session have direct influence over how the conflict is likely to unfold at that moment and throughout the entire session [Folger, 2001, p. 57].

---

ever, it is important to introduce here a few important principles that should guide the mediator in supporting empowerment and recognition shifts—all of which grow out of a proper understanding of the dynamics through which these shifts occur.

First, these are shifts that the parties, and the parties alone, can make. No mediator can "get" parties to shift out of weakness or self-absorption, nor should he try. Parties gain strength and openness by making decisions by and for themselves, in their own way and at their own pace. A mediator who tries to "get" shifts to happen actually impedes this process by removing control of the interaction from the parties' hands. In other words, this mediator violates the defined goal of supporting empowerment by *supplanting* party decision making.

Second, the mediator should expect that parties do not normally begin to shift out of self-absorption until they have first shifted out of weakness and gained greater strength in some degree. Simply put, people are unlikely to extend themselves to others when they are still feeling vulnerable and unstable. Empowerment shifts are therefore usually the first to occur, as the desire and capacity for strength reasserts itself, and supporting them is where the mediator's help is likely to be needed first. When such shifts do occur, however, they are often followed quickly by recognition shifts, as the desire and capacity for connection reasserts itself. Thus gains in strength often lead directly and quickly to gains in responsiveness. This dynamic is clearly visible in both examples of conflict transformation discussed in this chapter—Jim and Susan's family business case and the highway accident story. In each, interactional change begins with a party calming down, getting clear, and thus regaining strength; with this renewed strength, the party then begins to open up to a different view of the other. This pattern is very common in the dynamic that unfolds in a transformative mediation session.

Add this into our conceptual picture of conflict transformation: in the graphic representation of conflict change in Figure 2.2, one might draw a third arrow moving diagonally back from "strength" to "self-absorption," so that together with the "empowerment" and "recognition" arrows, it forms a "Z" across the figure. The diagonal represents the dynamic of the empowerment shift prompting a recognition shift, which is the full meaning of the virtuous circle discussed earlier.

Third, even though there is likely to be a dynamic interplay of empowerment and recognition, the move toward conflict transformation is unlikely to be smooth and even. Rather, empowerment and recognition shifts are often followed by retreats back into weakness and self-absorption, as the interaction reaches new or deeper levels; and the retreats are then followed by new shifts into strength and openness, and so on. In pursuing the goal of supporting shifts, the mediator has to be prepared for this back and forth, in order to follow along and be ready to provide support for new shifts as the opportunities for them arise. Ultimately, the cycling shifts and retreats tend to move forward, and the overall interaction changes in quality from negative to positive—but great patience is required of the mediator in *allowing* that movement rather than trying to "move" the parties forward.

Fourth, even though the mediator's job is to support empowerment and recognition shifts, the transformative model does not ignore the significance of resolving specific issues. Rather, it assumes that if mediators do the job just described, the parties themselves will very likely make positive changes in their interaction and find acceptable terms of resolution for themselves where such terms genuinely exist. Consider the strong logic of this claim: if empowerment and recognition shifts occur, and as a result the parties are interacting with clarity and confidence in themselves (strength) and with openness and understanding toward each other (responsiveness), the likelihood is very high that they will succeed in finding and agreeing on solutions to specific problems, without the need for the mediator to do that for them. More important, they will have reversed the negative conflict spiral and will have begun to reestablish a positive mode of interaction that allows them to move forward on a different footing, both while and after specific issues are resolved and even if they cannot be resolved. Research on transformative mediation has shown that it can and does produce both of these impacts—resolution of specific issues and, even more important, interactional change—just as the theory predicts (Antes, Folger, and Della Noce, 2001; Intrater and Gann, 2001; Bingham and Nabatchi, 2001; Bingham, 2003).

A study of mediation cases that were conducted at the U.S. Postal Service REDRESS program documented the changes that can occur when conflict is transformed through mediation:

The manner in which participants express themselves changes from strong emotion to calm, from defensiveness to openness, and from speaking about or at the other party to interacting with the party.

Participants interact more confidently and competently as the mediation progresses.

Interactions between participants that are negative and difficult often lead to discussions that are positive and productive.

Participants establish or reestablish personal connections with one another.

Participants gain new understandings during the mediation about the other party and their actions.

Participants gain new understandings during the mediation about the situation.

> Participants gain new understandings during the mediation about themselves and their own actions.
>
> Discussion of a specific incident often leads participants to talk about larger issues that are significant to their relationship and the workplace [Antes, Folger, and Della Noce, 2001].

Finally, it is important to point out that to focus on and successfully pursue the goal of supporting interactional shifts, two fundamental things are required of the mediator (apart from various specific skills to be discussed in Chapters Four and Five). The first requirement is that the mediator never lose sight of the overall point of his or her mission: to help the parties transform their conflict interaction from destructive and demonizing to positive and humanizing. Maintaining this clear perspective is not all that easy in a professional culture that generally views attainment of agreement or settlement as all important. One thing that can help is to have a firm mental anchor that keeps the mediator on course, and our suggestion is that the picture of conflict transformation presented in Figure 2.2 can be one such anchor. Holding that picture in mind can be a great help in keeping on task.

The other requirement is a deep acceptance of the premises about human motivation and capacity that constitute the ultimate foundation of the transformative theory. It will be very difficult for a mediator to stop trying to get the parties to make shifts, unless the mediator is firmly convinced that doing so is not only impossible but *unnecessary*—because the parties have both the desire and the capacity to make those shifts for themselves. Indeed certain hallmarks of transformative practice show how a transformative mediator's approach reflects the premises about human nature that underlie the model, including these: leaving responsibility for outcomes with the parties, refusing to be judgmental about the parties' views and decisions, and taking an optimistic view of the parties' competence and motives (Folger and Bush, 1996).

Holding in mind clearly both the picture of the conflict transformation mission and the premises about human nature that underlie it, the mediator can steer clear of a few serious missteps that are easy to make. First, she is reminded that empowerment is independent of any particular outcome of the mediation. If a party has used the session to collect herself, examine options, deliberate, and decide on a course of action, significant empowerment shifts have occurred, regardless of the outcome. Whether the outcome is a settlement that the mediator finds fair and optimal or unfair or even stupid, or a decision not to settle at all, the goal of supporting empowerment shifts has been achieved. And as a result, the party has gained increased strength of self from the process of self-awareness and self-determination enacted in the mediation session.

So even if a mediator is tempted to think, "Perhaps steering the party to what I know is a better outcome is really more empowering," the clear understanding of empowerment as a shift from weakness to strength reminds the mediator that even a "poor outcome" produced by the party's own process of reflection and choice strengthens the self more than a "good outcome" induced by the mediator's directiveness or imposition. That is, such "good outcomes" do not engender strength of self, unless accompanied by the process of empowerment. Solving problems *for* parties is not transformative mediation, because it fails to support—and probably undermines—genuine party empowerment. It is the concrete steps toward strengthening the self within the session that constitute empowerment, not the nature of the outcome or solution.

In addition, we put "good outcome" in quotation marks in the foregoing discussion, because even beyond the empowerment effects of the process, the quality of an outcome must itself be measured not only by its material terms but also by the process through which it was reached. Outcomes that are reached as a result of party shifts toward greater clarity, confidence, openness, and understanding are

likely to have more meaning and significance for parties than outcomes generated by mediator directiveness, however well-meant.
Early research on mediation's impacts supported this conclusion
(McEwen and Maiman, 1984), and there is no reason to suspect that
this is not still the case—a point discussed further in Chapter Six.

Similarly, clarity about mission, premises, and goals can help avoid
missteps in supporting recognition. As discussed earlier, recognition
is not recognition at all unless it is freely given. It is the *decision* of the
party to expand his focus from self alone to include the other that
constitutes the recognition shift. If that decision is itself the result of
pressure, cajoling, or moralizing, it represents nothing but self-preser-
vation. Forced recognition, in short, is a contradiction in terms.
When parties have made only slight recognition shifts, the mediator
may be tempted to push for more, especially if he thinks he can get
the party to see things differently. Yet when force is applied, recognition vanishes altogether. The key is for the mediator to understand
that the goal of supporting recognition shifts is fulfilled through whatever degree of recognition the parties are genuinely willing to give.

This actually points back to the critical point made earlier about
the interplay between the two kinds of movement: recognition
shifts are almost always based on empowerment shifts. Until the
point is reached where parties are consciously choosing their steps,
recognition is unlikely to occur or to be genuine or meaningful.

Clarifications

Some of the terms central to this chapter's discussion of the transformative framework deserve additional clarification so that the
framework is understood fully and accurately.

Conflict Transformation and Moral Connection

At various points in this chapter and in Chapter One, we have
made reference to a *moral vision* of society, the human *moral sense*,
and the sense of *moral connection*, in explaining the value of con-

flict transformation. In other places we have similarly used the terms *moral growth* and *moral development* (Bush, 1989–1990; Folger and Bush, 1994). Our use of this terminology might be taken by some readers as suggesting that the mediator's role in the transformative model is to improve the parties' moral character. However, it should be clear from the overall description of the theory in this chapter that this is not at all the case. We have written elsewhere about this point, clarifying the difference between mediation's potential effects and the principles by which it should be conducted:

> Some take the view that the transformative theory of mediation . . . encourages mediators or other intervenors to actively engage in efforts to "transform people's character." This misinterpretation confuses and conflates the transformative theory's claims about mediation's potential *effects* with the theory's suggestions about how the mediation process can and should be *conducted*. . . . Furthering party empowerment is one of the very cornerstones of this approach to practice. If third parties were to consciously try to "transform" disputants, or pursue any "agenda" beyond the parties' own wishes, this would directly negate the goal of empowerment. Attempting to change or transform the parties would be as directive as attempting to construct settlements for them. Clearly, this cannot be (and is not) what the transformative theory suggests for practice. . . . The distinction is between the possible effects of mediation and the concrete goals and processes of a transformative approach to practice. As pointed out earlier in this article, if mediators follow an approach that concentrates on the specific *goals and processes* of *empowerment and recognition*, the experience of the mediation process itself offers the *possibility* of transformative *effects*. The focus of practice is on establishing and sustaining a context which allows parties to

make clear and deliberate choices and to give consideration to other disputants' perspectives if they decide to do so. The third party is not there to *insist* on transformation, but to *assist* in identifying opportunities for empowerment and recognition, and to help the parties respond to those opportunities *as they wish* [Folger and Bush, 1996, p. 277].

Beyond the distinction between the goals of the mediator and the effects of the mediation process, one further clarification may be helpful. Any use of the term *moral* might be read by some as if it referred to certain religious or spiritual qualities that mediators were supposed to inculcate in the parties. This is the inevitable result of the use of a highly charged word in a culture not accustomed to its usage in practical, professional contexts. However, we hope that we have been clear in assigning a very specific meaning to this term, which is entirely consistent with the use of the term by relational thinkers like those referred to in the previous discussion of changing conflict interaction.

Many theorists use terms like *moral development* or *moral discourse* to denote a particular kind of response to the tendencies in human interaction, especially in conflict, toward weakness and self-absorption (Gilligan, 1982; Burns, 2001; MacIntyre, 1981; Sandel, 1982; Etzioni, 1996). In the work of these thinkers, overcoming those tendencies by asserting the capacities for strength and connection is the very essence of what is meant by moral connection or moral discourse (which they often associate with conflict). It is, of course, also what is meant here when discussing changing conflict interaction or conflict transformation, so that for us these terms are different ways of expressing the very same phenomenon. The use of the word moral in this context connotes the balancing of the claims of self and other and the relation of the two—nothing more, nothing less.

Empowerment and Recognition:
What the Terms Do and Do Not Mean

Clarification is also called for regarding the key terms empowerment and recognition, although some of this was also spelled out in the first edition. Mediator goals such as finding good solutions or ensuring fairness, even if they sometimes prove elusive to define and measure in practice, are familiar enough that people can discuss them without worrying that they will be totally misunderstood. Not so for empowerment and recognition. Even though they are based on ideas that have been around for a very long time in the mediation field, the ideas themselves have rarely been presented in succinct and precise form to define concrete objectives for mediation. As a result, it is important to distinguish our use of the concepts and terms empowerment and recognition from other usage with which they might be confused.

Before clarifying what empowerment and recognition do not mean, it is important to add here one very essential clarification of what they *do* mean. As should be clear from the earlier explanation of conflict transformation (and Figure 2.2), empowerment and recognition are not end states or products of the conflict transformation process. They are *dynamic shifts* from one mode of experiencing self or other to a different mode. In fact, we make it a point today to always use the words empowerment and recognition as adjectives attached to the word *shift*. In an *empowerment shift*, the party moves from weakness to greater strength. In a *recognition shift*, the party moves from self-absorption to greater understanding of other. This clarification is important because, as in any process, a mediator wants and needs to know if she is succeeding. Success in transformative mediation is measured by the *delta factor*, the occurrence of shifts and changes in the parties' experience of self and other and, as a result, in the quality of their interaction. In fact, the ability to notice such shifts as they occur is an important skill for a transformative mediator, because it gives her the confidence that comes from seeing the effects of her interventions. Furthermore research methods are being developed and tested to document the effectiveness of transformative mediation in producing interactional shifts, rather than simply surveying for party satisfaction levels.

Beyond this initial clarification, it is important to distinguish our usage of the primary terms, empowerment and recognition, from other usage. *Empowerment* is a term used currently to mean so many different things that it is important to clarify what we do *not* mean by it. As we are using the term, supporting empowerment does not mean "power balancing" or redistribution of power within the medi-ation process itself in order to protect weaker parties. In fact, sup-porting party empowerment is always practiced with both parties. Of course, empowerment shifts by both parties may indeed change the balance of power, if one party starts off with greater self-confi-dence and self-determinative ability. That, however, is an effect of supporting empowerment and not a conscious mediator objective.

Similarly, supporting party empowerment does not mean con-trolling or influencing the mediation process so as to produce outcomes that redistribute resources or power outside the process from stronger to weaker parties. It does not mean using the media-tion process—and the substantial powers of the mediator to influ-ence how problems are defined and how solutions are chosen—to give more power to those who are members of defined weaker groups. Even though some mediators may in practice see this as their role, we do not endorse it, and it is not what we mean by sup-porting empowerment.

Finally, supporting empowerment does not mean adding to the strength of either party by becoming an advocate, adviser, or coun-selor. We acknowledge that the distinction between supporting empowerment and advice giving or advocacy is sometimes difficult to draw in practice (Bernard, Folger, Weingarten, and Zumeta, 1984; Folger and Bernard, 1985; Bush, 1992). Still, supporting empowerment does not require—or involve at all—the mediator's taking sides, expressing judgments, or being directive, all of which are central aspects of advice giving and advocacy. In fact, supporting party empowerment in a transformative approach to practice requires avoiding all of these behaviors. Therefore, even if there are questions at the borders, the general concept of empowerment remains quite distinct from advice giving and advocacy.

Recognition, unlike empowerment, is not a term in wide use, so confusion over language is less likely here. However, a number of concepts common to discussions of mediation and dispute resolution may be confused with recognition in the transformative sense. Most important, a party who makes a recognition shift gives recognition *to* the other, rather than getting it *from* the other. Beyond this, several other distinctions are important.

Recognition, first of all, does not mean reconciliation. Of course, a recognition shift may sometimes go so far as to bring about reconciliation. But this need not happen for the recognition shift to be significant. This distinction is very important, because if reconciliation is the goal, it is very easy to argue that it is simply unattainable in all but a tiny fraction of cases. Although that may be true, it is certainly not true for the movement of recognition. A recognition shift is a much more modest, practical, and attainable event. In effect, an increase in understanding or openness to the other party, in any degree, constitutes a recognition shift.

At the other extreme, recognition does not mean the mere realization of one's enlightened self-interest, the experience of interdependence in instrumental terms. When one party sees how she can get more of what she needs by giving the other some of what he needs, this is a fundamentally self-referential awareness and experience. In it, the consideration of the other stems essentially from concern with oneself. The hallmark of a recognition shift is *letting go*—however briefly or partially—of one's focus on self and becoming interested in the perspective of the other party as such, concerned about the situation of the other as a fellow human being, not as an instrument for fulfilling one's own needs.

This discussion brings up a broader point. The phenomena of empowerment and recognition are considered important today in many fields outside mediation. Management experts in both the private and public sectors stress participatory measures that empower individual employees and citizens as the key to effective enterprises (Osborne and Gaebler, 1992; Rosen and Berger, 1992). Educators see students' achievement of confidence and self-reliance, not just acquisition of knowledge or skills, as a key objective of the teaching process (Bouman, 1991). Political theorists observe that in order for democratic institutions to be healthy, individual citizens must develop the power to define and address their own needs (Lappé and DuBois, 1994). Public health professionals document the importance in treating serious illness of fostering empathetic recognition through patient support groups (Spiegel, 1993). Social theorists argue that connection and empathy in everyday life are crucial in maintaining healthy social institutions (Putnam, 2000; Kohn, 1990; Bellah and others, 1991; Scheff, 1990). In sum, there is widespread acknowledgment across many fields that empowerment and recognition shifts are concrete and important events. This acknowledgment reinforces our suggestion that they deserve greater attention in the mediation process, where there are such rich opportunities to support them.

The Value of Conflict Transformation: Private and Public

A final and important clarification concerns the value or benefits associated with conflict transformation. Various views of the benefits of mediation are found in the literature, and discussion of private and public benefits of the process generally mixes the two together, not differentiating between them. Questions have been raised about why disputing parties themselves—as opposed to public policymakers—would find this approach to mediation useful. We hope that most of those questions have been implicitly answered by the discussion of this chapter, and the value of conflict transformation was also discussed at the end of Chapter One. It is nevertheless useful here to "unpack" the transformative view of mediation's benefits, separating private from public as clearly as possible.

Disputing parties themselves want and value conflict transformation and regard it as a benefit, because they want to escape the negative personal impacts of destructive conflict interaction, and they want to reestablish the positive experience of competence and connection that is found in constructive conflict interaction. Transformative theory posits that the greatest benefit mediation offers to parties in conflict is that it helps them conduct conflict itself in a different way. It helps people find and take the small but meaningful opportunities for empowerment and recognition shifts that arise. It supports the virtuous circle of personal empowerment and interpersonal recognition that de-escalates and "de-embitters" conflict, so that even if conflict continues, it is no longer dehumanizing and demonizing. It helps turn conflict interaction away from alienation, from both self and other, toward a renewed connection to both, restoring strength of self and understanding of other, even while conflict continues. Transformative mediation thus helps disputing parties move on with their lives, with the capacity for living those lives restored—including a sense of their own competence as well as confidence in their ability to connect to others.

These claims all relate to private benefits that according to transformative theory are sought and valued by disputing parties themselves. In fact, there are two kinds of private benefit involved—short term and long term. The short-term benefits relate to the specific situation that brought the parties to mediation. In that situation, conflict transformation allows the parties to reestablish their sense of self-confidence and common humanity, thereby allowing the parties to reach closure on the matter and move forward, with or without specific issues having been resolved in mediation. At the same time, when conflict transformation occurs—because empowerment and recognition shifts were made during mediation—there may also be long-term benefits to the parties. These are what some have called *upstream effects* of conflict transformation: impacts of the mediation experience that carry over into future situations (Hallberlin, 2001). For example, from having made empowerment shifts from confusion to clarity in mediation, parties may carry forward an increased confidence in their ability to clarify and express their views in future situations. Or having made recognition shifts from suspicion to greater openness, parties may be more willing and able, in other situations, to withhold judgment and give others the benefit of the doubt. The result is that they are more likely to avoid the negative conflict spiral in the future or to have greater ability to reverse it on their own—important long-term benefits of mediation for the parties themselves. In the REDRESS Mediation Program at the U.S. Postal Service, the likelihood of such upstream benefits for both managers and employees was one significant reason for the decision to use the transformative model, and research is under way to study these effects (Bingham, 2003).

In addition to these benefits to the parties themselves, conflict transformation has important public benefits, effects that advance the goals of society generally. Identifying these distinct public benefits is especially important in formulating public policy on mediation. If all mediation's benefits are private, there is no value in establishing public policies to promote or support its use. Private users can be counted on to make their own decisions about whether to use the process, based on its benefits to them. However, if using mediation creates value for society, public policy should encourage disputants to use mediation even when they might not do so for the private benefit alone. Indeed the widespread adoption of court-ordered mediation is one example of the kind of policy that can *only* be justified by mediation's public benefits. In general, discussions of the public benefits of mediation have focused on its value in saving public resources, especially court resources, when cases are settled (Galanter, 1985). Specifically, mediation is seen as reducing court backlogs and facilitating speedier disposition of cases, thereby allowing more efficient use of limited public resources, as noted in Chapter One.

The public value of conflict transformation is overlooked in most discussions of the public benefits of mediation. The reason for this omission may be the fact that the Transformation Story itself received less attention until recently than other views of the process. However, the public benefits of conflict transformation are quite important, particularly in debates over the value of mediation in comparison with the formal legal process, debates that were quite intense some years ago and have resurfaced more recently (Bush, 1989–1990; Hensler, 2002). Indeed, some fifteen years ago, one of the authors of this volume explained the public benefits of mediation— beyond systemic efficiency—in the following terms:

> Parties to mediation [are affected] in two ways: in terms of their level of self-awareness and capacity for self-determination, and in terms of their level of other-awareness and their capacity for consideration and respect for others. And *that itself* is the public value that mediation promotes. In other words, going through mediation [is] for both parties a direct education and growth experience, as to self-determination on the one hand and consideration for others on the other. . . . Simply put, it is the value of providing a moral and political education for citizens, in responsibility for themselves and respect for others. In a democracy, that must be considered a crucial public value and it must be considered a public function. . . . The experience of the mediation process and the kind of results it produces serve the public value of civic education in self-determination and respect for others. . . . Let me clarify that I'm not talking about a religious function here— unless it is what has been called the civil religion of the traditional civic virtues that is now being rediscovered in many quarters [Bush, 1989–1990, pp. 14–17].

Of course, the public benefits described here are benefits of conflict transformation. That is, they are the results of experiencing empowerment and recognition shifts within a mediation process aimed at supporting these shifts, thereby supporting conflict transformation. In our contemporary society, citizens increasingly suffer from learned dependency—whether on experts, on institutions, on addictive substances, or otherwise—and from mutual alienation and mistrust, especially along lines of race, gender, and class. The resulting civic weakness and division threaten the very fabric of our society (Etzioni, 1996; Handler, 1988). Personal experiences that reinforce the civic virtues of self-determination and mutual consideration are therefore of enormous public value—and this is precisely what the process of conflict transformation provides. This is the public benefit of conflict transformation, and it is critical to discussions of the public value of mediation, in comparison with the formal legal process or other alternative dispute resolution (ADR) processes.

Interestingly, the efficiency arguments for mediation's public value have long been given great weight, yet it increasingly appears that those arguments have been overstated and that they lack evidentiary support. That is, according to the most recent and thorough research, the use of mediation actually has little impact in reducing the time and cost of case disposition in the legal system (Hensler, 2002). If that is so, then what justifies public policy ordering—or even encouraging—parties to use mediation? This question has resurfaced recently with considerable force, and it cannot be answered except by pointing to public benefits of mediation beyond efficiency. Those are the very benefits just discussed, and they are all connected to conflict transformation, and to the practice of mediation as a transformative process.

Nevertheless this clarification is not intended as an argument that *only* the conflict transformation benefits of mediation matter—whether to private parties or to public policymakers. Parties may indeed be interested in other kinds of private benefits, especially those related to expeditious settlement of the dispute on favorable terms, and public decision makers may also be drawn to mediation for other reasons, including efficiency. The point here is rather that conflict transformation should also be seen as an important benefit of mediation, sought and valued by both private parties and policy-makers charged with furthering public, societal interests. The question of how to accommodate possible differences about private and public benefits is taken up in depth in Chapter Seven.

The Promise of Mediation as a Transformative Process

The transformative view of what mediation can and should offer to parties and to the public, as demonstrated by this chapter, is both practically and theoretically based. From the insights of psychology, communication, philosophy, and other fields, we have understood why conflict transformation matters to people and how it can theoretically occur through mediation. From the insights of political and social theory, we have learned why conflict transformation benefits not only private parties but society as a whole. From the parties, groups, and mediators that we have worked with and studied over many years, we have learned that this theoretical promise of what mediation can offer is real. It is not a magical vision, nor naive; its belief in human strength and decency carries the deepest truth within it. The promise that mediation offers for transforming conflict interaction is real, because skilled mediators can support the parties' own work, create a space for that work to go on, and—most important—stay out of the parties' way. Transformative mediators allow and trust people to find their own way through their conflict—and even more important—find themselves and each other, discovering and revealing the strength and understanding within themselves.

In Chapter Three, we offer a wide range of examples of how the transformative theory of conflict and mediation has taken hold and affected the field in the decade since it was articulated in the first edition of this book—because of the increasing recognition of the value of conflict transformation. Then, in Chapters Four and Five, we illustrate and discuss many of the specific practices that transformative mediators use to do this, by presenting a case study of a full mediation session, with accompanying commentary.

3

Gaining Sight of the Goal of Transformation

The transformative vision of conflict and mediation has existed since the field of dispute resolution began expanding in the late 1960s and early 1970s. As noted, some early supporters of mediation were proponents of the Transformation Story and sought to practice in ways that were consistent with its goals, even without a fully articulated practice framework. But these practitioners were relatively few in number, and their voices within the field were somewhat muted because transformative practice was not employed widely, nor was it supported by many mainstream mediation programs, which sought only efficient case management. As suggested in the first edition of *The Promise of Mediation* a decade ago, the prevailing and most widely adopted forms of practice were aligned with the Satisfaction Story. Research demonstrated that most practice tended to be directive and settlement driven; and as such it had little or no emphasis on the transformation of the parties' interaction or the core elements of empowerment and recognition, the shifts that produce such transformation.

But where do things stand now? How much has changed over the past ten years? Are the voices supporting the transformation story louder and more articulate? Are there signs in the mainstream of theory and practice that point to greater support for transformative mediation? Is the institutional climate within traditional or nontraditional arenas of practice more receptive to the premises behind, or the actual practice of, transformative mediation? Although there is no way to accurately quantify answers to these questions, there are useful indicators that suggest what has and has not changed. Overall our sense is that although there is still substantial institutional resistance to transformative mediation in some traditional arenas of dispute resolution, the value of transformative practice has been increasingly acknowledged over the past ten years. There are indications that the Transformation Story is viewed as increasingly important and valued and that transformative mediation is now practiced in a much wider array of settings than it was a decade ago. To a significant extent, the increasing acceptance of transformative practice has been due to the work of many people who have articulated and developed this approach to practice.

This chapter summarizes events and trends that suggest shifting ground in the mediation field—toward ground that supports the values and practices of the transformative model. We characterize some of this ground and discuss its implications for the evolution of transformative practice across dispute resolution settings. Specifically, we discuss three important trends that we have seen over the past decade. First, we point to a *shift in the rhetoric* in the field at large, which suggests that there are an increasing number of voices expressing concern about the value and impact of the Satisfaction Story, and its approach to practice. Second, we identify a *range of practice shifts* in the mainstream of the field that place increasing emphasis on conducting mediation in a way that works with and focuses on parties' conflict interaction. Finally, we look at some of the *major developments* achieved by those working within the transformative framework itself—developments that have advanced knowledge of practice, institutionalized transformative mediation in some settings, and extended the core values of transformative mediation to nontraditional arenas of conflict intervention. All of these trends and shifts ultimately suggest that the mediation field and the clients it serves are more receptive to and supportive of the transformative model.

Waking Up to What Is Being Lost

Over the past decade, an increasing number of theorists and practitioners have voiced their concerns about the prevailing models of mediation practice. More people within the field have expressed dissatisfaction or have been openly critical that mainstream practice overemphasizes settlement and ignores the potential for interactional shifts and conflict transformation. These commentaries come from a wide range of scholars and practitioners, many of whom are not specifically aligned with transformative practice. Some have questioned the value of mediation altogether because of the flaws they see, whereas others continue to practice mediation and support or administer mediation programs but remain troubled by the tendencies they see in practice.

Concerns About Diluting Party Self-Determination

Some of the sharpest questions are raised about the way mediation is practiced in court-connected programs. For example, Nancy Welsh (2001a) argues that the institutionalization of mediation in the courts has created an increasingly "thinning vision" of the role of party self-determination in the mediation process. The instrumental pressures that courts place on the process—to provide greater efficiency and economic savings for the system—have increasingly diluted the fundamental principle of party self-determination, in much of court-based practice. Welsh finds that mediators often practice "by engaging in very aggressive evaluations of parties' cases and settlement options . . . with the goal of winning a settlement, rather than supporting parties in their exercise of self-determination" (p. 5). The ultimate consequence is the erosion of the unique benefits that mediation can provide. As practice drifts toward an emphasis on efficiency and settlement, mediation becomes less and less recognizable as an alternative dispute resolution process. Welsh contends that if the courts do not change course, "self-determination will become a largely irrelevant relic from the early days of the contemporary mediation movement" (p. 93).

In effect, Welsh is saying that something of core importance in mediation is now on the verge of being lost almost entirely. Her concern about the erosion of self-determination in mediation practice reflects growing skepticism about the goals of practice within the mainstream of court-based mediation. Forms of practice that primarily pursue the Satisfaction Story's view of mediation's public benefits—efficiency and case disposition—are increasingly questioned by those familiar with mediation in court settings, including some leaders in the development of court-based mediation programs. Sharon Press, director of Florida's statewide court-based mediation program, commented on a study of court-ordered mediation (in another jurisdiction), noting that the goals of the mediators were primarily to reach settlements and clear the court's calendar. As a result, she worried, "Self-determination of the parties, which is . . . a foundation of mediation, is removed," and the mediator practices involved are not "consistent with the role of the mediator and the process of mediation" (Press, 1998, pp. 368–369). James Alfini, an early pioneer in court-based mediation, recently studied the emerging law on enforcement of mediation agreements. Reaching conclusions very similar to those of Press and Welsh, he stated that "the general policy favoring settlement, while advancing the goal of judicial economy, may not always be consistent with mediation principles and values. In particular, allegations of settlement coercion raise troubling issues relating to mediation's core values of party self-determination" (Alfini and McCabe, 2001, p. 173). Cynthia Savage, director of the Colorado state judiciary's dispute resolution office, and Louise Phipps Senft note that "as more and more courts have embraced mediation, they have done so primarily based on the promise of increased efficiency. . . . Mediation in a significant number of court-annexed programs has begun to look more like the traditional pre-trial settlement conference, and less like the alternative process originally intended" (Senft and Savage, 2003, p. 335).

Concerns About Missing the Opportunity for Party Engagement

Beyond the context of court-based mediation per se, well-known figures in the field have raised a broader set of criticisms about mediation and conflict resolution practice in general. For example, Bernard Mayer (2004) points to a developing crisis in the dispute resolution field and to specific inadequacies in the practice and use of mediation across various settings. Part of his criticism about mediation is that its practice has contributed to this broader crisis, in that mediators often rely on manipulative techniques that clash with the values that many in the field believe should be at the core of the process. He suggests that some approaches to mediation practice fall short of important expectations for what the process can provide—they do not fundamentally change the way conflict is addressed. He also believes that too much emphasis is placed in mediation practice on resolving conflict rather than on supporting disputants' ability to engage each other in their emerging conflict. Like Welsh and the others just cited, Mayer sees the practice of mediation restricted by the heavy focus that much of mediation places on settlement. However, whereas Welsh and others point out how this undermines the value of self-determination, Mayer stresses that this undermines the benefit that mediation can provide in helping parties engage with each other. Taken together, these commentators are saying that *self-determination* and *connection*—the core elements of conflict transformation—are the key values that have been put at risk by the field's increasingly narrow emphasis on settlement.

Concerns from the Community Setting

Dissatisfaction with settlement-driven models of practice has also been expressed by administrators of mediation programs that respond to requests for mediation not only from courts but also from their local communities (Della Noce, Folger, and Antes, 2002). Many of these community program administrators have stated that prevailing models of mediation practice did not adequately address their own vision of what mediation should provide and did not meet their clients' needs and expectations. They argue that models of practice that focus heavily on settlement often miss other potential impacts of the process, and as a result, they do not provide the outcomes that they and their clients value most. The Greenwich Mediation Centre, a community-based program in England directed by Patricia Gonsalves, described dissatisfaction with prevailing models of practice in a statement that characterized that program's goals, as well as its considerations in choosing among practice models:

> "Listening, talking and working together to reach agreement about disputes" was the mission statement quoted in the Centre's first annual report in 1996. It is reflective of the agreement-driven approach to mediation in which the Centre's initial group of mediators were trained, an approach so widely used in mediation programmes throughout the United Kingdom that to mediate any other way is almost unheard of. This approach to mediation makes a basic assumption that what parties in any mediation want most is to get their conflict settled and to reach some sort of agreement about how they will coexist in the future. There is a logical sense to this notion of mediation, but only if one views conflicts as problems that need to be resolved.
>
> From our earliest experiences with clients, we began to realize that this approach to mediation was simply too limited in terms of addressing what was important to parties who are experiencing conflict. We saw that while our clients were indeed interested in working out agreements to problems, this was by no means their only concern. In fact, the use of a mediation model that emphasized a continuous drive toward the goal of agreement seemed to give short shrift to our clients' needs to fully work through the

complex layers of interaction that so often characterize interpersonal conflict. Put another way, we began to see that mediation needed to address not only the "what" of conflict, but also the "why" and "how" of conflict inter-action. . . . The agreement-focused model we were using emphasized identifying tangible issues and solving prob-lems and, though our mediators had become adept at using it and could indeed help people find solutions, the most significant aspect of their difficulty was missed if the interaction between the parties was not addressed [Gon-salves and Hudson, 2003].

Thomas Wahlrab, director of the Dayton, Ohio, Mediation Cen-ter, also commented on his concerns about existing models of prac-tice and his aspirations for the program he leads. He was disturbed by the inconsistency he saw between the mediation field's rhetoric about the goals and values of the process and the way prevailing models of practice actually treat those goals:

Research throughout the 1980s and 1990s shows that even the formal role of mediator includes a pattern of practices that hardly distinguishes mediation from the authoritative enforcement roles inherent in courts and police departments or the supportive expert roles found in most psychological and counseling services. Commu-nity mediators are not acting as attorneys, bus drivers, engineers, etc. They are citizens who want to give back to their communities. Whatever authority they have in their personal or professional lives is not expected to carry over into the role of mediator. However, without a clearly articulated theory that fits with a community mediation center's values, this often is exactly what happens. . . .

[M]y mediation practice—and how I taught media-tion [at the Dayton Mediation Center]—did not fall in line with the values that were being articulated within the mediation field. I was noticing a trend, in the practice of our mediators, to focus on getting parties to agreement. The implication is that, although values were stated, they did not translate congruently into practices. I was beginning to understand that this inconsistency was problematic and in an article I wrote for our Center's monthly newsletter, . . . I attempted to point out this lack of congruency between values and practices. . . . We needed worldview, theory, and principles laid out so that we could develop congruency between purpose and practice. Without this clarity, our community mediation center was producing "citizen mediators" who practiced their "professions" while calling themselves mediators. Hence the police officer's principal intervention was to ask "why" questions. The lawyer only asked questions no matter how much we stressed "active listening techniques" [Wahlrab, 2004].

Concerns from the Workplace

Program administrators outside traditional court and community mediation programs have also expressed their dissatisfaction with prevailing modes of practice, as they considered possible models of practice for the institutional programs they were leading. Cindy Hallberlin, the founder and first director of the U.S. Postal Service REDRESS Mediation Program, explained the weaknesses she saw in the models of mediation with which she was originally familiar. Her goals for the REDRESS program went beyond settlement, and this led to her dissatisfaction with what she saw in much of existing practice: "I knew almost any type of mediation could result in 'settlements' but the Postal Service wanted more. Postal management wanted to improve the workplace environment by enhancing employees' communication skills. I needed more than 'deals.' I was looking for improved relationships" (Hallberlin, 2001, p. 378). Hallberlin indicated that she wanted the mediation program adopted in the Postal Service to capture the opportunity for *upstream effects*, as discussed in Chapter Two. That is, she hoped that employees' experiences in mediation could have a positive impact on their interactions with coworkers long after their involvement in the process. For most mediation with which she was familiar, she did not see the potential for this upstream impact. The focus of practice was too settlement oriented and mediator centered and did not allow for the possible changes in the interaction between coworkers or managers and employees when they returned to the workplace.

Concerns from Professional Organizations

The concern for losing sight of mediation's transformative benefits is also evident in the policy deliberations of mediator organizations, including one of the field's major organs, the Association for Conflict Resolution (ACR). When an ACR committee published a draft report on the tension between mediation and the unauthorized practice of law, Sharon Press, a committee member and a former president of ACR, wrote to the board:

> Mediation is not a process that we should allow to be defined as whatever anyone wants to do. . . . Here are some of the concerns I have about the blurring of evaluative processes with mediation. . . . I predict that if we don't take a stand on mediation now, it will go the way of arbitration. Specifically, mediation will begin to look more and more like a trial (we are already seeing hints of movement in this direction) and the benefits of informal resolution will be lost. Mediation was supposed to give parties the opportunity to resolve a dispute in a manner that *they* deemed to be acceptable—not necessarily how a judge would rule or the law would decide it. It seems to me that it is only a matter of time before someone really gets harmed in a "mediation process." . . .

> I urge the Board to take the bold stand which is needed
> now to carve out mediation from the evaluative processes.
> . . . No less than the future of mediation hangs in the bal-
> ance [Press, 2003].

Clearly, these are strong words expressing strong concerns that in the name of efficiency and settlement the core value of self-determination and the distinctive nature and benefit of mediation are at risk of being lost.

Questions About the Significance of Efficiency Benefits

Interestingly, apart from the questions being raised about the narrow focus on efficiency and settlement benefits, questions are also being raised about whether mediation actually produces those benefits at all. For example, Deborah Hensler (2001), a prominent empirical researcher of the effects of mediation and other ADR processes, argues that even the prevailing settlement-oriented model of medi-ation may not be accomplishing what many thought it was. There is convincing evidence, she contends, that court-based mediation programs may not be as economically beneficial as commonly assumed. Research studies of mediation of civil cases in court sug-gest that the process is not significantly less costly, or more time effi-cient, than other available means for addressing the same disputes. This finding is particularly surprising because research also demon-strates, according to Hensler, that most of the court mediation pro-grams studied rely more on evaluative than facilitative practice. Mediators conduct their practice in ways that place their opinions and influence at the center of the process. Evaluative practice would presumably have the best chance of meeting the purely instrumental goals of programs that are heavily geared toward case management. However, Hensler's analysis and critique suggests that mediation practice—even when designed specifically to produce the public benefits envisioned by the Satisfaction Story—may not be produc-ing the instrumental benefits it promises. From this evidence and reasoning, some have concluded that mediation has relatively little utility, and they are now turning to other forums of intervention (such as settlement conferences and hearing panels), which are more likely to achieve the economic benefits sought.

Regaining Sight of Transformative Benefits

In sum, across the mediation field—whether in court, community, family, or organizational settings—significant concerns have been raised about the prevailing, settlement-oriented approach to mediation practice. Most important for our discussion, the core of these concerns is that the focus on settlement has put at risk a set of values and benefits, private and public, that are even more important and that are now being more widely identified as the core benefits of the mediation process.

Those benefits are *self-determination* and *party interaction* or *engagement*—the core elements of the transformative model. Hence the growing dissatisfaction with the field's overly narrow focus on settlement simultaneously expresses a growing awareness of the importance of the benefits of conflict transformation and the capacity of mediation to provide them. Whether or not it is stated explicitly, many in the mediation field have come to view the transformative dimensions of the process much more seriously over the last decade. Likewise, as explored in the next section, many have begun to work more seriously on how to shift mediation practice in ways that pursue transformative benefits more intentionally—without necessarily identifying with the transformative model.

Shifts in Mainstream Mediation Practice

The shifts in attitudes about mediation's impacts have been accompanied by a second trend that became apparent over the last decade. This second trend has emerged within the realm of mediation practice itself. New and substantially different ideas and recommendations have been proposed by a wide range of people, about how mediators should conduct their practice. Although few of the proponents of these recommended changes have explicitly linked them with the transformative framework, the changes themselves, if adopted, would move practice increasingly away from settlement-driven approaches and toward approaches that place conflict interaction and its possible transformation at the center of mediators' work. In other words, these changes are aligned, at least implicitly, with the core values of the transformative framework and are in some ways a response to the concerns about the impacts of mainstream practice discussed previously. Taken as a whole, they also reveal emerging ground in the field that supports transformative practice.

In general, practice methodology in the mediation field tends to shift as practitioners and theorists make recommendations about how practice should be conducted. These recommendations are made in conference sessions, training programs, and published literature about the way mediators perform their work. For the most part, these suggestions are viewed as possible additions to a mediator's "toolbox"—contributions to a repertoire of alternative approaches or techniques that mediators can use as they work with parties during mediation sessions (Welsh, 2001a). Rarely are these specific suggestions about practice viewed from a broader theoretical or ideological perspective, and relatively little discussion is generated about what underlying assumptions about conflict support these suggestions, or whether certain practices are consistent with the assumed objectives that mediators set for themselves in conducting mediation (Della Noce, Bush, and Folger, 2002). As a result, the purpose behind the use of any particular mediation technique or tool is often not identified or explained. Therefore many of the recent suggestions for changes in practice are not explicitly discussed at the level of underlying principles, values, or goals. Nevertheless these practice recommendations often have clear parallels to the transformative framework. We suggest that many of the shifts in practice that have been suggested recently can well serve the goals of transformative practice or at least create a basis of support for those who have adopted this framework.

Shifts in the Definition of Mediator Competence: Performance Tests

One place where shifts in the field's view of good practice are evident is in the skill sets listed in certification procedures and performance tests for mediators. Most testing protocols that assess mediator competence are based on identification of a wide range of practice skills and techniques that mediators need to master to be considered proficient or to attain certification. The tests reflect the techniques of practice that are identified and recommended by various practitioner organizations and certification agencies, as well as the concepts of *core skills* that are presented by influential articles and books on mediation. Until quite recently, the skills and practices included in these performance tests were geared almost entirely to the goal of containing conflict through directive, settlement-oriented practice (Bush, 2004). That is, the tests most often assess whether mediators consistently try to move and direct parties toward points of agreement, common ground, and possible settlement. The behavioral methods for achieving these objectives are specified in the tests and are then used to evaluate whether a mediator's behavior acceptably aligns with this focus. As a result, the tests typically assess whether mediators perform well in controlling and structuring the process, identifying parties' underlying needs and interests, emphasizing common ground and areas of agreement, deemphasizing disagreement, steering parties to focus their discussions on the future and to disregard the past, as well as discouraging and limiting expression of negative emotions. Clearly, these behaviors are inconsistent with the goal of supporting interactional shifts and conflict transformation, as described in Chapter Two.

However, even though these kinds of mediator skills still dominate many of the existing proficiency tests, what is noteworthy is that a different set of skills and practices is now finding its way into performance and certification tests. Many of the new criteria being included are more consistent with transformative objectives, and they capture some key elements of the process that unfolds within a transformative mediation session. Although most tests are still not aimed at assessing the overall strength of mediators as transformative practitioners per se, the range of skills listed includes an increasing number of specific behavioral practices that are consistent with the approaches taken by transformative mediators.

For example, the Family Mediation Canada National Certification Program has developed a Family Mediator Skills Assessment Checklist. This checklist includes a diverse set of behavioral objectives that are assessed as mediators are tested. Included in the test are the following performance objectives:

- Works with participants to promote mutual understanding, insight into and empathy for the other

- Works with the parties to develop their communication guidelines

- Seeks clarification and direction from the participants in the process design and makes procedural changes as necessary

- Promotes participants' ability to define their own outcomes or solutions

- Helps participants identify principles and criteria that will guide their decision making

- Works with participants to develop their own principles to evaluate their solutions

Unlike the skills included in most prior performance tests, all of these behavioral objectives are potentially consistent with transformative practice. They support mediators' focus on empowerment and recognition in both the process and content dimensions of conflict. Other mediator performance tests, including tests used by the Pennsylvania Special Education Mediation Service and the Maryland Council for Dispute Resolution, also specify a wider range of mediator practices than have traditionally been included, and at least some of the specific behavioral elements included in these tests are consistent with the goals and practices of the transformative framework. That is, like the Family Mediation Canada test, they assess whether mediators focus on and work with the parties' conflict interaction as they conduct the process (Bush, 2004).

The documented changes in these competency tests are important markers of movement within the realm of mediation practice and in the field at large. They reflect the fact that an increasing number of professional organizations are identifying different mediator behaviors—ones that are not so exclusively focused on settlement and control of conflict—as core elements of practice. In other words, they point to a shift in what the definition of "good" practice is—a shift that is clearly a turn toward transformative practice, whether or not identified as such.

Shifts in Recognition of Mediation Models: Mediation Organizations and Texts

Another marked change in the field, over the past decade, has been the willingness of both mediation organizations and experts to recognize that there are different models of practice in use—one of which is the transformative model. At the time our first edition was published, the common view was that all mediators followed the same basic model of practice and that differences among them were matters of style rather than principle (Bush, forthcoming; Della, Bush, and Folger, 2002). In fact, our contention in the first edition that transformative mediation represented a distinct model was met with considerable skepticism (Menkel-Meadow, 1995; Williams, 1997).

However, beginning in the last several years, the view that there are indeed different and distinct models of mediation—not just stylistic variations—has been explicitly and increasingly accepted. In the literature of the field, major instructional texts on mediation acknowledge that "the facilitative, problem-solving approach to mediation is not universally adopted. The other two major schools of thought on mediation are transformative and evaluative" (Alfini and others, 2001, p. 140; also see Folberg and others, 2004). Professional articles also note that "mediation literature and practitioners commonly refer to three mediation models" (D'Alo, 2003, p. 205), one of which is the transformative model (also Neilson and English, 2001). This recognition of transformative mediation as a distinct model of practice is indeed one of the developments that led to the changes in the composition of mediator performance tests.

Apart from the literature of the field, the recognition of distinct models of practice, including the transformative model, has also become evident in the activities of major professional organizations in the field. For example, the ACR, one of the field's key organizations, recently sought to develop a policy on mediation and the unauthorized practice of law, and its report at least implicitly recognized the differences between the facilitative and evaluative models of mediation (Task Force on Mediator Certification, 2004). ACR has also worked on developing criteria for an "advanced mediation practitioner" status, and the committee doing so recommended that "criteria should neither exclude nor privilege one model of mediation practice. . . . Care should be given not to create additional requirements that restrict membership access to particular models of and approaches to mediation practice" (Advanced Practitioner Membership Work Group, 2003). Even more recently, in planning for its current annual conference, ACR altered the categories under which presenters could submit proposals for workshops, adding to the list a category for transformative mediation—in part because of the success at its previous conference of a "track" of workshops on the transformative model. All of these examples are evidence that the transformative model has gained recognition as a viable, distinct model of mediation.

Shifts in Proposals for Practice Changes: Practitioner Literature

In addition to changes in mediator performance tests and changed attitudes toward recognizing distinct mediation models, shifts toward greater openness to transformative mediation are evident in the increasing number of theorists and practitioners calling for specific changes in mediation practice. The important point here is that many of the changes called for are aligned with core goals and practices of the transformative framework. Mayer (2004), for example, has argued that mediation's strict focus on conflict as a problem-solving process has jeopardized the ability of mediators to work constructively with parties' conflict. Mediators have traditionally been encouraged to move parties away from their initial positions, because this allows a better understanding of the problem to emerge before parties become entrenched in one particular solution. Mayer argues that mediators should support disputants' articulation of their positions and not move parties from them so quickly, because each person's ability and willingness to state positions allows for a fuller expression of viewpoints and opens up the possible exploration of what the conflict is about for the participants. Beyond this concern about moving parties away from their positions, Mayer also suggests that mediators should step away from the problem-solving practice of steadily moving participants toward win-win solutions. His concern is that when mediators adopt a solution focus, and they allow this focus to shape their behaviors during the mediation, it often restricts the parties' own engagement in the conflict.

Along similar practice lines, Domenici and Littlejohn (2001) call for mediators to avoid focusing prematurely on specific outcomes or possible terms of settlement of a conflict from the beginning of a mediation session. They contend that "mutual agreement is only one possible outcome" of the mediation process, implying

"Focus on the future" is a valuable phrase of the mediator, but it is another basic principle of mediation that may conflict with empowerment. Talking about the past may actually be empowering and lead to recognition. A community mediator found that the key to unlocking a difficult mediation was to invite one participant to discuss a difficult and emotional situation from the couple's past [Pope, 1996, p. 292].

that mediators should practice in ways that allow for and support other outcomes, including the possibility of outcomes not typically prescribed by the problem-solving framework (Domenici and Littlejohn, p. 32). Stephen Schwartz places a similar emphasis on self-determination in his characterization of the core purpose of the process. He says, "The underlying objective is to restore the client's central role in both participation and responsibility for resolution of the conflict. A fundamental method for fulfilling this objective is to permit the client to tell the story and contribute directly to proposing and deciding upon options for settlement. If the client is not involved in this way, whatever is going on is not mediation but some other process" (Schwartz, 2003). For Schwartz, mediation practice that focuses on party self-determination is an essential defining characteristic of mediation as a dispute resolution forum.

In a similar call for practice change, Ahrens (2002) asks mediators to be comfortable with periods of silence during a mediation session and not to feel immediately compelled to talk to the parties when silence occurs. Ahrens makes this suggestion because he believes that the mediators tend to be uncomfortable with silence. The tendency to say too much and not allow lulls in the interaction can stand in the way of the parties' thoughtful deliberation and decision making during the process. He suggests, "Silence is precisely the time when people are often engaging in careful reflections about how they should proceed, how they can contribute to the process of dispute resolution." He also warns, "When the mediator talks, people listen, they don't speak, and they have very little opportunity to reflect." Ahrens, like Mayer, places an emphasis on supporting the parties' full involvement in the conflict interaction as it unfolds during a mediation session. Anything mediators do that obstructs or impedes party engagement in the conflict is seen as negative from this critical viewpoint of practice.

In addition to these calls for specific changes in practice, there are an increasing number of voices in the discourse about mediation practice that encourage mediators to acknowledge and work with a broader and more realistic conception of conflict interaction as they mediate. Of particular note are the recent calls from theorists and practitioners for mediators to allow for parties' expressions of emotion during mediation. Barker (2003), Mayer (2004), and others recognize that mediators have generally been uncomfortable with the emotionally expressive aspects of conflict interaction. They suggest that mediation practice should accommodate this important and inherent dimension of conflict interaction. Barker, for example, instructs mediators to "stay with the heat. Allow each person to have his feelings straight out, without stifling or interfering with them." Similarly, Mayer (2004) suggests that in conflict "the fundamental need that people have is to express strong feelings in strong ways." He warns, "We may have spent too much time creating formulas for communication and norms of interaction and not enough time figuring out how to help people express themselves passionately, forcefully, and powerfully or how to hear such expressions from others without shutting down or unwisely escalating conflict" (p. 130).

Moving Toward—or at Least Making Room for— a Focus on Conflict Transformation

All of these explicit shifts in the vision of mediation practice—both those documented in certification and performance tests and those in published or highly circulated discussions of practice—head in the same general direction. In a fundamental sense, they call for

mediators to focus on the nature of conflict interaction and its transformation, as led by and developed through the parties. All of these
practice suggestions generally support the sense that mediators
should do their work in a way that allows them to follow, rather
than lead, parties through the expression and management of the
unfolding conflict. These are markedly different practices than have
traditionally been prescribed in many prior discussions of how mediators should perform their work. The type of changes that have
been proposed could, if implemented, significantly redesign the
nature of mainstream practice. Taken as a set, they establish a different vision of mediation practice, one that moves away from some
of the core tenets of prevailing models of practice.

It is important to note that calls for these kinds of changes in
practice were not being made in the mediation field at large a
decade ago. In fact, the concerns raised in *The Promise of Mediation*
about the evolution of problem-solving practice, and the calls for
change to address these concerns, were rejected by many at the
time. At that time, there was a widespread sense that the prevailing technology of practice—as reflected in the performance tests
discussed earlier and the literature on which they were based—was
acceptable and effective (Bush, 2004). That is why we see the calls
for change that are advocated now—many of which are consistent
with the way transformative mediators currently practice—as sig-
nifying important potential movement in the field, movement that
is based on growing dissatisfaction with directive, settlement-driven
practice.

It is not yet clear how much impact these calls will have on the
nature and character of mediation practice across the field. However, based on our observations of the route many have taken in the
recent past, we predict that the recognition of difficulties with current practice, and the specific suggestions being made on how to
change it, will give rise to a broader impulse to change the core nature of the way mediation is conducted. In any event, regardless of
how the expressions of dissatisfaction with current practice evolve,

the voices that call for change in practice have opened the field up considerably—they have created substantial new ground for those interested in practicing the transformative model.

Developing Transformative Practice: The Reality Today

Perhaps the most visible signs of support for transformative practice can be found not in the criticisms and calls for change within mainstream practice but in the articulation and development of the transformative framework itself, and in the increasing use and adoption of transformative mediation across diverse practice settings. Significant new developments within the mainstream of transformative theory and practice have clarified the alternative nature of this framework for practice. This work has, in turn, enabled program administrators and practitioners to make clear choices about whether and why they want to adopt this framework as the basis for their mediation practice. Most of these developments have emerged in three areas: the translation of theory into practice, the adoption of the model within a range of institutional and program settings, and the extension of core principles of the transformative framework into new arenas of practice.

Articulation of Practice Technology—Steps Forward

Over the past ten years, there have been enormous strides in developing and refining the methodology of transformative practice. These strides have been made by people who have worked on a wide range of both funded and unfunded projects that have focused on practice, training, and research within the transformative framework. Three large initiatives in particular helped establish the methodology needed for transformative practice to become easily understood and widely accepted.

In 1996, the Training Design Consultation Project was jointly funded by the Surdna Foundation and the William and Flora

Hewlett Foundation. This project was specifically aimed at the development of new training resources for transformative practice. After the publication of *The Promise of Mediation*, many trainers and practitioners contacted us to inquire about possible training sessions for transformative practice. We kept a list of these requests, and as the numbers grew, we realized that it would be beneficial to seek outside funding for such a project and to draw from the years of training and mediation experience that already existed in the field. As a result, we used the Training and Design Consultation to bring together those individuals who had a potential interest in developing the model. We facilitated a series of think-tank weekends to share ideas about best practices for transformative mediation. These meetings were attended by over forty practitioners and scholars from the United States and Canada. We used the foundation funding as seed money for those participants in the project who wanted to develop and assess new practice ideas and training materials. Upon completion in 1998, this project "supported the development of twenty-four pilot projects, a wealth of new training materials, exercises and models, and new insights on the transformative model" (Della Noce, Bush, and Folger, 2002, p. 52). Some of the core ideas about how to translate a focus on empowerment and recognition into practice were generated by this work.

A second major project that contributed to the development of transformative practice was the assistance provided to the U.S. Postal Service in the development of their REDRESS Mediation Program. "This was the first time a mediation program was built on a specific, articulated theoretical framework from the ground up. Training programs and materials, trainer development programs, research protocols, and mediator evaluations were all created specifically to support the goals and values of the framework" (Della Noce, Bush, and Folger, 2002, pp. 52–53). The training programs developed and delivered for REDRESS provided an invaluable laboratory within an important institutional setting to develop and refine the skills needed for effective training and practice within the transformative framework. Over three thousand mediators received training in the transformative model for this program, although only about half of these mediators became part of the REDRESS roster (Bingham and Nabatchi, 2001). Valuable feedback was provided from the trainers, from the mediators who attended the trainings, and from the Postal Service REDRESS specialists who observed the mediators in their initial mediations for the program. The insights gained from this widely studied, nationwide workplace program provided a sound basis for designing transformative practice across diverse institutional settings (Bingham, 2003). This project also gave transformative practice much greater visibility in the mediation field and sparked considerable discussion of its potential merits. This project, more than any other over the past decade, put transformative mediation on the alternative dispute resolution map and made it the center of intense scrutiny in and out of the mediation field. It became a model for other institutions who were looking to mediation to address disputes and to have possible upstream impacts on organizational life. As of today, the REDRESS program has conducted over sixty thousand mediations using the transformative model, and it continues to flourish. In addition, the REDRESS program has inspired several other federal agencies to use transformative mediation to address workplace conflict, including the new Transportation Security Administration.

A third project that advanced the development of transformative practice was the Practice Enrichment Initiative. This project, also funded by the Surdna and Hewlett Foundations, engaged a group of ten practitioners and researchers who were experienced in working within the transformative framework to advance practice through three main efforts: the development of illustrative videos of transformative practice, the creation of research-based methods for assessing and supporting mediator competency in transformative practice, and the development of insights about how various mediation policies enhance or inhibit the institutionalization of the transformative framework. These three projects, completed in 2000, moved beyond articulation of the methodology of practice to assessment and institutional policy development. In doing so, the Practice Enrichment Initiative created a strong platform for overcoming some of the broader challenges that the transformative model faces when it is implemented in various dispute resolution contexts.

In addition to the work of this project, other practitioners have developed their own training approaches that are built on the core principles of the transformative model but have been tailored to suit the needs of particular programs and clients. The creation of alternative methods for achieving the same underlying goals and purposes is a sign of healthy development in the evolution of transformative practice. As we have noted, "There are many possible ways that the specific elements of training can be designed and still be consistent with the underlying goals and accomplishments of transformative practice. There is not one model, but many models of training for this framework" (Folger and Bush, 2001b, p. 182).

Specific Developments in the Methodology of Transformative Practice

In Chapters Four and Five, we illustrate transformative practice in detail by providing an extended case example and offering commentary on the choices and approaches that the mediator took during a complex conflict between members of a homeowners' association. What the mediator chooses to do as the session unfolds, and the reasons behind these choices, reflect and embody the many ideas and contributions that have helped to translate the transformative framework into a coherent and understandable practice methodology. Much of this translation was done by the people who contributed to the successful completion of the projects we have just described.

What is obvious from the case study in the following chapters is that this approach to practice is quite different from many current models of mediation that are described in research and prescribed in trainings and how-to books. This is because the transformative view of conflict, as described in Chapter Two, leads mediators to adopt practices that focus on the potential transformation of the parties' conflict interaction. The mediator's mind-set shifts, and this shift translates into different ways of working with people in conflict. The rhetoric of transformative practice translates into substantially different decisions about how to engage the parties during mediation sessions. Although we cannot offer a complete survey of practice methodology here, we will point to four short examples that provide a glimpse at some of the key elements of transformative practice.

The Opening Conversation

In the transformative approach to practice, the mediator thinks of the opening of a mediation session as a conversation among the parties and the mediator, rather than a statement by the mediator to the parties. This means that "the mediator invites the parties to use the mediation to have a conversation about whatever is important to them . . . and asks the parties to talk about their goals for the mediation" (Pope, 2001, pp. 86–89). The mediator also discusses with the parties whether they would like to suggest guidelines or ground rules for the session that might be helpful in having the discussions they want to have. The mediator lets the parties know that they can design the process as it unfolds, based on what they feel will be most useful. The mediator also inquires what the parties' expectations are about confidentiality between them and what other commitments they might like to make to each other at the outset of the session (Pope, 2001).

Structure of the Mediation Process

Transformative practice moves away from a linear, stage model of the process that typically instructs mediators to help the parties progress through a series of sequential stages. Instead, in transformative practice, the mediator conceives of the process as emergent— resulting from the ongoing interactions of all the participants (including the mediator) during the mediation session. "Conflict becomes understood as created, constituted and transformed in the mediation process through the ongoing communicative interaction of the parties and the mediator" (Della Noce, 2001, p. 77). During a session, parties spiral through several different spheres of activity that arise in no specified order. The parties may cycle through these activities several times, as new information and context is created by them during the session. These activities include creating the context, exploring the situation, deliberating, exploring possibilities, and making decisions. All of these activities contribute to the transformation of the parties' conflict, with the assistance of the mediator proactively following and supporting the activity and interaction among the parties (Della Noce, 2001).

> The focus of the transformative framework on discourse and social interaction in a dynamic, moment-by-moment social process explains why traditional stage models are inadequate, and indeed counter-productive. . . . This model also reflects the premise that structure and order need not be imposed, but will emerge from the interaction of the parties and the mediator, as the mediator attends to empowerment and recognition. This requires a certain amount of trust that social processes can take shape on their own, without a need to force them into any particular shape, which is contrary to the popular assumption that if mediation is to have a "form" the mediator must impose it [Della Noce, 2001, pp. 77, 81].

Identifying and Working with Empowerment and Recognition

In the transformative approach to practice, mediators sustain a focus on the parties' interaction. This means that the mediator looks for places—or opportunities—to support possible empowerment or recognition shifts. As parties speak and talk with each other, there are numerous places where parties can get clearer about their views, options, or resources. And there are also numerous places where parties can gain greater understanding of each other's perspectives and points of view. It is up to the mediator to recognize these opportunities and to work with them as they arise, so that parties can gain greater clarity about their own and each other's perspectives and choices. Opportunities for empowerment and recognition shifts arise in different ways and at different times as the conflict unfolds during a mediation session. Paradoxically, opportunities for positive shifts are often embedded in party comments with a markedly negative character, including expressions of weakness, disempowerment, and demonization. Transformative mediators are attuned to the many ways in which such opportunities emerge and offer verbal and nonverbal responses that help the parties work with these opportunities (Moen and others, 2001; Jorgensen and others, 2001).

Reliance on Core Communication Skills

In working within the transformative framework, mediators rely on a set of key communication skills that allow for and support parties' efforts to move through the substance of their dispute and shape the process in ways that they find necessary or useful. These skills are ones that allow the mediator to follow the parties through their conflict and to proactively support the potential positive shifts in their interaction as they arise. The mediator's goal is to attend "to the exchanges between the parties in a whole new way, on a new level, and in a new language—the language of conflict transformation" (Bush and Pope, 2004, p. 61). Mediators recognize important verbal and nonverbal markers of possible shifts in the parties' interaction and are then able to support them with several kinds of responses, which are discussed in detail in Chapters Four and Five. These skills, when used with the goals of transformation in mind, support shifts in the way the parties interact and as a result allow the parties to make decisions and achieve the outcomes they desire through qualitative changes in their interaction with each other (Bush and Pope, 2002).

Adoption of the Transformative Model in Diverse Contexts

Along with greater articulation of the methodology of transformative practice, the last decade has seen an increasing number of mediation centers and organizations adopt the transformative model as the basis for practice. To date, nearly three dozen centers and organizations have adopted or are in the process of adopting transformative practice for their programs. The reasons for adopting transformative mediation vary, but they generally center around aligning mediation practice with the underlying values and objectives of the programs. For many programs, transformative benefits are what clients identify as important and valuable about the use of mediation. In this sense, they echo the findings of numerous studies, summarized in Chapter Two, that point to the value clients place on the outcomes transformative practice can offer. The following excerpts illustrate the reasons that have motivated many program leaders to adopt the transformative model for their programs.

Thomas Wahlrab, director, Dayton Mediation Center, Dayton, Ohio:

Our clients are appreciating our comfort level with how people "do" conflict because our practices support the development of their unique way of talking to each other. . . . Unique realities produce unique ways to manage conflict, and our clients appreciate our practice of being patient with and supportive of the development, within the mediation, of their process for managing conflict. . . . Our practice of being present in the moment or "following" the parties translates into a respectful way of being with people. Based on my observations, exit interviews, and debriefing processes with mediators, our clients notice that our way of mediating responds to con-flict in a different and a positive way: they feel respected and they appreciate our patience with them. These char-acteristics are being consciously developed within our mediation practice and are directly related to our under-standing of the transformative model. . . . An important impact of [our] transformative mediation practice has been to understand that mediation has a unique role in society, one that is not to be confused with any other roles. Its unique societal role is one whose actions (inter-vention strategies, activities, etc.) imply "no judgment" of others' ways and are respectful of others' humanity, capabilities, processes and decisions [Wahlrab, 2004].

Kristine Paranica, director, North Dakota Mediation Center, Grand Forks, North Dakota:

Experienced and new mediators alike see the benefits [of transformative practice] for clients. Experienced media-tors often report that it is great to see people figure out the problems for themselves, having an "aha" moment, and offering "sincere apologies" without the resistance we felt before. [Mediators] often comment on the amaz-ing movement the parties make between sessions, due at least in part, to fostering empowerment and recognition at the table. One of my clients who just volunteered to appear [in a promotional video for alternative dispute resolution in North Dakota] said that mediation "taught us how to have these difficult conversations ourselves— it sort of empowered us to make better decisions and to grow up a bit so we could be better parents." Mediation had not taught them parenting skills. They just picked up on what the mediator was doing and began to recog-nize what was going on for themselves and the effect it had on each other and their kids. This motivated them to begin to change what they were doing and create positive results for themselves. Transformative mediation has allowed us to develop training that gives people a language for understanding and talking about conflict that has become a first and foundational step to better manage conflict daily, both for themselves and as intervenors in the conflicts of others [Paranica, 2004].

Patricia Gonsalves, director, and Donna Turner Hudson, Greenwich Mediation Centre, Greenwich, England:

As we began working from the transformative orientation, mediators started to look differently at mediation and at the role of the mediator. Mediators began to attend more to what seemed to really matter to the parties—their interactions—and less to what they'd been trained to focus on: outcomes, agreements, and solutions. Moreover we often found that when our support led to improved party interactions, the parties themselves were quite capable of making their own decisions and resolving whatever issues existed between them. One of the important lessons we have learned about the role of the mediator in supporting difficult conversations is that while mediator support may lead to eased tensions and even conciliation between parties, it is also true that such changes may not occur. Respecting party interaction and party choice means leaving all outcomes up to those who are involved in the conflict.

We discovered, too, how important the focus on party interaction was in terms of allowing conversations related to race and class unfold. Because mediators working from the transformative framework do not identify issues or move the parties through mediator-driven agendas, parties are free to discuss whatever is important to them, whenever and however it comes up. While this naturally means the conversation is unpredictable and may be uncomfortable, it also means that, usually for the first time, parties are supported in their efforts to talk about deeply held feelings, assumptions, and beliefs that may have played a part in the difficulties they have had relating to one another. Furthermore, because of our adherence to transformative principles, our mediators do not use the mediation process as a way of advancing their own notions of justice and equality. Rather our appreciation that each party's reality is his or her own informs our practice to support both sides of any conversation the parties are willing to have [Gonsalves and Hudson, 2003].

Janice Fleischer, Pro Se Family Mediation Project, Dade County Florida:

The transformative approach inspires problem solving through the growth of the individual. In any conflict context, but especially in the family arena, fostering self-determination and inspiring parties to see the situation through each other's eyes (recognition) lead to deeper communication and harmony with the family—even if the family is split. . . . If what mediators work on in mediation is the "human" side of the parties, the rest will fall in place. The problems will be solved because everyone involved sees the benefit to themselves and others in resolving the conflict.

. . . preliminary findings reveal that for those parties who appeared for their mediation sessions, in most cases a full marital settlement agreement was reached. These were parties who were unable to communicate and come to agreement prior to being assigned to the project. Even more significantly, postmediation surveys seem to indicate the parties' appreciation for the opportunity to keep control of their lives and decisions despite having to be involved, ultimately, with the court for final orders [Fleischer, 1996, pp. 301–303].

At some mediation centers, adoption of the transformative framework has led to important and unusual innovations in particular arenas of practice. For example, in the area of family conflict, mediation of cases involving domestic violence has long been a highly controversial issue. Generally, because of concerns about the capacity of battered spouses to participate in mediation, as well as the risks to them of doing so, the common practice has been to screen for domestic violence and then refuse to mediate cases where it has occurred. However, as a result of its adoption of the transformative model, one mediation center instituted major changes in its approach to cases involving domestic violence issues—both as to screening and mediation—as explained by the following excerpt.

Jody Miller, director, and Sara Jane Wellock, staff member, Dutchess County Mediation Center, Poughkeepsie, New York:

The Mediation Center's transition to the transformative orientation impacted many aspects of our work, not simply the way we mediated cases. Intake, or pre-mediation discussion, was influenced and changed due to our new understanding of party capacity, self-determination, and a commitment on our part to follow, rather than lead. Although consistently trained on the dynamics of Domestic Violence, our "screening" techniques were also influenced by transformative practice. The intake process evolved into a more comprehensive approach including a unique and trusting relationship with local domestic violence advocates. The Mediation Center's partnership with Battered Women's Services [of Dutchess County] is based on firm and fundamental similarities in our principles and practices while recognizing and appreciating the differing roles of mediator and of advocate.

Our intake process as transactional practitioners involved phone conversations prior to scheduling mediation sessions, where Center staff asked a number of questions, ultimately determining whether or not parties were appropriate for mediation. We asked each party for demographics, relationship history, the nature of their interactions when disputing, concerns regarding child abuse, and safety. The Mediation Center would deem high-risk cases unamenable—inappropriate for mediation.

After embracing the transformative orientation, we found ourselves asking fewer questions during intake, being more open-ended and present with parties, moving from "active" to "deep" listening. We also trusted the parties more, believing in their capacity to both raise important issues and/or determine for themselves if mediation was appropriate for their situation. We no longer screened out cases, regardless of circumstances, as we no longer felt expert; we were trusting the parties to be the experts on their own lives. We trusted the ability of parties, when met with non-judgment and reflection, to move from confusion to clarity and to make informed decisions about their participation in mediation.

After a year of working with Dee DePorto, associate director of Battered Women's Services, we jointly developed a domestic violence "protocol" for all cases involving intimate partners. We realized that the transformative model and the domestic violence community's model of working with victims is the same—they both honor voice and choice. The Battered Women's Services learned that what often held true about mediation and domestic violence victims was different [in our Center] because the goals of transformative mediation were different from the goals of other mediation models. Early in the discussions it was clear that the roles had to remain as they were—mediators could not act as advocates and advocates could not act as mediators because blurring the roles weakens each. A partnership was necessary so that victims could be identified and supported in their choice safely. The collaboration works exceptionally well. Weekly meetings are held to case consult, provide safety assessments and safety planning, as well as further develop the protocol through training mediators and educating referral sources.

The most exciting and rewarding aspect of the program has been the effect of the process on victims. For some, it is the first time there has been an acknowledgment of their experiences as victims of domestic violence. For others, it is validation of their voice in their safety by accepting their decision not to mediate. For still others, the preparation for and participation in the mediation session has strengthened them to take actions and make needed plans. Women are not, as sometimes reported by domestic violence experts, feeling coerced into mediation, and victims are being connected to necessary community resources. Both in deciding about and participating in mediation, victims are transforming from unsettled, fearful, confused, unclear, to more clear, settled, capable of decision-making, co-parenting, and seeking safety.

Although we are still struggling to continually educate the courts about domestic violence and the potential for some kinds of mediation, and the court system, to put abuse victims at risk, our new protocol has highlighted these controversial issues, making them easier to address. The partnership between Battered Women's Services and the Mediation Center, essential for the success of the protocol, demonstrates a smooth and respectful fit between two diverse disciplines [Miller and Wellock, 2004].

The program leaders quoted here, like others who have adopted the transformative framework—including many private practitioners—emphasize that doing so has aligned their mediation practice with the core ideals and objectives of their programs. The implementation of the transformative model in these programs, and the explicit rationales given for its adoption, illustrate how various sectors of the mediation field are becoming increasingly receptive to and supportive of this approach to practice.

Adapting Core Principles: New Forms of Transformative Practice

Most of the work on the development of transformative mediation has been explicitly constructed on one foundational principle. This principle is best captured by the phrase "purpose drives practice"—a phrase that is often quoted at the outset of transformative mediation trainings. An understanding of one's goals for the process—one's purpose in interacting with disputing parties—is essential for understanding what a mediator can and should do during a mediation session. Although the emphasis and clarity placed on underlying purpose has sometimes raised difficult questions about values and ideology, it has helped to ground mediators in their work. It has clarified their role and helped them to be able to articulate their purpose to clients and program stakeholders.

But this emphasis on underlying goals has also had an important secondary effect. In being so explicit about the premises and goals of the process, proponents of transformative mediation have sparked new ways of thinking about where and how transformative practice can be done. The discussion of core principles has opened up and guided new formats for intervention that are not limited to the arenas in which mediation is traditionally practiced. It has allowed practitioners to work with their core ingredients rather than being limited to a favorite recipe. This has been of real value because it supports those who are looking for a wider array of venues in which to provide conflict intervention services. There are relatively few mediators in the field at large who can work full time as private practitioners within traditional mediation venues. The possibility of applying core principles of transformative practice to other settings has been a valuable secondary result of keeping the core premises of the model in the forefront of training and practice.

Policy Dialogue

The extension of transformative practice is most evident in a range of practice arenas where the facilitation of dialogue or discussion is valued and needed. Almost immediately after the publication of *The Promise of Mediation*, members of the Public Conversations Project recognized key links between the transformative framework and the approach that they take to their work facilitating dialogue among people involved in intense controversy about public issues. Six members of the group expressed how they saw the core similarities between their dialogue work and the transformative framework of mediation:

> Nothing could be closer to our hearts than Bush and Folger's broad achievement: a conscientiously wrought and passionately expressed appeal to give priority to the quality of the relational experience, and to the enhancements of the relational skills required when dealing with human beings at impasse. We agree strongly with this priority and agree that it requires significant dedication and self-discipline. It requires that the third party be non-judgmental, resist creating solutions for clients, and care deeply about the quality of the process. Most impor-

tant, we must detach ourselves from the goal of settlement. Thus freed, our energies can help people reveal
and hear ambiguity, confusion, uncertainty, and other
elusive but critical human experiences that may seem
useless in a dash toward settlement, but that are vitally
important to our own work in fostering dialogue and to
the work of Bush and Folger in practicing transformative
mediation [Chasin and others, 1996, p. 340].

Multiparty Public Policy Disputes

The link noted in this statement by the Public Conversations
Project has also been seen by practitioners who work as intervenors
in multiparty, public policy disputes. Judy Saul, director of the Community Dispute Resolution Center in Ithaca, New York, has described
how the principles of transformative mediation have supported her
work in public policy settings:

Transformative theory has made a difference in the way
I facilitate interactions when working on multi-party and
environmental disputes. I have come to appreciate the
wisdom of groups and the importance of following the
participants' lead. Working closely with those who will
be present, I consider what activities may be helpful,
what skills to share with them, and how best to structure
time. Then I do my best to be totally flexible and responsive to what is happening in the moment. I am quick to
change the plan, turn attention elsewhere, to follow the
group when it begins down a different path. I check in,
note what I see and refer back to goals or earlier decisions. I depend on those present to decide whether and
when the path needs to change, and my trust in the
group's wisdom is seldom misplaced.

In the past I assumed responsibility for gathering information and developing a plan of action. Though this

included talking to some of those involved in the situation, I was making the decisions. Participants were left out. Now, when the size and structure allow, I suggest that a group use the initial session for discussing the issues they face, the information that will be helpful and ways to proceed. When groups are open (involving the public) or when processes are on-going, I put together a diverse planning team or advisory committee. This moves "behind the scenes" work to a place that is visible and participatory.

When a group's interactions break down, I avoid the role of enforcer. Instead I turn to the group for suggestions about how to proceed. I note what I see happening (e.g., a few people are dominating the conversation) and ask if that is of concern. Thus the group gets to weigh in on whether or not they agree that what I observe is a problem. Based on their sense of what is happening, I ask the group what they want to do in response. I put process decisions in participants' hands because I appreciate how closely process and content are intertwined [Saul, 2004].

Louise Phipps Senft, director of the Baltimore Mediation Center in Baltimore, Maryland, has also adopted the transformative model in her work with clients in multiparty situations, involving urban planning for example. She describes how she applies the principles of the transformative model to that setting:

My work in multi-party public policy interventions is guided by a transformative approach. In other words, it is about improving the quality of the interaction of those "at the table." My belief is that this change in experience then has wider implications beyond the persons "at that table" because those people will relate to conflict in a more productive way in the future. And this bears out repeatedly. Simply solving the policy crisis does not have the same systemic effects. I cling to the belief that people have what it takes to face conflict and work with it productively when given the chance to create the right environment for having safe dialogue. While I believe this is what people want, it is usually not what they say they want in conflict, and interventions that focus on quality of interaction in conflict are actually counterintuitive. I took a certain leap of faith years ago to practice in this way, and although counterintuitive, it makes sense from the way that I view conflict, and people in conflict. And it works.

One multi-party case I worked on is a good example. I was asked by the developers of a major urban site to facilitate a multi-party dialogue including the developers themselves, residents, merchants, preservationists, and government observers. The developers' presentations at community meetings had often degenerated into attacks and further alienation, and they wanted to stop this. They saw themselves as landowners with every right to develop as they chose, but also as publicly minded developers who went to great lengths to develop spaces in ways that complement existing neighborhoods. Regarding my role, I explained that my role would be to enhance the quality of their dialogue, not to take any one side in the discussion, but to instead offer a process where they can advocate for themselves and be understood by the community and where the community can do the same. They were a bit uncomfortable with this. One of the team had a number of experiences with facilitators, and assumed I would be pushing their agenda and would make sure that no one got out of hand. I clarified that that was one approach; however, it was not the one I would take. I said I believe people have the capacity to do that for themselves when given the opportunity, so I would ask the group itself how they might best have the conversation and spend some time on establishing these guidelines. What did they think about this? Good to some; a little too soft for others. I could see some members of the team squirming, possibly questioning my ability. But the overall view was, "You do whatever; that's why we're hiring you." I slowed down to talk about their own requests, since it appeared that it was important to them that boundaries be made clear about decision-making authority. They were in quick agreement on this; they asked why I couldn't just put people in groups, get their input in writing, end the meeting and let them see where the problem areas were. I said they could do that if they chose, but wondered about the consequences if their goal was to establish a better working understanding with the community. Again, they thought if I operated in this way the group would get "out of control." All this illustrates the type of work that it takes, even with well intentioned folks, to deal with conflict by design from the transformative framework. If all the members had not wanted this approach, after explaining, I would not have accepted the job. The conversation about the conversation is critical.

Fast forward: There were three meetings, each with 20 participant representatives, and the richness of the meetings was a result of the initial dialogue about how to have the conversation. True to the model's premises about people and their capacity, all those present responded beautifully and quite specifically about what a quality dialogue would look like. And the group came up with its own guidelines that allowed them to self-monitor. Part of that discussion included the community's history of feeling disenfranchised or disrespected or powerplayed and wanting to have information up front. Part of the dialogue included the developers clarifying their role as landowners and wanting input but also respect that they didn't have to be doing these public meetings, but chose to because they wanted a better working relationship. The participants established that they wanted to see progress and not get too sidetracked, but also that they wanted to be able to ask questions openly and to get responses, and that truthful information was easier to deal with, even when contrary to one's hopes, than fabrications or half-truths. Some of the requests and comments were sharp; I did not step in to reframe, stop or candycoat. Others were complimentary and seeking connection. Both were highlighted by me followed by checking in on how they saw such viewpoints and how they wanted to continue the conversation. They underscored the importance of this honesty and directness without having to be defensive, and how refreshing it was. *And all this occurred before they even began to discuss the plan or the expectations for the property.* This conversation was foundational, as it had to do with the quality of their continued and future interactions. They were growing more confident and more open and ready to tackle the potential substantive differences that lay before them.

This foundation led to the richness of dialogue over the next 4 weeks, in what became a posture of openness and desire to have the community's input into shaping the development. The developers decided after the first meeting to open up all possibilities to the community on how to develop roughly 11 acres of waterfront land. The community decided they wanted the developers to create a signature building for the city. The developers and community together found the most environmental and

"green" way to preserve open space, and were both ex-
cited about the development. And they decided to continue with the community dialogues every two months
for many years until all the phases of the project were
complete. Not surprisingly for the transformative model,
the dialogue had systemic effects [Senft, 2004].

Intraorganizational Facilitation and Team Building

In addition to the public policy arena, work that is built on the
core principles of the transformative framework has also emerged
within organizational settings. Because of the increasing recognition of the need for intervention in conflict within groups that work
together on a day-to-day basis, organizational settings offer an important venue for developing new models of intervention based on
the core principles of transformative practice. Although some organizations have established formal mediation processes as part of
their dispute resolution programs, most corporate, nonprofit, and
governmental organizations have no such program. Nonetheless
these organizations frequently have difficult internal conflicts to
address. In many instances, conflicts emerge and receive the attention of human resources or learning and development specialists
within the organization. The need for conflict intervention may not
be explicitly identified as such, but the skills needed are essentially
the same.

Many calls for team building or team development, for example,
stem from differences or conflicts within groups that are not adequately addressed by team managers or by the employees themselves.
These conflicts can be addressed with an approach to intervention
that stems from the same core principles of transformative mediation. The setting for the intervention and the label for the work is
different—it may well be called "team building" and the conflicts
may not be acknowledged explicitly by the organization—but the
need for conflict intervention is essentially the same. The ability to
support empowerment and recognition through the facilitation and

transformation of the team members' interaction often lies at the heart of successful team intervention in organizational settings. The principles of the transformative model drive the possibility for effective practice in this context.

Much of the team-building work in organizations conducted over the past ten years by one of the authors of this volume, Joseph Folger, has been based on the core principles of the transformative framework. Folger has worked with a wide variety of teams in different organizational settings, from Wall Street firms to small manufacturing and service organizations. The size of the teams varies considerably, from six or seven members to upwards of fifty people. Some teams have members who all work at the same geographical site, whereas other teams have been composed of members working remotely in different parts of the country or world. Across these diverse team-building projects, the overall objective is essentially the same: to design formats that allow team members to discuss difficult issues related to morale, productivity, roles and responsibilities, or leadership. In designing the process for these sessions, the goal is to allow the team members to identify the conversations that they believe are needed or would be useful to have. The design for the actual team-building session emerges from the suggestions made by team members through individual interviews conducted early in the process. At the team-building sessions themselves, agendas and discussion activities are suggested, with considerable feedback and modification from team members as the agenda unfolds. In all cases, the design of the sessions is aimed at allowing people to say what they want to say about the topics that team members have identified, but never forcing people to talk when they are not comfortable doing so. Discussion formats are frequently designed that allow people to raise issues or topics in ways that are comfortable or safe for them to participate, sometimes anonymously.

The role of the third party in these team-building sessions is to facilitate dialogue among the team members as the agenda unfolds, supporting the opportunities for empowerment and recognition shifts that occur as the discussions unfold. Sometimes the facilitator is not actively involved in the discussions but is enabling people to participate in predesigned formats and building on what is occurring to shape the unfolding session. The entire event is viewed as malleable and emergent, based on where the team feels it needs to head.

One particular team-building session was a two-day event involving sixty people from different human resource divisions that were being merged into one department. Toward the end of the session, the manager of one division came up to the team-building facilitator and commented on the process. She said, "This is pretty amazing. It is like you are not in the room but incredible conversations are going on—conversations I never thought we could have with each other." This observation about the role of the third party is characteristic of transformative practitioners in general and was viewed as a valued compliment by the third party involved in designing and facilitating the team-building session.

These team buildings are not training events. Nor are they about the third party who designs and facilitates the sessions. Rather, the focus remains on the team members' interaction and their ability to have the conversations they need to have, with the ultimate goal of transforming the team interaction in ways that the team finds useful or valuable for the work it needs to accomplish and the relationships that need to be sustained. This type of team-building work offers transformative practitioners many opportunities to use this framework and its skills in diverse organizational settings, in ways that are valued by management and employees.

The extension of the core principles of the transformative model to public policy and organizational settings suggests that this framework provides a potentially useful vision of intervention in many settings where significant conflicts occur. In focusing on core elements of productive conflict interaction, the transformative model has shown itself to be widely applicable and valued by practitioners and clients in an increasing variety of settings.

The Transformative Model in Concrete Practice

The preceding descriptions of program directors and practitioners using the transformative model attest to the viability of the model in a wide variety of contexts, and to its appeal to both institutional and private clients. In the short few years since its first articulation, the model has developed specific methods and practices, has attracted a growing "market" of users, and has demonstrated its ability to provide the kinds of benefits they are seeking from a conflict intervention process. In sum, the transformative model has begun to fulfill concretely the promise of mediation that inspired its articulation to begin with.

Conclusion

All of the shifts in the mediation field discussed in this chapter have supported the development and use of the transformative model of conflict intervention. The ground on which transformative practice rests today is far stronger than it was ten years ago, for the many reasons this chapter suggests. More professionals within the field have expressed dissatisfaction with the prevailing forms of practice. More practitioners and program administrators have turned to this model to guide their practice. And the core elements of transformative practice have become much clearer and more accessible.

Although all of these developments point to the increasing appeal and practical viability of transformative mediation, the real value of this approach to practice cannot be appreciated by cataloguing its features or by summarizing the reasons for its adoption. The impact of transformative mediation can only be felt, and the nature of transformative mediation practice understood, by looking closely at the very heart of this work—that is, by focusing on conflict interaction and its transformation. In the next two chapters, we offer an opportunity for the reader to see how the practice of mediation can support the transformation of difficult conflict when the elements of practice are aligned with the values and processes outlined in Chapter Two.

4

Putting Transformative
Theory into Practice
The "Purple House" Mediation,
with Commentary—Part One

As more practitioners and programs have moved toward the
transformative model—in the kinds of developments described
in the previous chapter—we have found that one crucial step in moving from theory to practice is actually observing a transformative
mediation session. Prior to observing the model in action, many mediators who resonate with the principles strongly believe that their
own practices follow the model. This is often true to some extent; but
when mediators see the model in action, they often find many of its
practices quite different from what they are familiar with—and from
what they expected to see. They begin to see that there are truly distinctive interventions used in this model, so that ultimately it makes
sense to see it as a unique model of mediation, not simply a stylistic
variation of other approaches to practice (Della Noce, 2001; Della
Noce, Bush, and Folger, 2002). In short, it turns out that a picture is
indeed worth a thousand words when it comes to getting a real grasp
of what transformative mediation entails in practice.

For this reason, we are including here, as a concrete example of
transformative mediation in practice, the complete transcript of a
simulated mediation conducted by one of the authors—Baruch
Bush—that was videotaped as part of the Practice Enrichment Initiative. The simulation was produced on videotape by Sally Pope
for the Institute for the Study of Conflict Transformation; and both
the videotape and the transcript represent a complete, live session,

without anything edited out. The simulation is based on a real case, but the parties are played by professional actors. The session itself was completely unscripted and unrehearsed, with the actors playing out their roles spontaneously, working from basic information about their characters and the facts of the dispute, summarized in the following discussion. Though simulated, this mediation gives a very good sense of the dynamics of a transformative mediation session, including both the parties' interaction and the mediator's interventions. It is not offered here as an "ideal" model of practice, because even within the transformative model there are different styles, and a different mediator might have made different interventions consistent with the model. It is nevertheless a good example of thoughtful, well-crafted practice of the transformative model. In training sessions, we have found that this tape conveys very effectively how transformative mediation is practiced. We believe that including the case here will provide the reader a good exposure to the concrete experience of "observing" a transformative mediation session—to the extent possible in a written volume.

To give the reader a feel for the parties and the case, here is some brief background information: the parties are homeowners in an exclusive (and expensive) housing development, The Trees. Julie is a woman in her forties, white, who has been a resident of the development for about eight years. She is chair of the development's architectural control committee. Elizabeth is also in her forties, an African American woman, who bought a home in the development within the past year or so. She resides there with her daughter, Bernice, a young woman in her late teens or early twenties, an art student, who accompanies her mother at the mediation. Both Elizabeth and Julie are well-dressed, well-spoken women. Elizabeth comes to the session dressed elegantly in tailored suit and matching hat—which she wears throughout the session. Julie is dressed in a businesslike pants suit. And Bernice is wearing the normal jeans and sweater of a young person her age. The mediator is wearing coat and tie.

The basic facts—and the only information given to the actors prior to the simulation—are these: shortly after moving in to their home, Elizabeth and Bernice repainted the house. The color they chose for the repainting was one that the development's architectural control committee found objectionable, and the committee claimed that the use of this color violated a covenant in the development's standard homeowner contract. When the committee and Elizabeth could not agree about the matter, the parties' lawyers recommended that they contact a mediator to see if this would help. The mediator, a private practitioner, spoke with both parties by phone before the session to explain the nature of the process but otherwise has minimal information about the situation. The mediation session is being held in the mediator's office, and the transcript begins with the very opening of the session. As noted previously, the simulation was totally unrehearsed, and the mediator had no advance knowledge of what the parties would say or do; it was as close as possible to a genuine, live mediation.

The transcript is presented here in six segments, each followed by a brief commentary highlighting aspects of the parties' interaction and the mediator's interventions that offer particularly good examples of the way the model works. The entire session lasted about seventy-five minutes. For readers interested in getting a more immediate feel of what the session was like—the parties' personalities, the tone of the conversation, and so forth— the videotape from which the transcript was made can be ordered from the Institute for the Study of Conflict Transformation, whose address is found in the Acknowledgments.

The Purple House Mediation: Segment One

MEDIATOR: Good afternoon to everybody. I just want to sort of review. I think I've spoken with you all on the phone before today, but I'm not sure I know who's who in the room, so maybe it would be helpful if everybody tells me who's who. [looks from one party to the other]

BERNICE: I'm Bernice.

MEDIATOR: [*looks at Bernice*] OK.

ELIZABETH: I'm Elizabeth; this is my daughter.

MEDIATOR: OK, very good. I'm glad to meet you.

ELIZABETH: And we own the home.

MEDIATOR: Right. Good to meet you in person and you can call me Baruch if that's OK.

BERNICE: OK.

MEDIATOR: And . . . [*looks at Julie*]

JULIE: I am Julie, yes, and I'm chairman of the architectural control committee in our homeowners' association.

MEDIATOR: OK. And that would be the Trees Development?

JULIE: That's correct.

MEDIATOR: Well, we spoke a little bit on the phone about what mediation is, what it means to come to a mediation meeting or session. Would it be helpful to review that a little bit now, or are you all pretty clear on that? How do you . . . What's your view on that? Should I, in other words, sort of go over a little bit what we spoke about before, just to bring it back up? Or are we ready to just sort of jump in? [*looks from party to party*]

ELIZABETH: Yes, would you please, please, go over it a little bit.

MEDIATOR: [*looks at Julie*] That's OK with you?

JULIE: That would be fine.

MEDIATOR: [*looking back and forth from party to party*] What I see happening here is basically a conversation between all of you about the concerns that you have, the issues that have come up. And my role in the process is to be helpful to you in having, uh, the most productive conversation you could have about that stuff, including, uh, understanding the way you see, each of you, the situation, uh, the decisions that face you, what you want to do about those decisions and also how you . . .

JULIE: [*interrupts mediator, who stops to let her speak*] Well, I want it resolved, that's what I want to do.

MEDIATOR: [*directly to Julie*] OK, OK, and clearly that's one of the, one place that those decisions can lead to, Julie, based upon what decisions you make along the way. All of that is basically in your hands. [*resumes looking from party to party*] And also part of what can happen in the conversation is for you to, for you to review and assess how you see one another and how you see one another's situation and positions. So in the conversation, all of those kinds of things can surface, uh, and as you sort of walk through that and make decisions along the way, it will lead you to whatever ultimate point all of you decide you want to get to. I'm not going to, uh, make decisions for you in any way here really, uh, whether decisions about how to have the conversation or what to talk about or where to wind up. I see my role as helping you to have the conversation, listening to you, helping you listen to yourselves in a way, as well as to each other, uh, and that's, that's sort of a general way of describing the mediation process, at least as I practice it. So does that seem like it might be helpful to you to proceed as we spoke about before? Is that . . . ? [*looking from party to party*]

ELIZABETH: Yeah.

JULIE: I guess we won't know until we try.

MEDIATOR: [*to Julie*] Well, that's true, but you have to be willing to try at least. . . . [*waits for Julie to respond*]

JULIE: I'm here.

MEDIATOR: OK. [*resumes looking from party to party*] And I guess one place to start, uh, to see how you want to handle that is just to ask you if there is anything you want to say about, sort of guidelines for the conversation itself, uh, in terms of, you know, the way the talk goes, taking turns, or just having the conversation in a free-flow way. What feels most comfortable to you about guidelines? Or do you need to talk about that at all?

JULIE: No, I don't think so.

ELIZABETH: No.

MEDIATOR: Just see what happens basically. OK. Fine. Just one thing that I want to say in terms of my guidelines, that when I work with people, I do so on a basis of confidentiality. So what that means is that I'm not going to discuss anything that any of you talks about in here with anyone outside of this room. I don't know why that should come up anyway as far as I can see, but I just want to reassure you that in that sense you're having a private conversation, as far as I'm concerned, and there's no way that it's going to become public through me, um, so I want to reassure you about that. [*pauses*] I sometimes take notes just to keep track of where I am, but this is essentially, you know, for convenience, for me just to keep track of where things are going. OK. Where would you like to start? How would you like to begin? Do any of you feel like it would be useful to, uh, jump in to start off? [*looks back and forth*]

JULIE: Certainly.

MEDIATOR: [*looks at Julie*] Do you want to start off?

JULIE: [*speaks first to Elizabeth*] Would that be OK with you?

[*Mediator looks to Elizabeth and she nods her assent; mediator looks back to Julie, who now addresses herself to him, and he continues looking at her as she speaks.*]

JULIE: I am, as I told you, the chairperson of the architectural control committee in our Trees Development, and it is the concern of not only the committee itself but also several members of the community that when Elizabeth and Bernice moved into their home, they opted to paint it, um, purple. Um . . .

BERNICE: [*interrupts*] Mauve, I'm sorry . . . mauve.

[*Mediator looks at Bernice when she speaks, then back to Julie when she responds, and continues in this fashion, looking at whichever party starts to speak, and giving them undivided attention as long as they keep speaking.*]

JULIE: Ah, mauve, purple, mauve, whatever. This is not in keeping with the colors of the other homes in the community, and, uh, we do have a policy in place that says any homeowner who's going to make major changes in, uh, his or her home has to get prior approval from the architectural control committee. And they did not do that; they just went ahead and painted their home purple. And, uh, honestly, if you could see it, it stands out in—my apologies [*Julie glances at Elizabeth here, then turns back to mediator*]—but in a way that is just not really, not in keeping with the rest of the community. And we want them to, uh, repaint the home. [*pauses, as if finished*]

MEDIATOR: OK. [*speaks directly to Julie at this point*] So . . .

JULIE: That's basically it.

MEDIATOR: [*stops to allow Julie to interrupt him (here and in next few comments) and then continues*] So what I'm hearing from your point of view, Julie, is . . . uh, and you're, you're here not just as yourself but in effect representing some, uh, committee from the development . . .

JULIE: That's correct.

MEDIATOR: . . . that from your point of view the choice of color that Elizabeth and Bernice chose for the house that they bought in the development—um, and you're describing it as purple—is out of keeping with the rest of the character of the development.

JULIE: Correct.

MEDIATOR: And the committee, again I'm assuming you're speaking for this committee, would like to see, uh, see them repaint the house. And that that would put it more in keeping, as you see it, with the, with the . . .

JULIE: . . . the tenor of the community, yes.

MEDIATOR: OK.

ELIZABETH: [*interrupting*] May I speak?

[*Mediator stops, looks back and forth between Elizabeth and Julie—who is now looking at Elizabeth; then mediator turns full attention to Elizabeth, as she speaks to mediator.*]

ELIZABETH: First of all, I believe that we have a document of, I don't know, it might be fifteen or twenty pages, that outlines the parameters that are involved with the maintenance and the control of the property—and nowhere in any of those pages does it talk about painting. We are well within our rights. [*gradually gets louder and more emphatic*] Secondly, I believe I can give a list of at least, what, ten or twelve neighbors and various community members who have no objection. Thirdly, it is a *pastel* color. And fourthly, I could name you at least five to seven other members of the community who have painted their homes other colors than gray, tan, or yellow, that it says in the . . . is so typical of the architectural *control* committee . . . [*by this time, Elizabeth's voice is loud and angry*]

BERNICE: I like purple myself. I think it's a nice color.

JULIE: Well, I think it's a nice color, too, Bernice, but not for a house.

ELIZABETH: [*directly to Julie, quickly and sharply*] It's not your house.

JULIE: No, it's not my house, but I do have a responsibility as . . .

ELIZABETH: [*interrupts, cutting Julie off*] And you've met your responsibility, and we disagree.

BERNICE: There's other colors . . .

JULIE: [*ignoring Bernice and responding to Elizabeth*] That's why we're here.

BERNICE: There's other colors the other homes are trimmed with, you know. It might not be mauve, but there are other colors.

JULIE: Speaking of trim, you've got some sort of turquoisey blue trim. It's, it's . . .

ELIZABETH: [*leans forward and interrupts angrily*] Because you don't like it? You've been on a campaign for the last six months, and you don't like it!

BERNICE: [*speaking slowly, as if to calm the conversation*] I've been to art school. I read a book in school in history class about living in color, and it's, it really does work, you know . . . you know. I'm an artist.

JULIE: [*looking to Bernice, confused*] What does that mean? "Living in color" works?

ELIZABETH: [*gesturing to Bernice to stop, and responding sharply to Julie*] She doesn't have to define it. We like the color! We have paid, what, $650,000 for this house, and I think we can paint it any color we want to—polka dots—if it's our choice! We don't have to defend our taste to you! [*almost spitting out her words at Julie*]

JULIE: [*with some sarcasm*] Actually, polka dots would not be acceptable either.

ELIZABETH: [*very angry now, speaking rapidly, pointing and gesturing at Julie*] And show me the page! You got the contract? Show me the page.

[*During this entire exchange, mediator is sitting back, remaining silent but following the exchange intently, looking from party to party as each one speaks.*]

BERNICE: [*leaning over and trying to calm Elizabeth down*] Ma . . .

JULIE: [*speaks past Bernice to Elizabeth, in cold, aloof tone*] My dear, I told you . . .

ELIZABETH: [*interrupting, mocking Julie's tone, still very angry*] "My dear . . ."

JULIE: [*trying to continue*] . . . major changes . . .

BERNICE: [*stepping back in, still trying to calm things down*] What my mom is trying to say, she's just a little emotional right now, but my mom, she's speaking from the truth. [*Elizabeth sits back, lowers her head, and frowns as Bernice continues*] But she's saying that, you know, why shouldn't we be able to paint the house the color that we choose, because in our contract it doesn't say, "Do not paint your house mauve." Other neighbors have painted theirs with a teal and beige and white, and a hint of blue. . . . I didn't see anything in the contract that stated that we could not paint it. . . . [*pauses*]

MEDIATOR: [*steps in to speak as Bernice pauses, first glancing from party to party*] If I can just say what I'm hearing from you, Elizabeth [*looks at Elizabeth*], from you and Bernice [*Elizabeth looks up when mediator addresses her*]—and part of that is a sense of, you know, pretty strong feelings about your choices and your freedom to make those choices, having bought the house—that you don't see, in any of the formal agreements that were made in purchasing the house, any restriction on the way the house is painted.

ELIZABETH: [*immediately nods her head and interjects*] No, right, other than it doesn't suit her taste. [*moving her head in Julie's direction but not looking at her*]

MEDIATOR: [*stops to allow Elizabeth's interjection (both here and in the next few comments) and then continues*] OK, and so you don't see this as being, you don't see the paint that you chose, the color that you chose, as violating those agreements in any way.

ELIZABETH: [*again interjects, emphatically, gesturing with her head*] In no way, no how!

MEDIATOR: Right. And that having paid a substantial price for the house, that you're really free to paint it any way that you choose. But that I also hear you saying that there's a considerable number of people in the development, your neighbors, who have expressed to you they have no problem with it.

ELIZABETH: [*still emphatic, but a good deal calmer*] None whatsoever.

JULIE: [*interrupts to speak, less cool now, more perturbed and defensive*] Well, I do think I could match the number of people that have said to you that they have no problem with it—which when you think about it, is kind of a negative way to say it—uh, with people who have come to us as the control committee and said, "You have to do something about that house." [*getting more exercised as she speaks, and gesturing dramatically*] It's like a neon light in the middle of the community! It's like having a great big McDonald's sign right there!

BERNICE: [*in a calm, casual tone, as if to ignore the anger in the conversation*] Is it possible that we could find out who they are, 'cause I go to school with about five or six other, you know, kids who live in the block, you know. We go to art school together, and their families don't have a problem with us, so I'd like to know who they are.

JULIE: [*calmer*] That would be possible.

BERNICE: Yeah.

ELIZABETH: [*leaning forward, gesturing to Bernice to back off*] It really doesn't matter, Bernice. It doesn't matter. [*turning to face Julie directly, with angry and challenging tone*] You know, Julie, ever since we have moved into this community, I think it's because the house is what, four or five doors from yours, you have been on a, it seems like a personal vendetta. [*pauses for emphasis*] Is it because we're the only blacks on your block?

JULIE: [*reacts as if stung, sitting back and shaking her head*] Absolutely not!

ELIZABETH: [*responding quickly, not letting up*] I beg to differ.

Commentary: Segment One

The conversation about the "purple house" has clearly become very heated very quickly. How that heat is dealt with and how the conversation evolves are evident in the following segments of the mediation. First, however, here is some analysis of the mediator's interventions in this opening segment of the session:

1. Notice first how the mediator opens the session. He avoids making an opening statement as such and instead has an "opening conversation" with the parties. He sets an interactional tone from the very first moments of the session, rather than simply launching into a formal opening statement.

   - In talking about the process and explaining his role as mediator, he explains that he will support the parties in thinking about what they want to do, considering how they want to see each other, and making decisions about what to do in the situation. These are some of the simple-language ways of expressing what we described in Chapter Two as "supporting empowerment and recognition shifts," in terms that parties can understand.

   - In talking about the possible outcomes of the mediation, the mediator notes that resolution is one of the possibilities but also points out that other useful things can result for the parties, such as gaining clarity in their assessment of the situation and what they want to do. From the beginning, the process has a broader focus than agreement.

   - The mediator describes the session as a conversation—not as a mediation, not as exploring resolution, not even as a session! Conversation is something that everyone understands, so parties sense right away that this is something they can do, increasing their sense of competency and control. In addition, the conversation metaphor is in tune with the focus of the model on party interaction rather than settlement per se.

2. A second important element of the mediator's practice in this segment is that he allows and supports party control and choice, from the earliest moments of the mediation.

- He begins by asking them if they want him to review how the process works, immediately giving them control over what is and is not discussed.

- When the parties show no interest in setting up specific guidelines for the conversation, the mediator accepts their decision right away and moves on, not imposing on them a discussion about ground rules that they are not interested in.

- As the opening conversation finishes, the mediator asks the parties themselves to determine who should speak first, instead of making this decision for them.

- When the parties interrupt him, or each other, the mediator draws back, not trying to control the interruption; similarly, when the parties begin to get angry, he does not step in to defuse or control their anger.

Thus the mediator starts from the very beginning of the mediation to turn control of the process over to the parties and to follow their lead. Further examples of this are noted in the commentary on the next segment of the case.

3. The third major point in this segment is that the mediator uses of one of the specific forms of intervention that are characteristic of the transformative model—*reflection*. In reflection, the mediator "mirrors" back to the speaker what the mediator believes the speaker has just expressed, capturing both the substance and the emotional tone of what the speaker has said.

- Reflection is one of the most powerful things that transformative mediators do to help parties make interactional shifts. It is a move that supports both empowerment and recognition shifts, for both the speaking and the listening party.

- For the speaking party, the mediator's reflection allows that party to hear herself speak, and then to have a kind of "conversation with herself."

  First Julie and then Elizabeth, each in response to the mediator's reflection of her comment, nods her head emphatically, saying something like, "Yes, that's right, absolutely." In effect, each one hears herself in the room and draws strength from this itself.

  In addition, in hearing herself each gains in clarity, confirming that "yes, that's what I wanted to say, that's the way I see things." Or she modifies her statement slightly, becoming clearer by doing so.

  The impact of reflection for the speaking party is to help her gather her sense of clarity and decisiveness about what she wants to say, how she wants to present herself, and to grow stronger in the process.

- At the same time, the mediator's reflection to the speaker allows the other party to "listen in" from a safe distance, considering more fully what the speaker has said.

  When the mediator reflects the speaker's comment, the listening party often hears the comment for the first time, because she has been "filtering out" the speaker's voice. The mediator's reflection, in a new voice, allows the listening party to hear things she may not have heard clearly before and begin getting new information about the situation—an empowerment shift toward greater clarity.

  This happens here as Julie listens to the reflection of Elizabeth's comment about her view of the contract. The effect is that Julie begins to realize more clearly how strong Elizabeth's opposition is going to be, and why.

• Reflection can also help the speaker make recognition shifts, by allowing her to hear when she has "gone too far" and reconsider and retract negative comments. And it can help the listener make recognition shifts by allowing the listener to hear the speaker's comments "for the first time" or "in a different way," because of the reflector's voice. This emerges in later segments.

In general, reflection acts as an amplifier of the conversation for each party: it makes what is being said more audible and intelligible to both parties. To accomplish all of this, the mediator must follow certain guidelines in reflection, as demonstrated in this case.

• In his reflections, the mediator engages *directly and only* with the speaking party, whose comments he is reflecting. The mediator does not move back and forth: he does not speak at all to Elizabeth when he is reflecting to Julie. He is fully and directly engaged only with Julie at that time. Similarly, when reflecting to Elizabeth he is engaged only with Elizabeth and not bringing Julie in.

This mode of direct, exclusive engagement helps both parties. Beginning with the first reflection to Julie, it helps Julie really listen to herself, through the mediator, becoming clearer and stronger in what she is saying. And it helps Elizabeth, when the mediator is reflecting with Julie, because it allows Elizabeth to have private space and not be put on the spot, as she would be if the mediator were to ask what she thinks of Julie's comment.

Reflection means mirroring to the speaker whatever she has expressed. The mediator *does not carry* the speaker's message to the other party because this would both make the mediator the speaker's advocate and put the listener on the spot.

- Other guidelines for reflection are also demonstrated by the mediator here.

  Providing an undistorted mirror: a reflection is most effective when it's inclusive, capturing the full range of what has been expressed—without editing, softening, or filtering what the speaker has said.

  Including reflection of emotions expressed by the parties: this means not just what has been said but how the speaker appears to be feeling. What is being reflected is any and all communication or expression, not just speech.

Reflection usually carries its own confirmation. An effective reflection will usually evoke an immediate confirmation response from the speaker, like the parties' responses to the reflections in this segment. Even if a reflection misses the mark, it usually evokes a response from the speaker that "cures" the mistake. ("That's not it at all, here's what I said" or "I'm not just mad, I said furious!") In other words, the positive empowerment effects of reflection can occur whether the speaker confirms or corrects the reflection—in either case, the speaker is gaining clarity and strength, as occurs in this case.

The Purple House Mediation: Segment Two

ELIZABETH: Is it because we're the only blacks on your block?

JULIE: [*reacts as if stung, sitting back and shaking her head*] Absolutely not!

ELIZABETH: [*responding quickly, not letting up*] I beg to differ.

JULIE: It has nothing . . .

ELIZABETH: [*interrupting Julie*] Ever since you have become head of the committee, this control committee, you have been out . . .

JULIE: [*protesting*] It has nothing to do with . . .

ELIZABETH: [*talking over Julie*] . . . on a vendetta! Now four doors or five doors down, Mr. Wataski painted his house what, that salmon color, or blue with salmon color. Nobody objected to him!

JULIE: [*getting increasingly flustered*] Oh, please, Bernice, I mean Elizabeth, excuse me. I'm so sorry.

ELIZABETH: That's right. [*turns to Bernice, who has placed a hand on her arm*] What? I am just tired of her. It is a racist . . . They've got five families I can name, five families, what, gold . . .

JULIE: [*interrupting and finally getting out her answer, spoken forcefully*] It has nothing to do with your color. It has to do with the color of your house, and it is very different. And I am not alone . . .

ELIZABETH: [*disregarding Julie's response, very persistent and angry*] We are the only ones. We are the only family that you are attacking, the only ones.

JULIE: The only purple house.

ELIZABETH: Because you don't like purple?

JULIE: It isn't because I don't like purple. I represent a committee!

ELIZABETH: Well, there is nothing, there is nothing. We have met the . . . We have met all of the dictates of the contract and that is it. There's nothing more to talk about. Because you don't like purple. Because you are a racist, that's what this is really all about.

JULIE: Listen, you knew when you . . .

ELIZABETH: [*talking over Julie to repeat the accusation, pointing her finger at Julie*] You are a racist. You are the one!

JULIE: . . . moved into this community that there were certain rules and regulations that you had to abide by.

ELIZABETH: And none of them were met until you got to be chairman of this committee.

JULIE: And major changes in the structure as evidenced by this purple paint . . .

ELIZABETH: [*very loud, protesting*] We did not change the structure! To put paint on a surface is not changing the structure!

BERNICE: [*trying again to calm Elizabeth*] Ma! It's not . . .

JULIE: [*ignoring Bernice and responding directly to Elizabeth, insistent and offended at the same time*] Well, of course it is . . . and I really have a problem with your calling me a racist. [*sits back hard in her chair, folding her arms across her chest, scowling*]

BERNICE: [*once again intervening, seemingly to interrupt her mother's growing anger and calm things down*] It's not . . . I think we're here to talk about the house. And, like I said, my mom might be a little upset.

ELIZABETH: [*turning to Bernice and speaking to her as if privately*] You'd better say something to them because I'm getting very upset! [*sits back, head down, while Bernice continues*]

BERNICE: I haven't found any complaints, you know, like I said, from the families that surround us and on our block. Because I go to school with them and like I said, they have other colors and their trimmings of their houses also. [*pauses*]

ELIZABETH: [*starts to speak but stops*]

MEDIATOR: [*steps in tentatively as Bernice pauses, first glancing from party to party*] Let me just ask all of you, and, and . . . obviously, there are some very strong feelings about not just the house but, Elizabeth [*looks at her*], you feel that there are some issues about the position that Julie is taking based upon her attitudes towards you as an African American.

ELIZABETH: I really do. [*pauses*]

MEDIATOR: OK. And . . . [*starts to continue, but then stops as Elizabeth resumes speaking, to allow her to go ahead*]

ELIZABETH: I'm sorry to say that. I moved into the community. It's an interracial community. It's, it's . . .

JULIE: [*interrupts and speaks directly to Elizabeth*] Then why am I not picking on all the others?

BERNICE: But, but, um, Miss Julie . . . [*begins to respond, but is cut off by her mother*]

ELIZABETH: That's what I want to know. That's really what I want to know. The other four or five homes that are not what, white . . .

JULIE: Then why am I not picking on all the other African American families in the community?

ELIZABETH: Because I guess their houses . . . I think they are . . . Mr. Williams has a white house . . .

JULIE: [*interrupts to answer her own question*] Because their houses conform to the rules and regulations!

BERNICE: But, what are the rules and regulations? Look at the Hendersons, they have that salmon and with that deep bluish trim.

ELIZABETH: That's right, thank you!

BERNICE: I don't see the difference between that . . .

JULIE: It's just not a purple house.

BERNICE: . . . and the trim . . .

Elizabeth: They're not on that street.

BERNICE: . . . in a deep blue. It seems like a personal thing with you. You don't like purple. Someone might say they don't like blue,

you know. You know, I don't think there's anything wrong . . .
[*begins to trail off*]

MEDIATOR: [*steps in as Bernice's comment trails off*] I just want to just sort of frame what you're talking about in terms of the different issues that you're discussing, if it's helpful at all. [*pauses to see if they will allow him to continue, then goes ahead when no one else speaks*] One issue is, is what the colors actually are. And [*looking at Julie*] you're characterizing the colors one way, and Bernice and Elizabeth are [*looking at them*], you're characterizing them differently. That's kind of, I guess, a hard thing to have an objective measure of, but certainly you're seeing the actual colors that are involved here differently. Um, but it sounds like you're also disagreeing about what the rules actually are.

[*Throughout this comment, when he mentions one party's view, the mediator looks to that party as he speaks; otherwise, he looks back and forth to both.*]

MEDIATOR: Um, and Julie, you're saying that there are some clear rules that apply here, and, Bernice and Elizabeth, you're saying that there are rules, but that this is an area that they don't really cover, uh, that's, you know, it's left to your choice basically. Um, and, and you're also disagreeing about the responses of other people in the community. Elizabeth, you and Bernice are saying there's really no problem that people are having with this, um, as you've experienced it; and Julie, you're saying that there really are numbers of people who have a problem with it, and that you are essentially speaking for them.

JULIE: Well, but I'm not denying that some people may be supporting you [*looking at Elizabeth*] and saying, "I have no problem." I'm not denying it.

[*After stopping to allow Julie to comment, mediator continues speaking, explaining his purpose in doing so.*]

MEDIATOR: What I just am trying to do is sort of point out to you some areas where you have some pretty strong disagreements. Um, and also on the issue of what's the motivation. Obviously, Elizabeth, you said that you feel very upset because of what you see as a racial dimension to this, and Julie, you're saying that there's really none of that involved, um, and this has to do with the specifics of the situation. So there's a number of differences that, that in the way the situation looks from . . . your perspective . . . [*is about to add something else, but stops when Elizabeth begins speaking*]

ELIZABETH: [*starts speaking very quietly and slowly, with very different tone than before, not really angry but still sounding upset, almost wounded*] Every other person on her block, I was told, when they moved in, got baskets of welcoming. Our family did not. She was at that time just, I think, made chairman of the control committee. We were the only blacks on her block. That was the first. I didn't think too much of it. . . . [*pauses; Julie is sitting up straight, listening intently, as if hearing something for the first time that she doesn't quite understand*] Um, I think the second incident was where the car was parked in a place, and there was an anonymous complaint about it and it came to us—of course, that was hearsay through another party—that it was her complaint. . . . [*pauses again; no one else speaks, and as Elizabeth continues she gets more and more emotional*] Um, I have tried to get on several of the, uh, committees myself, and Julie has said, "Well, I don't think so, maybe not at this time." But there has just been one thing after another, and I really believe it is racist. [*says this with emphasis, but not anger*] I'm sorry, but I do. I've faced it all of my life. I have tried to shield my daughter from it, and I was hoping that . . . [*pauses, sighs heavily*] moving in this community . . . [*starts to cry, then sobs*] . . . I'm sorry [*through the sobbing*] . . .

MEDIATOR: [*quietly*] No, you don't have to be sorry. [*then sits quietly while Elizabeth continues to cry*]

[*Elizabeth continues sobbing for some moments, gradually stopping.*]

BERNICE: [*steps in again, seemingly to take attention off her mother's emotion*] My mom, basically, you know, she says one thing after the next. I know we're here to discuss the house, but she's just full right now because of the other things that she feels have gone on. But, you know, clearly I don't see, you know, why this is really the issue. We all are homeowners, and everyone seems to have color trimmed on their house, whether it be blue or mauve or teal or salmon. And, uh, because Miss Julie doesn't like purple as opposed to someone's, um, ultramarine blue or, or cobalt blue, whatever. That just seems like a preference, like a personal thing, and, and to me it shouldn't even be an issue. That's what I see here.

Elizabeth: [*calm again, having regained her composure while Bernice was speaking, looks up and turns to the mediator*] Where do we go from here?

MEDIATOR: [*shrugs his shoulders, looking first at Elizabeth and then Julie*] Well, that's sort of what I was going to ask you after talking about those differences that you have, and, uh . . . I don't know. What do you think?

JULIE: [*speaking directly to Elizabeth, looking at her*] Well, I just want you to know, Elizabeth, that my son-in-law is African American. . . .

[*Elizabeth avoids looking back at Julie, laughs nervously and dismissively.*]

JULIE: . . . and I bet you didn't even know that.

[*Elizabeth laughs again, still looking away from Julie.*]

JULIE: And I do not . . .

ELIZABETH: [*now interrupts Julie, speaking quite sarcastically*] The one you don't speak to, or that you don't have over to your home?

JULIE: [*leaning forward, both offended and defensive*] Oh, I've had him over to my home many times! They live a long way away.

ELIZABETH: [*dismissive and impatient*] Oh, please! Listen, Julie, that is like saying, "My best friend is black." Please!

JULIE: [*insistent, but still defensive*] But it's my son-in-law; it's my family. It's not the same at all! And I just . . .

ELIZABETH: [*cuts Julie off, and turns away from her to the mediator, determined and businesslike*] Anyway, the house. Let's get back to the house, because we will never resolve this . . . four-hundred-year-old issue.

Commentary: Segment Two

As noted earlier, the parties' conversation gets heated quite quickly, and this intensifies in Segment Two. At the same time, the substance of the discussion gets more complicated and tangled in this segment. The mediator's interventions are geared to both of these developments in the dynamics of the parties' interaction.

1. First, notice how the mediator responds to the escalating anger and emotion, and the rapid-fire party exchange, that characterize the first part of this segment, including what the mediator does and does not do.

   • Despite the parties' angry, emotional exchange, the mediator does not intervene to defuse or contain the emotion. This is intentional, and it is a clear reflection of his commitment to party choice and control.

     Supporting party choice, in the transformative model, includes not only choices about outcome but also choices about process; indeed, the model rejects the conventional distinction between the two (Folger, 2001).

     For parties, choosing *how* they want to talk about things, including expressing strong emotions, is an important decision—and one to be left within their control.

     The mediator here works hard—though it isn't visible in the transcript—to remain calm and unperturbed even

when high emotions flare. Doing otherwise might implicitly discourage emotional expression.

- The mediator is careful not to cut off the parties' conversation, whether emotional or not. When they speak, he
rarely interrupts; when they interrupt him, he quickly stops.
He supports their conversation without taking it over.

    His challenge is to find a place to enter, to know when it
    is "his turn." To do this, he listens to the rhythm of the
    conversation, waiting for lulls when the parties' talk slows
    down, as occurs late in this segment.

    He also notices that Bernice tends to speak only when the
    primary interaction between Elizabeth and Julie falters,
    and he uses her comments as signals that it is possible for
    him to step in after her.

- In reflecting, after a party has spoken emotionally—as with
Elizabeth in this segment—the mediator supports her by
not filtering out the emotion or "heat" in what she has
said. He does his best to help her—and Julie—hear the full
range of what she's saying.

    He includes reference to the *tone* and *feeling* of her com-
    ments, not just the substance. He also includes reference
    to her accusation of racism, even though this is obviously
    an inflammatory statement.

2. In this segment, the mediator uses another form of intervention characteristic of the transformative model—a *summary*.
In a summary, the mediator organizes and condenses what the
parties have talked about into the *topics of discussion* that were
introduced. Like reflection, summary can be a powerful tool
for supporting empowerment and recognition shifts for both
parties, depending again on how it is used—as illustrated in
this case.

- Summary can help the parties see the "big picture" of their conversation, get clear, and make choices. Conflict conversation often unfolds so rapidly and intensely, covering so much ground, that parties lose track of what they've said, where they are, or what they want to do next—as occurs in this case.

   Elizabeth and Julie get bogged down in this kind of confusion during this segment, going from the race issue, to the rules about painting, to the facts about the paint colors, back to race, and so on.

   The mediator's summary helps "part the fog" of this confusion, displaying all of the topics they've covered, and allowing them to see a kind of "map" of what they've discussed, assess where they now stand, and choose for themselves the most important area to address next. Elizabeth does this, with her clear choice, after the summary, to focus on the race issue.

- Summary can also help parties express and appreciate how differently they see things, helping to support both empowerment and recognition shifts.

   The mediator's summary reveals that there are sharp differences between Elizabeth and Julie in almost every area they've talked about.

   As a result of the summary, Elizabeth expresses her perceptions of racism more fully, gaining in clarity; and Julie begins to realize how Elizabeth sees things—even tries to respond, though her response is rejected.

Like reflection, summary has an amplification effect, but now at the level of conversation rather than individual comment. It makes the conversation as a whole—including the differences revealed and the choices offered—more visible to the parties, so they can make clearer choices about what to do. To accomplish this, certain guidelines for summary should be followed, as demonstrated here.

- The mediator's summary, unlike his reflections, directly involves both parties—that is, he includes what both Julie and Elizabeth have said during this chunk of the conversation, and he delivers it in a way that addresses both parties together.

- His summary is not a "playback" of everything they've said, but rather a thematic condensation of the topics of discussion that have emerged from both parties' comments.

  Topics summarized should include not only those that the parties agree about but also and especially those that they disagree about—the *topics of disagreement*. This summary is entirely topics of disagreement, because that is what the parties discussed, as is often the case early in a mediation.

  The summary includes the views that each side expressed on each topic, which helps the parties see what their differences are and decide what to do about them.

  The mediator's summary is full and undiluted. It uses party language where possible and does not omit any topics brought up. Most important—it does not soften or dilute Julie's and Elizabeth's differences. On the contrary, it highlights and even sharpens differences, in order to support clarity and choice, including the choice to give recognition or not.

As with reflection, summary often produces its own confirmation of effective practice. After a summary, parties will usually move the conversation in a direction that the mediator could not have predicted. The unpredictable movement is the sign that the summary was effective in supporting party choice, unaffected by any mediator judgment or agenda. In this case, Elizabeth's choice to focus on her experience of racism was just such a decision, entirely of her own making.

3. Finally, at the very end of the segment, the mediator uses another characteristic transformative intervention—a *check-in*.

- Having made the choice to focus on her concerns about race, and unhappy with Julie's response, Elizabeth is uncertain of what to do and looks to the mediator for direction. His response is simply to offer that decision back to her, checking in to see what *she* wants to do.

- She then makes the decision and returns to the topic of the house, also by her own choice, unprompted by the mediator at either point. This conversation is being driven entirely by party choice, supported by the mediator's interventions—a classic characteristic of transformative mediation, which continues in the following segments.

The Purple House Mediation: Segment Three

ELIZABETH: [*turns to mediator*] Anyway, the house. Let's get back to the house, because we will never resolve this . . . four-hundred-year-old issue.

JULIE: [*trying to respond to the points Elizabeth raised before she began crying*] I did not report anything . . .

ELIZABETH: [*interrupting and ignoring Julie's response*] The house . . .

JULIE: . . . about a car or any of these . . .

ELIZABETH: [*still interrupting*] . . . the house is . . .

JULIE: . . . things. And who sends those bouquets and welcome packages?

ELIZABETH: [*persistently ignoring Julie's response to her earlier points*] We are well within our rights to paint our house any color we want. There is nothing in the twenty or fifteen or twenty pages that we have signed that we are violating any rule, and we are *not* repainting the house. It has cost several thousands of dollars to have it painted. We stand, and you have to do what you have to do. [*folds her arms as if the matter is closed*]

JULIE: [*frustrated, trying to get through to Elizabeth*] Did it ever occur to you that maybe the color of your *house* was the cause of some of these incidents—alleged—that you've described, and *not* the color of your *skin?* Did it ever occur to you that maybe you weren't fitting in because of the choices you made?

ELIZABETH: [*reacts quickly, with anger*] Oh, we don't fit in! You are the first person who's ever uttered *those* words!

BERNICE: Miss Julie, fit in where?

ELIZABETH: *Please*, don't call her Miss Julie!

JULIE: I'm not, I'm just Julie.

BERNICE: Julie, you know, like I said, I would like to know who is complaining because I have a lot of friends in the neighborhood. Their houses are blue, salmon, different colors of trim.

JULIE: [*eager to talk to someone who will listen to her*] Well, do you know who's on the committee? Do you know who's on the committee?

BERNICE: Some of the people . . .

JULIE: You should know the names of those people. They've asked me to come to you and talk to you about it.

ELIZABETH: [*steps in and cuts off the discussion between Bernice and Julie*] Well, you've done that, and we disagree, and we're not going to change the color of our house. Now what?

JULIE: It is our belief that you are, uh, in violation of . . .

ELIZABETH: Well, it is our belief . . .

[Julie and Elizabeth talk over each other.]

JULIE: . . . the covenant . . .

ELIZABETH: . . . that we're not in violation of the covenant.

BERNICE: We didn't see anything in the covenant that said that we shouldn't paint our house mauve. Just like my neighbor didn't see anything in the covenant where they shouldn't trim their house in blue. And the difference between mauve and blue . . .

JULIE: Your trim is some kind of blue.

ELIZABETH: *[again cuts off the exchange between Julie and Bernice]* We don't need to go into that. We've already gone into that.

JULIE: We're talking about the color of the house.

ELIZABETH: We got it. OK, now what? We're not going to change it. *[succeeds in ending discussion between Bernice and Julie, and both parties sit back in silence]*

MEDIATOR: *[speaks here, after having been silent during the preceding back-and-forth between the parties, although following the discussion intently]* Again, I just, what I hear you saying to each other *[looks back and forth between the parties]* is that there is basically some serious disagreement about . . . , apart from what attitudes are involved and what motivations are involved—and you disagree about that too, uh, but you've said, let's set that aside. That's certainly up to you. Um, . . . there are some real strong disagreements about what, again about what the colors are and what needs to be done about them, um, from I guess the legal point of view. And you have strong disagreements about that. *[pauses, then continues]* Is there any way in the conversation . . . I guess one question to ask, is there any way in the conversation to resolve those disagreements about the meaning of the documents, for example, that you're disagreeing about?

JULIE: *[starts to say something, then stops]*

MEDIATOR: Or do you just disagree? Is that where you want to leave it today? [*pauses, looking from party to party*] Again, that's all up to you. Is there any way to work that through now, or it's . . .

ELIZABETH: You tell *us*. *You're* the mediator; you tell us.

MEDIATOR: [*starts to respond*] Well, . . .

ELIZABETH: [*interrupts mediator and continues her question*] What do you do when you meet a point like this? She obviously has her position, and we obviously have ours, and the two don't seem to be . . . What do you do in a case like that? I mean, we have a contract. I don't think we violated the contract. She says that we *have* violated the contract, so . . .

BERNICE: It's not in . . . It doesn't state in the contract about whether . . .

ELIZABETH: . . . about the painting of the house . . .

[*Elizabeth and Bernice talk to each other.*]

BERNICE: . . . you paint your house blue or whether your house is mauve. There are houses on the street that have a blue tint.

ELIZABETH: Exactly.

BERNICE: Ours just happens to be mauve.

MEDIATOR: [*addressing Elizabeth and Bernice, in response to what they've just said*] You see it's not all that different from what other people . . .

ELIZABETH: A disagreement, do you like green or do you like blue? I mean, *come on* . . .

MEDIATOR: And you're saying you see it as not all that different; and you said you put several thousand dollars into painting the house, so it doesn't seem to you to be reasonable, in effect, to ask you to repaint it when it's not that different from others.

BERNICE: Exactly. And if we repaint our house, I think that all the neighbors should repaint theirs too!

ELIZABETH: [*to Bernice*] No, honey; no, honey. Honey, we're not *going* to repaint it.

BERNICE: [*to Elizabeth, as if they are having a private conversation for a moment*] I'm just saying that if that's what she's telling, you know, asking us to do . . .

MEDIATOR: [*starts to follow up on his previous comments*] Let me ask you one thing . . . [*interrupts himself and looks at Julie*] and Julie, you're saying that again the way you see that and your committee sees it, the guidelines, they're clear enough to indicate that this would be over the line, and there *is* a difference from what other people have done. [*goes back to what he started to say before interrupting himself, looking now from party to party*] One way to, maybe, a suggestion I can make—is there anything that either of you wants to say, or could say to the other, um, that you think maybe they haven't thought of, that might change their view of the situation? Julie [*looking at her*], could you say anything beyond what you said so far to Elizabeth and Bernice that might change the way they're seeing this; or Elizabeth, Bernice [*looking at them*], is there something that you haven't said that you could say, that might change the way that Julie is seeing this? I don't know what will, you know, make a difference to you here. . . . [*speaks here very tentatively, with pauses*] This is really your situation, so I can't tell you, you know, what to do. . . . It's clear that you have some pretty strong disagreements. . . . Is there anything else that you might want to say to each other that you haven't thought of? Do you want some time to think about it? [*looks from party to party*]

[*Both parties are silent for several moments, Elizabeth and Bernice sitting back and looking down; and Julie leaning on the table, leaning her chin on her clasped hands; mediator starts to say something else, but stops himself when Julie begins to speak.*]

JULIE: [*begins speaking slowly, very calm and deliberate, with hands on the table and sitting forward*] I . . . would like to say a couple of things. Um . . . It is true that in the covenant there is nothing about painting. . . . That is absolutely true; you're right. [*Julie pauses here; Elizabeth and Bernice are silent but do not look up as she speaks*] It has been the interpretation of this committee that the language that I've referred to included what we perceived as, uh, color choices that are not in line with the color choices on other houses in the community . . . but we're just one committee. [*pauses, then continues*] I would certainly be willing to take this conversation to the board and see if they have another interpretation. [*finishes and sits forward awaiting a response*]

[*Elizabeth starts speaking while still looking down, also noticeably calm and deliberate; then picks up her head, sometimes speaking directly to Julie, sometimes seeming to address the room generally.*]

ELIZABETH: Julie, you know it's very interesting. There are no . . . There is no *diversity* on that board, or on the committee, and I find that rather curious. In this community that is really so very, *very* diverse, as we are well into the year 2000 . . . , and neither your committee nor your board reflects the diversity of this community. [*pauses*] So I am really [*short laugh, either nervous or dismissive*] at this point hard pressed to [*another short laugh*] really accept any, um, decision of your board or of your committee. I don't think a legal document is interpretive. [*her tone gets very businesslike, confident*] I think it's very precise. I think with fifteen or twenty some odd pages that you, your committee, and your board obviously paid thousands of dollars to draw up, had legal minds draw it up, that it is quite precise. And nowhere in this document does it say *anything* about *paint*, the color of the paint. We have not in *any* way changed the structure. We have not in *any* way violated what is in the document that *your* board and *your* committee has drawn up. And so it becomes a matter of *taste*. It becomes a matter of *culture*. It becomes a matter of *control*, . . . that I am simply at this point in time in my life not willing to . . . to *deal* with. Um, . . . I mean no disrespect. I mean no . . . animosity. I think we have gone as far as we can go. I believe you're talking about seeing a lawyer. . . . We certainly have consulted with ours; and I think perhaps we should let people who are not, as myself—quite frankly, I am very emotionally involved, obviously by our, this meeting . . . you're very emotionally involved—so perhaps we should let some legal minds really settle it from here.

JULIE: [*still sitting forward, having listened intently to Elizabeth's comment; now responds right away, persisting with her proposal, still calm, but also firm*] We certainly *could* do that. I've offered to go to the board. You've said that you don't think that would work, because it isn't a diverse board. It's elected by the community. It's not an appointed board. I can't speak to that. I mean, you're right, but it *is* an elected board.

ELIZABETH: [*responds hesitantly, seeming flustered by Julie's persistence*] I'm sure you haven't come this far, uh, [*short laugh*] to us without having, you know, some consultation with your committee and with your board.

JULIE: *Not* with the *board*.

ELIZABETH: [*quite skeptical*] And what would the *board* do?

JULIE: They might have a different interpretation of it. I don't know.

ELIZABETH: Why didn't you go to the board before we came here?

BERNICE: [*Bernice interrupts to add her own questions about the proposal*] Miss Julie, are you sure this is not an issue with *you*? Is it the board, or do *you* have a problem?

JULIE: It isn't *just* me. Yes, I *do* have a problem.

BERNICE: So it's you . . .

JULIE: I'm very comfortable representing the committee because I agree with this. But . . .

BERNICE: But, Miss Julie . . .

JULIE: [*correcting Bernice*] Please don't call me *Miss* Julie. I'm *Julie*.

BERNICE: I'm sorry. Julie, if you went to the board and you told them that you did not have a problem with our house, do you think they would agree with you?

JULIE: I don't think I would do it that way. I think I would say, you know, we disagree, we've gone to mediation; we weren't able to resolve it in mediation. Before we take the next step, I want to see what the board thinks . . .

ELIZABETH: [*interrupting to join the discussion of the proposal*] I would prefer . . .

JULIE: . . . about this language.

ELIZABETH: . . . I don't understand what going to the board would do, but I would really prefer a neutral representative. Because I do feel that whether *I* go to argue my case or whether *you* go to argue *against* my case, um, that we are partial. So I would, if we're going to—the emphasis and pitch, tone, and inflection would certainly inform position; so I would prefer, if you are going to do that, if that's going to be done, that we have perhaps some of our *peers*, and some of the community who do stand by us, who do certainly agree with us, to speak on our behalf, if you want to go that route. [*pauses; then continues, sounding tired, resigned*] Although I am, at this point [*sighs heavily*], I've been fighting all my life, and I have no problem taking it to the courts. [*after Elizabeth finishes speaking, there is a pause*]

MEDIATOR: [*steps in during this pause, speaking to Elizabeth*] I guess the question is, the general question is, does the idea of taking the matter to the board as a next step—in whatever fashion you described how you would like to see that done—does that seem like in general something that would make sense to you?

Commentary: Segment Three

In this third segment, the mediator's positive interventions are few; but—together with his continuing practice of allowing uninterrupted party exchange—they provide the fulcrum for some very powerful empowerment and recognition shifts by the parties.

1. First, this segment demonstrates again the concrete meaning of *following the parties* and *supporting party choice*, on multiple levels.

   - Elizabeth goes back to the concrete issue of the house and the covenant and turns away from the issues of race and relationship—and the mediator follows her and Julie right back into this narrower discussion.

     This illustrates clearly that the transformative mediator will support a *transactional discussion*, if that is what the parties want to have. There is no hidden agenda, on the mediator's part, to reach "underlying" issues about relationships, and the like. The mediator follows; the parties lead.

   - The discussion about the house quickly stalls, because their differences on this are very stark. Still, the mediator never makes the obvious suggestion that the parties simply look at the contract to clarify the matter. His intentional avoidance of this suggestion flows from the principle of supporting party choice making.

     Examining the contract is a step the parties themselves could raise; in fact, earlier on, Elizabeth mentions it but doesn't insist. Given that *they* are choosing not to take the document out, the transformative response is to assume that there is a reason for their choice and not to try to override it with a mediator suggestion.

     Given how this segment unfolds, it is clear that such a suggestion would have preempted Julie's subsequent choice to acknowledge the contract's terms voluntarily.

- When the discussion of the house and the covenant stalls, the mediator does a quick summary, and then he asks—a check-in—if the parties simply want to leave the matter in disagreement and end the session. This check-in is a response to the way the conversation is going: they disagree sharply and don't seem to have much more to say to each other.

  Such a situation is not a signal for the mediator to redouble his efforts to get a resolution; it is rather a time to simply highlight choices for the parties—and ending the session is clearly a choice at this point.

  When differences seem so significant that there may be no meeting of the minds, allowing them to come face-to-face with that moment of truth, and to realize that it is entirely their responsibility, offers them a powerful opportunity to gather strength, achieve clarity, and make choices.

  When the mediator asks here whether there is more that they can say, or is this where they want to leave it, it begins to bring home to Elizabeth and Julie the reality of this moment of truth. Then they begin to "step up to the plate" and make serious decisions, as discussed later in the chapter.

- Following a brief exchange with Elizabeth and Bernice—reinforcing the sense that a decision point is at hand—the mediator offers another check-in, in the form of a *process question:* He asks the parties if there is anything else they want to say that might change each other's views, and he also asks if they need time to think.

  As before, the check-in serves to highlight for the parties their own responsibility for whether the discussion continues or ends. In addition, the mediator here is giving the parties the opportunity to call for a time-out, if any of them feels the need either for time alone or for a separate meeting with the mediator.

This illustrates that meeting separately is certainly an option in the transformative model—if the parties wish to do so. Here, neither seemed interested in the option, and it is not the mediator's place to "call a caucus"—process decisions belong to the parties, not the mediator.

2. The second general area deserving comment pertains to the *shifts* the parties make in this segment, following the mediator's summary and check-ins. Both Elizabeth and Julie make empowerment and recognition shifts, and the shifts are clear and visible.

• First, it is clear that, beginning with the mediator's first summary, both parties—but especially Julie—are realizing that they have important choices to make and are deliberating about them.

Julie is silent from the mediator's summary until she begins speaking after his second check-in. She is obviously thinking things through, deciding what to do. She seems to realize that something needs to happen if there is to be any resolution, which she said was her goal. This *thoughtful deliberation* itself is an empowerment shift for her.

As a result, Julie makes a decision to admit that Elizabeth is right, that "in the covenant there is nothing about painting," which she states calmly and deliberately. Further, she explains that the committee acted based on its "interpretation" of the covenant and offers her proposal to go to the board. Her concise and articulate statement of all this shows plainly her increased calmness, clarity, and decisiveness.

Beyond this empowerment shift, Julie's admission to Elizabeth that "you're right"—like most admissions made voluntarily—also shows a greater responsiveness to Elizabeth, a recognition shift reflecting her *acknowledgment* that Elizabeth's views have validity. The same shift is implicit in Julie's board proposal.

Consider this: If the mediator had tried to steer the parties to look at the contract earlier, it would have largely preempted this self-determined decision making and acknowledgment by Julie.

- As transformative theory predicts, a shift in one party has impacts on the other. Here, following Julie's admission and offer, there is a corresponding shift in Elizabeth, who begins talking in a very different manner than before.

  First, Elizabeth speaks with a calmness and deliberateness that she has not displayed before this point. From here on, in this segment, her voice is neither raised nor hurried.

  Second, although it is clear she is considering Julie's proposal about the board, it is equally clear that she has her own ideas about it, and she immediately voices her concerns about diversity, fairness, and control. In short, she is standing up for herself with clarity and confidence.

  At the same time, in using phrases like "I mean no disrespect, I mean no animosity"—expressed without irony or edge—she is addressing Julie in a tone quite different from the earlier angry accusations. She seems also to be seeing something different in Julie and responding to it.

With both Julie and Elizabeth, the shifts that are evident in this segment seem to occur somewhat suddenly. However, without the steps made earlier in the session, these shifts would probably not have occurred at this point. Each of these women has been making choices from the beginning of the session on what she wants to talk about, what she thinks, how she wants to express it. *The cumulative impact of these choices, and the clarity and confidence gained through them, produces the "sudden" shifts here.*

Shifts like those made in this segment often seem to be fleeting rather than lasting changes in the interaction. That is, "retreating" from empowerment and recognition is common in transformative mediation. As with the sudden appearance of shifts, the mediator sees their sudden reversal as a natural part of the cycle of conflict transformation and is not discouraged by it—as demonstrated in the next segment of the session.

The Purple House Mediation: Segment Four

MEDIATOR: [*to Elizabeth*] I guess the question is, the general question is, does the idea of taking the matter to the board as a next step—in whatever fashion you described how you would like to see that done—does that seem like in general something that would make sense to you?

ELIZABETH: [*responding to mediator*] The challenge that I have with that is, we have reached an impasse—is that it? . . .

MEDIATOR: Um hm, whatever . . .

ELIZABETH: . . . much long ago, and why wasn't that done prior to our meeting with you? I mean, if that could possibly be a resolution, why is it addressed *here*? Why not *then*?

MEDIATOR: [*following her thought, to check her meaning*] Before coming . . .

ELIZABETH: Before coming *here*.

MEDIATOR: Before coming to mediation.

ELIZABETH: Exactly. That all means have not been exhausted, to solve this problem that they have.

MEDIATOR: Within the . . .

ELIZABETH: Yes. Then why not?

MEDIATOR: . . . within the association. [*Elizabeth nods, indicating this is her question*] You're saying you'd like an answer to this from Julie? [*Elizabeth nods again*]

MEDIATOR: [*turns to Julie*] Is there an answer to that, that would make, that you could offer?

JULIE: [*speaking directly to Elizabeth, but with less energy now, somewhat defensive*] Probably not one that would satisfy *you*.

ELIZABETH: Oh, *don't*, please, don't do that, just don't do that.

MEDIATOR: [*turning to Elizabeth, following her thought*] In other words . . .

JULIE: Don't do what?

ELIZABETH: Don't do that. Don't assume. Don't think for me. Don't, please. Just answer the question.

MEDIATOR: [*turning to Julie*] Do you want to answer that question?

JULIE: [*slowly, somewhat less defensively*] I hoped that the two of us, or the three of us, with a mediator, would be able to work it out, and where the committee stands on this is very clear. It seems like maybe we *aren't* going to be able to work it out, in which case I'm offering, you know, another option.

ELIZABETH: Why didn't you do that before?

JULIE: I don't want to go to *court*. I don't want the publicity . . .

BERNICE: [*interrupting Julie, stepping in again to make a different point*] You just want us to change the color of our house.

JULIE: . . . I don't want the expense. [*after finishing her thought, responds to Bernice*] Sure, I said that at the outset.

BERNICE: We would like a lot of *other* houses to change their colors also.

JULIE: What if you put up a hedge or something to mask or filter the color?

BERNICE: What if all the people that had their houses blue, teal, or salmon paint their houses all white?

JULIE: Well, we like a *little* color.

ELIZABETH: It's like a *personal* thing.

JULIE: We like a *little* color.

[*This exchange seems somewhat like bantering, not serious; mediator sits silent through all of this, following the exchange but not intervening.*]

BERNICE: It seems like a *personal* thing, whether you like blue or whether you like purple.

JULIE: It is partially personal, but I'm not . . . I'm not here as an individual.

BERNICE: It seems like maybe you got a *lot* of personal people.

ELIZABETH: You're feeling here . . . [*pauses to get the right words*], you're not a *neutral* person, you're not a neutral party [*shaking her head no as she speaks*].

JULIE: [*responds right away, sounding quite confident*] That's true, Elizabeth, but if I didn't agree with the position that the committee has taken, I would *still*, as chairman of the committee, have to come and fairly represent it.

ELIZABETH: But it's a double-edged sword, with your being chairman of the committee and your agreeing with the committee. [*looking squarely at Julie, quite forceful, even aggressive*] You're not arguing in a way that does at least, certainly, defend *my* rights as a home buyer or *our* rights. You're not, you know, you're not *impartial*, so it has a different . . .

JULIE: *Neither* of us is impartial . . .

ELIZABETH: [*comes right back, very assertive, with strong hand gestures pointing to herself*] I don't *have* to be, I'm not *on* the committee. *I'm* not *representing* the committee. I'm representing my *family*, so I don't *have* to be impartial.

JULIE: [*uncertain how to respond, confused by Elizabeth's argument*] I, this, this doesn't make sense to me. I mean, I'm *chair* of a *committee*.

BERNICE: [*picking up on Julie's words*] It doesn't make sense to *us*, we don't know why we're here today, to tell you the truth, Julie.

ELIZABETH: [*joining Bernice's line of thought*] And the more we talk about it, the more trivial it becomes, really. I mean it's so *ridiculous*, the color of our house—come on! [*shakes her head as if in disbelief*]

MEDIATOR: [*starts to speak as parties all sit back from table, seemingly stumped*] Well, I'm . . . uh . . .

ELIZABETH: [*interrupts mediator, frustrated*] I'm getting a headache. I really am. [*fans herself with paper*]

MEDIATOR: [*allows Elizabeth to finish, then continues, looking from party to party*] Just one question that I could ask you at this point—and if you're finding this unproductive, you know, it's your choice with how far you continue the conversation. Um, there were a couple of things, . . . [*interrupts himself to finish his first thought*] And so that, now, Elizabeth [*turns to her*], if you're ready to check out at this point; Julie [*turns to her*], if you're frustrated—you have choices to make about whether you want to go on with this or just, you know, see this as an opportunity that didn't work out and take whatever next step there is.

[*Mediator pauses, and when neither party speaks up, he returns to the other line of thought he'd introduced, again looking from party to party.*]

MEDIATOR: Um, there were some . . . before you do that, maybe it's worth just reaching some closure on the question of, does it make sense to follow up on the suggestion of going in some way to the overall board of the association? You had a notion, Elizabeth [*looks at her*], that if that were going to happen—I didn't get a sense that you were clear that you necessarily wanted it to—but if it were going to happen, you would be more comfortable with some sort of a different process than just having Julie or her committee bring this to the board. You'd want that to include some input from either yourself or other people. . . .

JULIE: [*interrupts mediator to speak directly to Elizabeth, suddenly sounding quite frustrated and angry*] I'm just *really* upset that you assume that when someone doesn't agree with you, it's *racial*. I'm really having a problem with that. I don't *understand* that. I told you I have a *son-in-law* who's African American!

ELIZABETH: [*puts her hand up, as if to stop Julie from going on*] Julie, please, Julie!

JULIE: [*determined to go on*] I am *not* a racist.

ELIZABETH: [*cool, unresponsive*] Julie, I am not going to deal with your guilt. I am not.

JULIE: I'm *not* feeling guilty. I think it's an unfair accusation!

ELIZABETH: I think a lot of it . . .

JULIE: [*interrupting Elizabeth to finish her thought*] Everyone with white skin does *not* have racial bias.

ELIZABETH: I'm not talking about *everybody* with white skin, I'm talking about *you*.

JULIE: So if I don't agree with something you've done, that makes me a racist?

ELIZABETH: I am not talking about your disagreeing with me.

JULIE: Well, then, how do you hook this into *racism*?

ELIZABETH: I really don't want to go into it. It's just too deep.

JULIE: [*persistent, intent on pursuing the issue*] *You* brought it up. You did, you *started* it. To me, this was an issue of *homeowners* and *colors* and *covenants*, and *you* threw the racism into this.

ELIZABETH: [*bitter, with irony*] That's right, I did. Yes, I'm sure I did.

JULIE: You *did!* You cited a series of events. . . .

ELIZABETH: And they are true.

JULIE: [*determined to get her point across*] I do not dispute that they're true. I *do* have a problem with your attributing them all to *me*. Is that OK, that I'm having a problem with that, and you call that *guilt?* It's not guilt. You've painted a *picture* of me and that's not an accurate picture, and I'm having a *problem* with it.

BERNICE: [*quiet and measured, by contrast to the others*] Well, Julie, I think what my mom is basically saying is that our house is mauve, our neighbor's house is blue. They are Caucasian and their kids are friends of mine, and we go to art school together. You don't have a *problem* with their blue, their deep blue, but you have a problem with our *mauve*. So she's wondering, yes, is there a racial thing?

ELIZABETH: In addition to several *other* things, which we've . . .

JULIE: [*calm again in talking about this issue, after her strong emotion before*] I *do* see a difference between a purple house and a blue house. I do.

BERNICE: That's a preference. That's a preference. It seems like a personal thing.

JULIE: It isn't just a preference, it's not a standard house color.

ELIZABETH: I do not want to go back over all the . . .

JULIE: How many purple houses have you seen?

ELIZABETH: What's standard?

JULIE: This is a community that has a certain . . .

ELIZABETH: [*beginning to get angry*] What are you trying to say? A certain *what*?

JULIE: A certain relatively conservative, visual predictable tenor to it.

ELIZABETH: [*with a tone of challenge, but also humor*] We're not conservative, and we're not predictable. Now what?

BERNICE: [*after a brief pause*] You have a *problem* with us, Julie?

JULIE: You personally?

BERNICE: Yes.

JULIE: No, I don't. No, no, I don't—except when your mother calls me a racist.

ELIZABETH: [*throwing the words at Julie, almost casually*] Yeah, you are.

JULIE: [*almost explodes in frustration*] How do you *know* that?! Because I don't like the color of your *house*, this makes me a *racist*?

ELIZABETH: [*in tone of disbelief*] Oh, please!

JULIE: Isn't that a simplification?

ELIZABETH: [*to the mediator*] Please, can we end this torment?

[*All the parties sit back, frustrated; mediator speaks after a few moments of silence.*]

MEDIATOR: You can end it any time you want to. You have, each of you, put issues on the table; and any time you want to, you can stop talking about them.

ELIZABETH: [*again, speaking to no one in particular*] Any racist I know says, "I'm not a racist. My best friend is black. I'm not a racist."

JULIE: [*raising her voice, not quite yelling, but almost*] I'm *not* a racist, I'm *not* a racist, I'm *not* a racist!!

BERNICE: [*speaking quietly, innocently*] I'm an artist. I love my neighbors' blue house. I love the salmon and the blue trim of the other neighbor's house. I'm an artist, and maybe Julie would like to come to art class with me.

ELIZABETH: [*laughs*]

JULIE: [*her tone totally different, looking at Bernice and smiling*] You have a *great* daughter.

ELIZABETH: I know.

JULIE: You have a great daughter.

ELIZABETH: [*looking at Bernice, also smiling*] I know I do.

[*Again, the conversation lapses; mediator speaks after waiting through several moments of silence.*]

MEDIATOR: [*looking from party to party*] Well, uh, where do you want to go, folks?

JULIE: [*quietly, calmly, looking at Elizabeth*] I've offered to take it to the board. I'm perfectly happy to come up with some neutral presenter if that would help. Um . . .

ELIZABETH: [*also quiet and calm, not meeting Julie's look but looking down*] If you want to take it to the board with a neutral presenter, fine, . . . [*pause*] . . . fine. [*long pause*] I want you to know that, irregardless, we are *not* changing the color of our house. So if you feel it will assuage you to take it to the board, fine.

JULIE: [*seeming to want to explain her logic*] Well, if I take it to the board, and they disagree with the control committee's, the architectural control committee's, interpretation of this particular clause, then it'll end there, right? So that would be a resolution. I can't say I'd be thrilled with it, but it would be a resolution. If I take it to the board and—or some neutral person takes it to the board—and they agree with the committee's interpretation of that clause, then we're where we are right now, and then we'll see where we go from there.

ELIZABETH: [*sounding bitter, still looking down*] I hope we go to a court of law with a jury of our peers.

MEDIATOR: [*looking first to Elizabeth and then Julie*] Um, Elizabeth, I just want to check out with you, and also with you, Julie: you know that there are limits whatever the circumstances are, and obviously you're not happy with all the circumstances. Are you comfortable with that as a decision where to take things and where to leave them today? In some ways . . . Again, I don't want to read things into what you're saying, Elizabeth [*looking at her*]. Just sort of listening to the way you describe that particular step, would you be more comfortable saying—I'm just thinking like in the opposite terms— would you be more comfortable saying, "You know what. It doesn't really make sense to delay things. You know, let's just, you know, let this go on to the lawyers and let the chips fall where they may." Is that more comfortable to you?

ELIZABETH: [*long pause, and then she begins slowly, a bit haltingly*] I feel . . . [*pause*] . . . that it will, . . . it may come to that, [*pause*] . . . but if we're sitting here thinking, "Oh, there is one more step that we can take by going to the board, and we have a, certainly, a neutral representative and we can perhaps, um, resolve it in that way," . . . then I am certainly, um, not unwilling to, uh, try that. [*gets more fluent, expressive, confident as she continues*] But I am mindful that neither the board nor the committee is diverse or reflects the diversity of the community; so—I almost say it with tongue in cheek— but I am willing to certainly be pleasantly *surprised* at a neutral outcome. But I do know that I do not foresee anything the board or the committee can say at this point that would make Bernice or I repaint our *home*. And probably before they would—or put a hedge up, and, and, um, with the beautiful *light* that we have coming in, with those beautiful *windows,* to obscure it with high bushes to hide because of somebody's obvious taste problem—I don't think we will do that either. So we are very clear that we are not going to change the house. We are very clear that—and, and, and *really* in our hearts and souls feel that—we have not violated the covenant of the archi-tectural control committee. So I'm going a long way to say, of course I will try, we will try that step; and if that step doesn't work, then they will do what they have to do.

MEDIATOR: [*to Elizabeth*] Um, hm. And does that . . . and it sounds like you'd have no problem. . . . You're sort of saying right now that everyone should know that your position is that you're willing to take that step, let this be considered again, but that if the decision is the other way, that you still feel strongly that this is within your, your rights.

ELIZABETH: Yes, I agree. We have our day in court.

MEDIATOR: [*to Julie*] And you know, given that that difference is still there, Julie, does that still seem to be a useful step, for whatever of your purposes?

JULIE: It might be a simpler resolution. The possibility is there that the board will make a different ruling, and if they do, then that would, you know, take care of it. So, yeah, sure. It's not ideal, but it seems like . . .

ELIZABETH: [*talking under Julie's comment*] What would be *ideal?*

JULIE: . . . a smart next step. [*to Elizabeth, as if not having heard her*] I'm sorry.

MEDIATOR: [*looking from party to party, speaking slowly and somewhat hesitantly*] Well, then, if you were going to take that particular next step, is it worthwhile talking more here about how that—and I'm mindful of the fact that, you know, again there have been other things as well put on the table, and you are certainly free to, to talk about those or not, as . . . as in terms of how you feel. . . . what you feel is appropriate to talk about in terms of the other issues that you mentioned. Um, that's a possibility. It also might be, . . . do you want to also talk further about, if you're going to take this next step, how that would work? I'm not exactly clear on what it would mean to have a neutral representative. *I* don't *have* to be clear about that, but *you* might want to. Uh, what does that mean? How would that next step take place? Is that something that it makes sense to spell out further, or are you comfortable just leaving it general?

[*Neither Elizabeth nor Julie speaks; then Bernice speaks up, not quite getting the mediator's question.*]

BERNICE: I think we kind of put it on the table. I mean I think if we have to go through the motions, which I don't think is necessary, but to court and everything. I think it's pretty clear it's a personal thing. It's not anything obscure as they're making it sound like it is.

MEDIATOR: [*clarifying his meaning*] Right. I'm actually asking about this notion of going before the board.

[*Julie and Elizabeth both speak at the same time, to Bernice, explaining the mediator's question.*]

JULIE: . . . the previous step, what are the pragmatics involved.

ELIZABETH: . . . he's asking about . . .

JULIE: [*taking the bull by the horns, leaning forward and speaking directly to Elizabeth*] Elizabeth, how would it be if I drafted a letter—and I know that I'm not a neutral, I understand that—and couched it in as neutral a way as I can, and I showed you the letter, and you edited it any way you wanted to, and between the two of us we came up with a neutral presentation of the two sides . . . for the board?

ELIZABETH: [*looking down, gesturing with her head toward Bernice*] I think . . . why don't you and Bernice do it.

JULIE: [*to Bernice*] Would you be willing to do that with me?

BERNICE: Sure. Sure.

JULIE: OK.

Commentary—Segment Four

In the early part of this segment, the interactional shifts evident at the end of Segment Three seem to disintegrate, as the parties get caught in a replay of their earlier disagreements about both the house and racism topics. However, by the end of this segment, not only have the parties regained a more positive interactional ground, they have also reached some fairly concrete plans to deal with the questions about the house.

1. This segment is an example of how, in transformative mediation, conversation tends to cycle in *nonlinear fashion*—up and down, forward and back—but nevertheless leads to *interactional gains* as well as *transactional resolutions*. As in the previous segment, note the work done not only by the mediator but by the parties.

    • The first indication of a seeming movement back occurs when the mediator checks in with Elizabeth about her commitment to the board proposal. In response, she expresses doubts about both the motivation and the fairness of the proposal.

      What prompts the check-in here is the signal that Elizabeth sends, at the end of Segment Three, in her acceptance of the proposal. Her words and tone suggest uncertainty about the decision, and the mediator's job is to help Elizabeth (and Julie) gain clarity and make decisions confidently—so a check-in is called for.

Seeing such uncertainty, the mediator is willing to have an "agreement" unravel in order to support Elizabeth in making choices clearly. He is highlighting her uncertainty for her, rather than ignoring or minimizing it in order to nail down an agreement.

- Just as forward shifts feed into each other, one party's retreat feeds the other's: after several minutes of Elizabeth expressing her doubts and suspicions of Julie's proposal, Julie returns to her angry rejection of the racism accusation—and they seem to be back where they started.

- Despite the apparent recycling and reversals, closer examination of the parties' exchange here shows that they actually make real gains, in terms of empowerment shifts. In effect, there is an overall forward dynamic, despite appearances.

  Elizabeth asks new questions about the process by which the matter was brought to mediation, as well as the process by which it would be put to the board. Julie makes new statements about why she can't understand the accusation of racism.

  Rather than going over the same ground, each goes more deeply into the points that concern her. They are not going around in circles but spiraling into the heart of the matter. They are gaining in clarity—about what's at issue and what their views are—an empowerment shift for both.

- In addition to gaining clarity about the topics themselves, another clear indication of empowerment is found in the quality of both Elizabeth and Julie's statements in this segment. Specifically, each one's statements are noticeably more articulate and powerful than earlier in the session.

In effect, Elizabeth and Julie both develop into strong advocates for themselves in this segment, making solid arguments to explain their views.

For example, when Julie says, regarding the possible "partiality" of a board review, that "neither of us is impartial," Elizabeth immediately answers, "I don't *have* to be," and she points out, "*I'm* not *representing* the committee, I'm representing my *family*." Communal representatives, not families, need to be impartial—a striking and powerful argument.

Here's another example: To explain why she is so upset by the charge of racism, Julie tells Elizabeth, "I do not dispute that [the events you mentioned are] true. I *do* have a problem with your attributing them all to *me*. . . . You've painted a *picture* of me and that's not an accurate picture, and I'm having a *problem* with it." This picture is not me!—a clear, powerful statement.

In short, both parties here are posing strong questions and offering powerful responses. They are speaking up for themselves more clearly and coherently than before—the empowerment shift in concrete form.

2. In this segment, the mediator's responses are very much geared to his awareness of the parties' empowerment shifts and his desire to support and not thwart them.

   • During most of this segment, the mediator intentionally "steps out" of the discussion. He listens and follows the parties' exchange closely but does not intervene.

     At the beginning of the segment, the mediator is briefly more involved in the question-answer between Elizabeth and Julie, probably because it grows out of his initial check-in with Elizabeth and her response to him.

     Then he sees the emerging empowerment shifts. He hears the parties talking over each other less and to each other more. Their tone is not friendly, but there is a sense of both strength and engagement on both sides.

He therefore stays out, because to intervene too much here would deprive the parties of opportunities to speak for themselves and to each other—the opposite of supporting party shifts.

- When the mediator does intervene in this segment, his interventions are almost all *check-ins*. In each instance, he is responding to either a signal that a party doubts the value of continuing the discussion or a signal that a party is uncertain about a particular decision.

  In general, a check-in highlights a decision point and asks one or both parties what they want to do, in order to support them in making deliberate, clear decisions. In form, a check-in may or may not be joined to a brief reflection or summary and often takes the form of a question.

  As noted previously, the segment begins with a check-in with Elizabeth about her acceptance of Julie's board proposal, prompted by her tone of uncertainty.

  The mediator offers two more check-ins when, at different points, Elizabeth complains of the "triviality" of the discussion and asks, "Can we end this torment?" In each case, the mediator takes the remark seriously and invites both parties to consider whether they want to end or continue.

  A transformative mediator is careful to make sure that the parties' option to end the mediation at any time is real, not fictional. So any statement of this kind is taken at face value and explored.

  Interestingly, after each check-in, Elizabeth decides to continue the conversation. But because of the check-in, her decision to do so is a clear and intentional one: in effect she is deciding, "I have more to say here."

- Toward the end of the segment, the mediator does another check-in, after the parties return to the board proposal, and Elizabeth accepts it—but again in a tone indicating misgivings. This check-in is more elaborate, actually inviting her to reconsider and perhaps change her mind and "go on to the lawyers."

   Note the impact of this check-in on Elizabeth: she pauses, reflects, gathers her thoughts, and comes to a clear decision to go ahead—and then explains herself in a very articulate and confident way, even using the *words* "very clear." In short, she makes a visible empowerment shift.

   The dynamic of her shift carries the discussion forward, so that by the end of this segment the parties have, for all practical purposes, made strong, clear decisions on how to deal with the question of the "purple house."

As this segment closes, it might appear that the discussion is done, and the mediator could "wrap things up." But in the transformative model, only the parties decide when they are done. As seen in the next chapter, they have not yet come to that point, and the mediator remains ready to follow the parties wherever they may decide to go next.

5

. . . .

Putting Transformative
Theory into Practice
The *"Purple House" Mediation,*
with Commentary—Part Two

At the close of the fourth segment of the Purple House mediation as presented in Chapter Four, it could have appeared that
the session was winding down and that the parties were on the
verge of concluding an agreement about how to approach the board
regarding the color of the house. Elizabeth and Julie moved through
some difficult conversation in Chapter Four, and although they did
not reach a final resolution of the house issue, they did reach an
agreement on how to proceed further, including some fairly specific
details about how to present the matter to the board. In getting to
that point, they also both made significant gains in clarity and calmness, beginning in Segment Three and continuing (if not always
smoothly) through Segment Four. Both parties seem to be making
decisions quite deliberately at the end of Segment Four. In sum, it
is entirely possible to imagine the session coming to a close at this
point, apart from some minor wrapping up.

At the same time, it also seems fairly clear, both from the parties'
tone at the end of Segment Four and from the recurrent bubbling up
of comments about the race issue, that Elizabeth and Julie might have
more to talk about—if they wished to do so. Some mediators might
decide, at this point, that such matters are much better left alone,
because "resolving" them in the course of a mediation session is
unlikely if not impossible, and because even trying to approach them
might reignite animosity and scuttle the agreement about the house.

. . . . .

In the transformative model, however, it is not the mediator's job to make such decisions—about whether the session is over, about whether certain issues are best left alone, about whether an emerging agreement should be put at risk by resurfacing contentious matters. It is not the mediator's job to make decisions of *any* kind, but rather to support the parties' decision making in every regard. So whether this mediation is over or whether it is simply turning a corner and going further is an open question for the mediator in this case, and one on which he is looking to the parties for direction. And he is prepared to follow them in whatever direction they decide to move. The significance of this readiness to follow the parties is evident as the rest of the purple house mediation unfolds in this chapter, with the mediator working hard to support the increasingly difficult discussion that Elizabeth and Julie decide to have. The ultimate impact of taking this transformative approach to the case can be assessed at the end of this chapter.

The Purple House Mediation: Segment Five

JULIE: [*to Bernice*] Would you be willing to do that with me?

BERNICE: Sure. Sure.

JULIE: OK . . .

MEDIATOR: [*starts to speak, then stops as Julie looks as though she has more to say*] And that would be . . . I'm sorry [*looking at Julie*], go ahead.

JULIE: No, I had another topic. [*sits back, indicating with a hand gesture that the mediator should go ahead*]

MEDIATOR: That's fine. [*follows up on Julie's previous comment about the letter to the board*] I'm just wondering is that, . . . that would be then be presented as a letter to the board, is that the way the board normally considers something like this? Through somebody submitting . . .

JULIE: [*interrupts mediator, who stops when she speaks up*] We could put a photograph of the house in, and a copy of the paragraph that's in question, and how each, how the committee feels and how you all feel and let them do it. [*sort of rushes through this, pauses briefly, and then starts speaking again more slowly, carefully*] And I keep going back to this racism and diversity, and I . . .

[*Elizabeth sighs, heavily and audibly.*]

JULIE: [*to Elizabeth*] You're sighing again, but it's really hard for me to let that go.

BERNICE: [*steps in, seemingly to protect her mother and keep Julie from going back to this*] Well, that seems like a personal thing, also. I know my mom brought that out and, but it seems it's really, she let it go; and you're still . . .

JULIE: [*to Bernice*] But she brought up something really important, that there's no diversity on the board.

BERNICE: We're *here* to talk about the *house*. And you're still being eaten up by it, you know.

JULIE: [*once again persistent, though calm and reasonable*] I'm also trying to respond to what she said. There *are* no African Americans, Asians—*she's right*—on the board. And I think that's very unfortunate. And I'd like to see if maybe there isn't something we can do to work on that, independent of this, because it is a matter of election, and elections are coming up soon, and there might be something that we could do to work on that.

[*Bernice nods her head in acknowledgment of this, but neither she nor Elizabeth says anything.*]

MEDIATOR: [*to Julie*] Is that something . . . and that's something you'd like to talk about here, Julie?

JULIE: Well, I'd certainly like to know what *Elizabeth's* response to it is. Bernice is nodding her head but . . .

ELIZABETH: [*sighs again, shaking her head negatively, then speaks, but very slowly, heavily*] I, I, I'm . . . spent, I'm sorry, but I'm absolutely, um, . . . I'm *spent*. [*lowers her head in silence*]

BERNICE: [*after a short pause, comes in as if to take pressure off her mother*] I think my mom would agree that we need more, um, you know, you know, different races on the board. I think we have it in our community, why shouldn't we have it on the board? And, um, I think if the issue was reexamined, and we had different races on the board, it probably would be a different, you know, resolution to all this, a more expedient one, and one that . . .

JULIE: Or whatever the resolution was, it would maybe feel *fairer*, because . . .

BERNICE: Exactly. I think so.

JULIE: [*to Elizabeth, who still has her head down*] If, if you're spent, then now isn't the time to have this conversation maybe, but . . .

BERNICE: [*talking over Julie, again trying to speak for her mother*] I think my mom is . . .

JULIE: [*finishing her comment very softly*] . . . I would *like* to have this conversation.

BERNICE: . . . a little tired of the issue, but I think she agrees with what I'm saying here. [*places her hand on her mother's arm, but Elizabeth still remains silent*]

MEDIATOR: [*speaks softly, looking from party to party*] Is it . . . Again, you know, that's something you could decide to pursue in the future. It's something that you, Elizabeth, [*looking toward her, though she is still looking down*], you said you're pretty much exhausted from the discussion today. And I don't know how you feel about continuing to talk about this, or have the conversation go on between Bernice and Julie about this now, or whether you would really like to table the whole thing and take it up at another time. All of you . . . [*stops immediately when Elizabeth suddenly interrupts him and starts to speak*]

ELIZABETH: [*picks up her head as she begins, speaking slowly but forcefully*] I just have such a *challenge*, . . . that it takes . . . [*pauses briefly*]

MEDIATOR: [*speaks to Elizabeth, following her words*] The challenge . . . ?

ELIZABETH: [*continues, speaking very emotionally and expressively, with gestures and voice inflections—but not looking directly at anyone, addressing the whole room as it were*] I mean, it's *wearying*, the challenge of dealing with racism in America. . . . And in one easy sentence or two, we're going to *correct* it and make everything all right? And it's not so *easy*. . . . And the *pain* that it inflicts, and, and . . . [*pauses briefly and then resumes as if she has a new idea*] OK, . . . why this community is quite, what it's got to be, what, at least fifteen or twenty years old? Even older than that? And *why* does someone have to accuse Julie of being what she *is*, a *racist*? . . .

JULIE: [*practically explodes in reaction to this, interrupting Elizabeth*] How do you *know* that?!!!

ELIZABETH: [*ignores Julie's interruption, continues speaking without looking at Julie*] And, and, and then, and then . . .

JULIE: [*talks over Elizabeth, repeating her question, though less explosively*] *How* do you know that?

ELIZABETH: . . . and after that, she goes into ooh, very conciliatory, "We can make the board *diverse*." [*suddenly almost spits out her words, contemptuously*] D-d-d- *duuhhhhhh!!!* Is this *news*?

JULIE: [*sits back in her chair, angry, emotional*] You *enjoy* living in a racist society. It sounds like you're trying to perpetuate it! It sounds like when somebody reaches *out* to you, the thought that something might *change* is so traumatic that you don't want to have anything to *do* with it!

ELIZABETH: [*starts to respond, but Julie interrupts her*] I, I, I . . .

JULIE: It's easier to accuse people!

ELIZABETH: [*continues her response, ignoring the interruption, looking directly at Julie now and speaking very forcefully and deliberately, as if having decided to take the plunge*]

No, Julie. Reaching *out* is when you move in next door, and somebody knocks on your door [*knocks on the table*] and says, "Welcome!" [*gestures with her arms open*] Reaching *out* is when you move in the neighborhood and they say, "You know, we've got this monthly meeting that we have, and would you come?" Reaching *out* is *inviting* us to the table [*slaps her palm onto the table*]—not being *forced* to invite us to the table, not because somebody called you a *racist!* But then you say "*Ooh*, I feel so *bad*, somebody called me a *racist*. I've got a son-in-law who's black. *Ooh*, well I'll tell you what we'll do. We'll get other people on the committee, other black people." And therefore you've reached out to me? Come on!!! And you want to solve it, in ten easy lessons—or two sentences with a mediator? You cannot cure four hundred years of racism in five minutes!!! You cannot do it! [*practically shouting by the time she finishes*]

JULIE: [*a bit overwhelmed by Elizabeth's statement, somewhat defensive, but still persisting*] I'm not *trying* to cure it in five minutes. I'm trying to take a *step*, OK? A little teeny, tiny step.

ELIZABETH: [*answers immediately, with sarcastic, almost mocking tone*] You've *taken* the little "teeny, tiny step," OK? You've taken it. Now *feel good*. You've taken the tiny little step. Thank you, thank you!!! [*putting her hands together and "bowing" in mock appreciation*]

JULIE: Oh, please!

ELIZABETH: I'm *sorry*, but I just . . . This is too much!

[*Silence follows for several moments; none of the parties speaks; Elizabeth and Julie are both leaning back from the table now, looking down or away, arms folded tightly, faces scowling.*]

MEDIATOR: [*speaks softly, breaking the silence*] I . . . and . . . so maybe this is a discussion that you really can't have . . .

JULIE: [*Julie interrupts him*] Clearly not!

MEDIATOR: [*after a slight pause*] . . . or that you don't *want* to have.

ELIZABETH: [*speaks up suddenly, with force, though not looking up*] It just *cannot* be resolved so easily. . . .

JULIE: [*starts to respond*] I'm not *trying* to resolve . . .

ELIZABETH: [*ignores Julie and continues, very forcefully, again address- ing the room at large and not looking at Julie directly*] And first of all, somebody has to *admit*—not deny, but admit. *That's* the first, that's when the healing begins. I heal if I say, "I have a problem." Then I can face the problem. But to deny that I have a problem? To deny that—if I'm an alcoholic, and I say, "I'm not an alcoholic?" The first step is when you stand up and you say, "I *am* an alcoholic!" That's when the healing begins. "Yes, I *am* a racist!" [*clapping her palm to her chest, and then slapping it against her other hand, for emphasis*] That's when the healing begins.

JULIE: [*responds to Elizabeth's statement with equal force and emotion*] I'm *not* a racist!! I just don't like purple houses! I don't like purple houses, and . . .

ELIZABETH: Ooh . . . [*sighs audibly and gestures, with sense of helplessness*]

JULIE: . . . to take that and translate it into *racism* is really limited vision!

BERNICE: It's mauve, it's mauve. [*her comment breaks the tension somewhat*]

JULIE: [*speaks to Bernice, much more softly and calmly*] You keep say- ing that, but where *I'm* sitting it's *purple*.

BERNICE: It's in the purple family.

JULIE: I believe that you go to art school, and you see distinctions that I don't see; but it's purple to me. And every other house is blue or yel- low or white or beige or gray—and then there's this *purple house*.

MEDIATOR: [*steps into a brief pause after Julie's comment, speaking to both parties*] Well, you see different colors. You see different colors, right? And you also clearly see different realities in terms of what's racism.

ELIZABETH: [*glancing at Bernice, calm, but in ironic and bitter tone*] Well, she said conservative. What did she say predictable? The only thing she left out was *white:* white, conservative, predictable . . . .

JULIE: [*to Elizabeth*] You're stuck!

ELIZABETH: [*refuses to look at Julie*] Um hm . . .

JULIE: You're *really* stuck.

ELIZABETH: [*repeats Julie's words in ironic, bitter tone*] I *am* stuck, um hm.

[*There's a long pause; neither party speaks, and mediator does not intervene; then Julie continues, her tone frustrated, somewhat defeated.*]

JULIE: I don't know what else I can do. [*addresses Bernice*] I'll write the letter; you'll vet it. Between the two of us, we'll work out a neutral presentation. We'll send it to the board, and we'll see what comes of that.

BERNICE: OK.

Commentary: Segment Five

The discussion at the end of Segment Four seemed to reach a conclusion, but that conclusion was only apparent—because in this segment the parties choose, or at least Julie does, to go back to "another topic." The mediator follows where the parties lead, and though they move into very difficult terrain, further positive shifts are still in evidence here.

1. The first noteworthy point is that this segment illustrates the real unpredictability of conflict conversations—when the parties are allowed to be in control.

- The topic of race has surfaced over and over, but each time it was dropped because it was "too deep" and the discussion went back to the house—at the parties' direction. Having directed the conversation away from race, they now direct it back to that subject, deep or not.

  Readers may wonder why the mediator "permits" the reintroduction of the race question: it puts the resolution of the house issue at risk, because this volatile subject may explode the whole conversation. Why risk the agreement to discuss an almost certainly insoluble, intangible issue?

  Also, why does the mediator consider racism a "mediable" issue to begin with? How can racism be mediated or for that matter negotiated?

  The answer to both of these questions is the same: in transformative mediation, *parties decide and mediators support*. What is worth discussing and worth exploding, what is mediable and what is not mediable—these are matters for the parties and not the mediator to decide.

- What is most surprising in this segment is how Elizabeth, who has resisted the race topic since she first introduced it—and here also begins by resisting it—now reverses herself and decides to talk about it. Why?

  First, when Julie brings the subject up again, the mediator does a reflection and check-in that allows Julie to elaborate that "I'd certainly like to know what *Elizabeth's* response to it is," followed by the statement that "I would *like* to have this conversation"—two very clear requests to talk about the subject with Elizabeth, made calmly and respectfully.

  Then, when Elizabeth rejects the requests ("I'm spent"), the mediator does a summary and check-in that invites all the parties to reflect on what to do with this topic.

It is after hearing these requests, and having the chance to reflect, that Elizabeth decides to take up the "challenge" and talk directly about race with Julie. Her decision may also reflect the strength and clarity she has gathered cumulatively through the session.

In effect, her decision to talk embodies two shifts: an *empowerment shift*—I am strong enough now to talk about this; and a *recognition shift*—I see you are sincerely interested in this, so I'll talk to you about it, despite the difficulty.

It is therefore possible to see, in this segment, the interplay between the mediator's interventions and the shifts that Elizabeth is able to make—and how the interventions support the shifts.

2. Another important point about this segment is that it shows both how *difficult* and how *powerful* conflict transformation can be—and how simple but difficult it is to support it.

• Once she decides to engage, Elizabeth's comments are both powerful and devastating. In effect, she finds her voice here and begins to speak passionately and eloquently. Listen to her words:

About the challenge: "It's *wearying* . . . dealing with racism in America. . . . and in one easy sentence or two, we're going to *correct* it and make everything all right? And it's not so *easy*. . . ."

About the need to make the board diverse: "Is this *news?*"

About "reaching out" to minorities: "Reaching *out* . . . is when somebody knocks on your door and says, '*Welcome*'!" "Reaching *out* is when you move in . . . and they say, 'You know, we've got this monthly meeting . . . and would you come?'" "Reaching *out* is inviting us to the *table*—not being *forced* to invite us . . . because somebody called you a *racist!*"

About dealing with racism: "First of all, somebody has to *admit . . . That's* the first, that's when the healing begins. . . . Yes, I *am* a racist! *That's* when the healing begins."

- These are hard things to say, particularly to another person face-to-face. In saying these things so strongly and clearly, Elizabeth demonstrates both her strength and her willingness to connect to Julie—despite their distance.

- The fact that the parties' conversation in this segment (and the next) gets so harsh, so difficult, illustrates a key point about conflict transformation: *conflict interaction usually gets worse before it gets better.* Reaching a turning point means going down to the depths, and then climbing back up.

  For both Julie and Elizabeth, this is very tough—*and* it represents positive change. The fact that they sense this is what keeps them at it.

- This last point is also relevant to the mediator's work at this point in the conversation, which has two distinct dimensions.

  One part of the work he does is simply to remain present with the parties through this difficult exchange—as he did when anger first surfaced in Segments One and Two.

  This intentional, calm presence provides support for the parties as they go into the hard conversation. His *lack of alarm* reinforces their confidence that whatever needs to be said can be said. At the same time, it allows him to overcome the impulse to "soften" things, which almost any person listening to such a conversation will feel.

  The second part of his work is to step in with a reflection, summary, or check-in, when one of these is needed to support the hard conversation.

  In fact, he does all three in this segment: *reflecting* for Julie ("That's something you'd like to talk about here")

and Elizabeth ("The challenge . . .); *checking in* when
they seem stumped ("So maybe this is a discussion you
really can't have . . ."); *summarizing* when they finish the
cycle ("Well, you see different colors. . . ." "And you . . .
see different realities in terms of what's racism").

Again, this segment shows how these interventions—
simple, modest, but not easy to deploy in the conversation as it unfolds—help support the parties' efforts to
gather both their strength and their sense of connection
and then have this very difficult exchange.

The segment also suggests, if the reader reflects on what
the mediator does here, that his working in this way *stems
directly from his belief* that the parties have both the desire
and the capacity for both strength and connection.

3. Again, at the close of this segment, it seems that the session is
at an end. The hard part of the conversation is, indeed, too
hard to continue. For the mediator, two insights are useful at
such a moment.

• First, if the conversation were to end here, the shifts
already made by the parties represent real "success," and
they have changed the interaction significantly. In other
words, success does not require total "transformation" any
more than "resolution."

• Second, it is still not for the mediator to step in and decide
that the session is over. Conversation is full of surprises, and
only when the parties stop talking is the conversation over.

The Purple House Mediation: Segment Six

JULIE: I don't know what else I can do. [*addresses Bernice*] I'll write
the letter; you'll vet it. Between the two of us, we'll work out a neutral presentation. We'll send it to the board, and we'll see what
comes of that.

BERNICE: OK.

MEDIATOR: That's, that's, that much you can agree on.

ELIZABETH: [*still quite bitter*] That much we can agree on. We can-not heal four hundred years of racism in one day.

JULIE: [*also ironic and bitter*] God forbid we should try.

ELIZABETH: Well, you *tried*, honey. You tried. You "*invited* us to the table." [*claps her hands, applauding Julie mockingly*]

JULIE: [*in a challenging tone, undeterred by the mockery*] And I would ask *you* to go home and think about why you rejected it!

ELIZABETH: I did *not* reject it. What I . . .

[*Julie interrupts Elizabeth to respond, and then they go back and forth very quickly, arguing intensely; the mediator remains attentive through this but does not intervene.*]

JULIE: You certainly did.

ELIZABETH: No, I did *not* reject it. I did *not* reject it.

JULIE: Yes you did.

ELIZABETH: What I rejected is trying to make you feel *better* about it.

JULIE: I, I . . .

ELIZABETH: That's what I . . .

JULIE: . . . I want to make *you* feel better!

ELIZABETH: I'm fine!

JULIE: No, you're not fine! You sat here for the last hour accusing me of racism. You're not *fine*.

ELIZABETH: It seemed to bother *you* quite a bit more than it both-ered me. *I've* lived with racism all my life.

JULIE: Yeah, right because . . .

BERNICE: [*interrupts them both, but speaks to Elizabeth*] Mom, we need to talk about the house.

JULIE: [*resisting the interruption*] But this is relevant.

BERNICE: Yeah, it's relevant, but . . .

ELIZABETH: [*also ignoring Bernice's interruption, and continuing to argue with Julie*] You cannot *solve* it. You want to *feel* better.

JULIE: No, I don't want to feel better. And stop imputing feelings to me!

ELIZABETH: I'm not! You *said* [*repeating her version of Julie's words, but with less mockery in her tone*], "I feel bad. It's unfair. You've been unfair to me. I'll tell you what I'll do to, to, to take a step in the right direction. What do you want me to do?"

JULIE: I said maybe we can work on something together! I did say that.

ELIZABETH: That is *what?* It's getting on the committee and inviting diversity to the board, inviting diversity to the committee. *That* was your step, yeah?

JULIE: Yes. Is that a *bad* thing?

ELIZABETH: [*sits back and, though still irritated, for the first time does not reject or mock Julie's proposal*] That's fine. You've taken it, we've accepted it. That's a good idea. My *daughter* said that was a great idea.

JULIE: [*also sits back, still disturbed, but calmer*] We'll write the letter. I'll write the letter. We can do that. We can do that.

[*After the parties have remained silent for several moments, the mediator begins speaking, looking from party to party.*]

MEDIATOR: It might be just worthwhile to, in terms of what sort of someone sitting over here hears you saying . . . that in terms of this larger issue of, of racism, relations between white and black, black and white, that—apart from the feelings, apart from the feelings, not that that isn't a major part of it—but in terms of your word *healing*, Elizabeth [*looks at her*], that you may have different ideas about what that takes, what that means, what that would take. Your comment [*still looking at her*] was first you have to admit to what the situation is and, . . . or, for example, you were saying, reaching out means coming over and knocking on the door. It means . . .

ELIZABETH: [*she interrupts to clarify*] Before we get here, right, . . .

MEDIATOR: [*allowing her to interrupt*] . . . um . . .

ELIZABETH: . . . before one *compels* you to do that.

MEDIATOR: [*continues, after Elizabeth finishes*] Right. Right. OK, and, Julie [*turning to look at her*], you're saying, uh, that in terms of what it means to talk about that, that your suggestion of addressing the issue . . . or, listening to Elizabeth's comment about the lack of diversity on the board, that whatever else happened before, acknowledging that *now*, and . . .

JULIE: [*talks over him briefly, but doesn't continue*] She's *right*.

MEDIATOR: . . . and responding to it—what I hear you saying from your side is that the way you see that is, it's *not* because you want to *feel good*, but because you acknowledged that, as you just said, "She's right."

JULIE: She's right. There *are* no African Americans or Asians or Hispanics on the board.

MEDIATOR: She's . . .

JULIE: She's right.

MEDIATOR: So what you're saying is . . .

JULIE: [*again, she interrupts him to add something*] And we should *fix* it.

MEDIATOR: [*pauses briefly to allow her interruption, then continues*] . . . separate from how you *feel*, she's *right*, and that situation is *wrong*.

JULIE: Right. Yes, I *am* saying that. I didn't use that word, but yes I am.

MEDIATOR: So in other words . . . but on the other hand, that part of what you're saying may not be responsive 100 percent, that may not be exactly the kind of thing that Elizabeth is looking for. [*looks now from party to party as he continues*] Again, that conversation is sort of, as you said, is a hard conversation to have. And it may not be possible to have it, you know, to, uh, uh, any kind of a conclusory point, you know, in this room today. You've clearly started to talk about it and I guess, I guess, the plans you made about writing the letter to the board concerning the house, um, are pretty concrete. Is there anything you want to do about pursuing in any way this discussion about diversity on the board, uh, the way in which new people to the community are, are welcomed into the community—or *not* welcomed? Do you want to talk about that, anything else, to go anywhere else with it?

JULIE: [*following a few moments of silence begins speaking; her head is down, her tone is low, tentative, vulnerable*] I can think of lots of ways to address the issue of diversity in our community; but if I'm going to be met every time with, "I don't want to make you *feel good*," "This isn't about *you*," and rejection of those ideas—then it's very hard to have the conversation.

ELIZABETH: [*speaks directly to Julie*] How long have you lived in this community?

JULIE: [*looks up to answer, her voice shaking a bit*] Eight years.

ELIZABETH: Eight years. And did you just discover today that it wasn't diverse on the committee? Did you just today decide to have these, uh, conciliatory steps? [*gets more aggressive as she continues, almost cross-examining Julie*] Was it just today? Was it just today, Julie? Did it ever occur to you eight years ago, or seven years ago, "Oh, my, I don't live in a sea of whiteness. I live in—there's some Asians over there, there's some Latinos over there, there's some African Americans. . . . I think there's even a couple of African and Haitian fami-lies." Did it ever occur to you. No, it *didn't!*

JULIE: [*confused, not understanding Elizabeth's charge*] Did it ever occur to me that there was a multiracial community? Of *course*, I *like* it. That's why I'm *here*.

ELIZABETH: [*continuing her driving questions*] That your committee . . .

JULIE: [*interrupts, but it doesn't stop Elizabeth*] Not that you would *believe* that.

ELIZABETH: [*persisting*] . . . that your committee, and your board, were not diverse, not reflective of the community? No! And *this* is all that I take exception to—not that you're suddenly saying, "Oh, yes, that's a good idea. Let's make it more diverse." [*leans forward and raises her voice for emphasis*] But to dare to say, on the one hand, "Oh, I am not racist. Oh no, no, no, I like the diversity." As long as we're *in our place??!!*

JULIE: [*speaking immediately to object*] No, that's not what I said.

ELIZABETH: [*mocking Julie's denial*] "No, no, no."

JULIE: That's *your* language. You're *imputing* it to me.

ELIZABETH: [*jumping in on Julie's statement, almost pursuing her*] Exactly! I am! But if seven years ago, Julie was a worker of the mind—"I'm going to make this community in all ways as diverse as I can possibly make it," and you had opposition—I could understand it. [*again, raises her voice, angry and indignant*] But for you to dare come in here, and in one or two sentences, "Oh, yes, let's take *steps*." And I'm supposed to be, what, *placated?!!!* Well, I'm not! Not yet.

JULIE: [*almost pleading*] Not placated, but willing to work with me. Let's make it better!

ELIZABETH: [*less loud, but still simmering*] Fine. Fine. [*gestures with her hand, as if to table the discussion*]

BERNICE: [*steps in to calm her mother*] Mom . . .

ELIZABETH: [*ignores Bernice; still finishing the exchange with Julie, though looking away from her*] Fine. [*pauses, seems to be done speaking*]

MEDIATOR: Well, . . .

ELIZABETH: [*looks back at Julie and questions her sharply*] But do you see my point?

JULIE: [*trying to follow what Elizabeth is saying*] Because I haven't been an *advocate*? Because I choose . . .

ELIZABETH: [*raising her voice, losing patience*] Not an *advocate*, honey, not an *advocate!!* You are the one who's saying, "I care. My son-in-law is African American. I moved in this community because I *wanted* diversity." And yet, in your very life, other than your son-in-law, is your world diverse? I don't think so!

JULIE: [*stung, offended*] You have no idea. You have no idea. Have you been to my church? Have you been in the city with me?

ELIZABETH: [*unmoved by Julie's response*] Judging by this committee? *You* can nominate. Have you ever nominated a nonwhite person to the board or the committee?

JULIE: I'm not on the nominating committee. That's an irrelevant question.

ELIZABETH: [*dismissive, fed up*] Julie, you always come up with excuses.

JULIE: I just think you think everybody who's white is racist.

ELIZABETH: [*warning her off*] Please, don't do that.

JULIE: [*defending herself*] "Please?" You're doing all these things to *me*!

ELIZABETH: I am speaking to *you*, specifically to *you*. . . .

JULIE: Yeah, OK, me. [*tired, seeming a bit stunned by Elizabeth's harshness*]

BERNICE: *We* aren't racist, Julie.

ELIZABETH: [*almost relentless*] . . . specifically to you, . . .

JULIE: OK.

ELIZABETH: . . . to you.

[*There is silence in the room, while the intensity of this exchange sinks in; after a fairly long pause, the mediator speaks, looking at Elizabeth.*]

MEDIATOR: [*to Elizabeth*] Can I ask you just a question? I'm not sure whether this will clarify anything, but in the way you're describing your . . . , the questions that you're asking, one of the implications that I'm hearing is when you use a term like *racist* in this context, one of the things you mean by it is: If you're living in a multiracial community but participating in a management structure, power structure, that excludes everybody but *one group*, then whether or not there's an intention behind that or not, it's discriminatory. It's, in your word, racist. It excludes. I'm not sure I'm getting that right, but it sort of seems like you're focusing on . . . the committee. . . .

ELIZABETH: [*interrupts the mediator*] In Julie's particular case . . .

MEDIATOR: [*a bit apologetic, explaining the reason for his questions*] I'm just trying to understand . . . [*stops when she goes on speaking over him*]

ELIZABETH: . . . in Julie's particular case . . . And I don't want as a mediator *you* to give this definition of racism now. I don't think that . . . that's an exclusion. It's certainly an exclusion that is question-able. Why is that exclusion taking place in a diverse community? Why? I mean, often people say they . . .

JULIE: [*interrupts Elizabeth; ironic, but on the defensive*] It's all *my* fault!

ELIZABETH: [*cuts Julie off; dead calm, almost icy, and intent on making her point*] Julie, I'm really not only addressing the committee and the board. I'm not holding you accountable for the committee and the board totally. There are several incidents in the community, some of which I have named, that you have been doing, I feel, that have been racist. That some of your actions . . .

JULIE: [*starts to speak but can't stop Elizabeth's flow*] That have been . . . what?

ELIZABETH: . . . have been racist, specifically. Your words and your deeds have been racist, specifically. So now you sit at a table with a mediator, and you say, "I'm trying to take a step to correct the situation." And I, my daughter, has said, "That's great. Take the step." [*spoken this time without any irony or mockery*] You know what you need to do. You've said you . . . you're not on the committee, you don't elect; but you're going to take steps to make it more diverse. Do what you can. And *I'm* saying to *you*, the reason I haven't turned on a dime and said, "Oh, thank you, thank you, great!" is because you've been here eight years, and what has it taken for you to make those steps? [*Elizabeth's calmness fades, and she begins to get more and more emotional*] Has your *heart* been open in the eight years, yes? You moved to this community because you wanted diversity. What, to *say* you lived in a diverse and multiracial community? Multiracial diversity means to me some kind of inter-action. It doesn't mean staying secular, integrated within your own separate groups! It doesn't mean the board after *umpteen* years of a community existing, that is still an *all-white* board. And an all-white *committee*, that *all* the committees that function in this . . . [*very worked up, tired of explaining*] Come on!!!

JULIE: [*frustrated, struggling to get Elizabeth's point*] So let's work to *change* it!

ELIZABETH: [*calmer again, but still very intense*] That's fine. That's fine. But you cannot, but you cannot . . . What you must understand . . . That now suddenly today the light bulb has gone on—for whatever reasons, and I suspect, I am certainly suspicious of the motive, but, OK, suddenly . . .

JULIE: [*interrupts, frustrated and offended at being "suspected"*] Are you going to change the color of your house because I do that? Of course not! So what would be my motive? What?

ELIZABETH: [*quite calm now, but intense—and determined to go on, even as Julie speaks over her for a few moments*] I don't believe you're hearing me. What I am saying . . .

JULIE: You said you were suspicious . . .

ELIZABETH: Please . . .

JULIE: . . . and I want to know . . .

ELIZABETH: Please . . .

JULIE: . . . why are you suspicious?

ELIZABETH: . . . Hear me!

[*This last plea brings Julie to silence; Elizabeth continues—and Julie listens intently*]

ELIZABETH: The fact that you sit at this round table today and say to my daughter and myself, "Let us now open up the committees. Let's do something to make the committees and the board more diverse"—that's fine. It will *not* suddenly make all these feelings— make your eight-year history of action, or the twenty-some-odd-year history of this community—suddenly disappear! [*suddenly raises her voice dramatically*] If the Ku Klux Klan came and *hung*, God forbid, *lynched somebody*—uh, uh, uh [*struggling for words, gesturing*]—and then today they want to say, "I'm sorry" . . . it's not going to erase the *horror*, the *hurt* and the *ugliness* of that period! *That's* all. The healing has begun, and I applaud you, thank you. [*now without a trace of irony or mocking gestures*] Yes, we will try to get in to take those steps. That's all I'm trying to say. [*finishes, breathes heavily as if relieved, and sits back in her chair; no one else speaks for several moments*]

MEDIATOR: [*after waiting some moments, speaks to Elizabeth*] What you're saying is that's not . . . you're not ready to let go, and you *can't* let go, of the feelings that you have that you've expressed here today and that probably haven't . . .

ELIZABETH: [*interrupts him*] It's not going to be so *easy*.

MEDIATOR: Not so easy, right.

ELIZABETH: [*ironically*] Oh, I'm on the *committee*; I'm on the *board*. Uh, no *problem!* [*gestures with her hand as if brushing off a fly, again with irony, and sits back in her chair, finished speaking*]

[*Julie has been listening intently to Elizabeth and her exchange with the mediator, sitting far back in her chair, slumped down, seemingly worn out; when Elizabeth finishes speaking, the mediator turns to Julie.*]

MEDIATOR: And, Julie, I mean . . . you've sat here and been going through this discussion, which isn't all that easy a discussion to have. Does that . . . I guess, you know, this has been an important discussion for you to have, because you brought it back up again, and you wanted to talk through some of this. [*Julie nods her head up and down slightly*] I don't know what your thoughts are about where the discussion is at this point and how you feel about what's come out, whether you think that's added to your clarity in this situation or understanding of it, and what Elizabeth's views of this are. [*Julie nods her head again*] Has that been, has that accomplished some of what you wanted to in having the discussion? And do you . . .

[*Julie interrupts the mediator and begins speaking—slowly, carefully, with vulnerability in her voice, and without looking directly at Elizabeth but rather looking at her own hands in front of her on the table; as she speaks, Elizabeth and Bernice both sit up in their chairs and lean forward, listening intently.*]

JULIE: I, I, I, can't say there was such clear intention in having it. [*pauses, then goes on*] Um . . . , I *do* hear Elizabeth saying that there's four hundred *years* of discrimination and that one gesture—or eight years in a community, whichever number you want to use—and one gesture doesn't fix everything. [*pauses*] And I *appreciate* that. Of *course* it doesn't. [*pauses again*] I guess, I guess, . . . I just, I just wish . . . I guess I just wish that . . . although it doesn't put everything to rest . . . I felt like that you were willing to be open to this anyway [*her voice starts to shake*], instead of just questioning my motives and . . . *dismissing* it. [*pauses*] That's what I . . .

[*Elizabeth interrupts Julie to speak, leaning forward on the table as she does. Julie looks up, though still slumped back in her chair.*]

ELIZABETH: [*speaks slowly and softly, firmly but gently*] Julie, . . . I am a woman of God. . . . And I don't want to *hurt* anyone. And as much as I may disagree with you, I don't want to leave you *hurt!* [*Elizabeth reaches her open hand across the table to Julie*] I am extending my hand. I don't want to hurt you.

JULIE: [*very much surprised by this response, has sat up in her chair, leaned forward and grasped Elizabeth's hand, face-to-face; when she speaks, her voice is still tentative, shaky.*] Would you work with me? Will you help me to work with you?

ELIZABETH: [*smiles and nods at Julie*] I will. Julie, I would like *you* to *help* me to work with you. I will work with you. I will do my best. I will do my best.

[*They nod to each other.*]

JULIE: [*seeming to joke a bit, lightening the very emotional mood*] Even though I don't like purple houses?

BERNICE: [*leans forward and puts her hand on Elizabeth's and Julie's*] I like purple houses. [*they all laugh*]

JULIE: [*to Bernice*] What color is it?

BERNICE: *Mauve, mauve!!*

JULIE: [*they all release hands and sit back; Julie speaks to Elizabeth*] You *do* have a *great* daughter.

ELIZABETH: [*puts her arm around Bernice's shoulder*] I *know* I do.

JULIE: [*to Elizabeth and Bernice*] Thank you. Thank you. [*they nod, smiling*]

MEDIATOR: [*after some moments of silence*] I don't think there's much to say after that. [*the parties all laugh*]

JULIE: [*to mediator*] Thank *you*.

ELIZABETH: [*her voice lighter than at any time during the session*] Well, we've started the healing of four hundred years of racism—but we still have a purple [*she corrects herself*] . . . *mauve* house!

MEDIATOR: You're not giving up that *mauve* house! [*the parties laugh again*] You've talked through a lot of stuff today, and, uh, that's part of what, uh, conversation is all about. So, um, I hope that the next steps continue as you intend them to, and, uh, if there are other ways in which this kind of process can be helpful, we're, I'm certainly willing to continue it, if that's useful, whatever happens next. Do you feel comfortable about where you're leaving this at this point? [*looks at each of the parties*]

BERNICE: Yeah, I do.

[*Elizabeth and Julie both nod their assent, without speaking.*]

Commentary: Segment Six

This final segment, and especially the way the session ends, is very powerful—but it could be seen as somewhat unexpected, even unbelievable. As noted in the Introduction, the simulation was unscripted and spontaneous; indeed, the actors who played the parties were so affected afterward that they took several hours to discuss what had occurred and its implications for their own lives. The important point here is this: understood in context, the conclusion of this mediation is not at all unbelievable; rather, it grows organically out of what has occurred throughout the entire session—especially when seen in the light of transformative theory.

1. As in previous segments of the session, it is very evident in this segment that *it is the parties, and not the mediator, who direct the conversation* into its deepest levels.

   - Consider how this segment begins. From the end of the previous segment, it would be hard to predict that the parties would go right back to the race topic, having just withdrawn from it with a sense of futility.

     The return to the issue is entirely party directed. The mediator does nothing to steer them toward this subject nor to steer them away. Indeed, he has done no "steering" of this kind at any point in the session.

     With the bitter back-and-forth at the start of this segment, some mediators might discourage the parties from going into this again. This mediator doesn't substitute his judgment for theirs, on this or any question.

   - In fact, the parties make a new choice in this segment: previously, whenever one party pressed the race issue, the other withdrew. Now, *both are committed* to see it through. This is *their* decision, and it carries the conversation to a new depth.

2. In the new depths that the conversation reaches, the parties themselves reach new heights of both strength of self and openness to each other. That is, their empowerment and recognition shifts *not only continue but accelerate*.

   - Elizabeth, having decided to discuss racism with Julie, does so with a *clarity, articulation,* and *forcefulness* that reflect clearly the strength she has gathered.

She makes clear that Julie's long inaction and unconscious-
ness about diversity is the heart of her grievance: "Did it
ever occur to you . . . [that you] don't live in a sea of whiteness?" "*You* can nominate. Have you ever nominated a
nonwhite person? . . . Julie, you always come up with
excuses."

She makes clear why she feels Julie's concern for diversity
is suspect: "You wanted diversity. What, to *say* you lived
in a diverse . . . community? . . . Diversity means to me
some kind of interaction. It doesn't mean staying . . .
within your own separate groups! It doesn't mean the
board after *umpteen* years . . . is still an *all-white* board."

She makes clear that her reluctance to trust Julie's over-
ture stems from her—and her people's—long struggle
with racial oppression: "It will *not* suddenly make all these
feelings . . . disappear. If the Ku Klux Klan came and . . .
lynched somebody . . . and then today they want to say,
'I'm sorry,' . . . it's not going to erase the *horror*, the
hurt . . . of that period! . . . It's not going to be so *easy*."

- At the same time, Elizabeth's very willingness to make
these statements to Julie and to make them so honestly,
represents a remarkable level of openness and willingness
to try connecting across the gulf of difference.

In fact, her words show clearly that she wants to connect
and believes this is possible—that Julie can "get it":
"What you must understand . . . I don't believe you're
hearing me. . . . Please . . . Please . . . hear me!"

By the very act of making these pleas for understanding,
Elizabeth is showing that she *recognizes a humanity* in Julie
that can respond to her and her daughter.

- For her part, Julie gets very clear about what it is that disturbs her so much—which is not only the charge of
racism—and finds the strength to express it.

She realizes and states clearly that what really hurts her is the suspicion and rejection of her overtures: "I can think of . . . ways to address the issue of diversity . . . ; but if I'm going to be met . . . with, 'I don't want to make you *feel good*,' 'This isn't about *you*,' and rejection of those ideas—then it's very hard."

Julie's empowerment shift is expressed not only in this clarity but also, ironically, in her willingness to say what she has realized even though it shows her vulnerability. She finds the *strength* to display vulnerability.

- At the same time, throughout this segment Julie expresses powerfully her desire—even determination—to connect with Elizabeth and her belief that this is possible.

  Regarding Elizabeth's argument that the board is not diverse, Julie repeats several times, "She's right. . . . and we should *fix* it," and affirms that the situation is "*wrong*." She directly recognizes Elizabeth's views as valid.

  Julie persists in the discussion despite Elizabeth's unsparing statements and clearly tries very hard to listen and understand what she is hearing—which in itself strongly expresses her openness to Elizabeth.

3. The empowerment and recognition shifts visible in this segment are produced by the parties' own efforts, not by the mediator. At the same time, the mediator's interventions *support* those efforts, and this is also visible at several points.

   - The mediator uses, in this segment, *all* of the forms of intervention discussed earlier in the chapter—reflection, summary, check-in—and a careful reading of the transcript will show that Elizabeth's and Julie's shifts often build from these interventions.

   - What is new in this segment is that—especially in reflections and summaries—the mediator is more willing to *go beyond* the parties' exact language. Here are some examples:

In his summary pointing out differences in their thinking about what it would take to "heal" the racial split, he refers to Julie's view that "separate from how you *feel*, she [Elizabeth] is *right*, and that situation [of no diversity] is *wrong*."

This goes beyond Julie's words—she never used the term *wrong*—and she points this out but agrees that she is saying this.

Later, in a reflection to Elizabeth after her bitter statements about the long years of an all-white board, the mediator says, "one of the implications that I'm hearing [in your] . . . term . . . *racist* in this context . . . is: If . . . a management structure . . . excludes everybody but *one group*, then whether or not there's an intention behind that . . . it's, in your word, racist."

Again, this goes beyond Elizabeth's words, and she rejects "this definition of racism" by the mediator—but this is followed by her clarification that "diversity means . . . interaction, [not staying] within . . . separate groups!"

- In each of these interventions, the mediator goes beyond simply mirroring or condensing what the parties said. He adds an element of *translation*—describing what he thinks they are trying to get across and thus helping to surface this, even though he's going beyond their words.

In doing this, there is a risk that the mediator will misinterpret what is said, steer the conversation away from the parties' real intent, and thus violate the principle of party control.

This risk is less if this is done late in the session, when close listening throughout has given the mediator a very strong feel for what the parties are trying to say.

The risk is even less if the mediator offers his statement as only a "draft" of what was said and backs off quickly if it is rejected—as he does here, when Elizabeth rejects his "definition of racism."

- This *enhanced form of reflection and summary*, offered as a draft of what parties are saying, can help parties express points that are hard to surface and articulate.

  In effect, the mediator's draft, even if rejected, provides a *platform* that the parties can use to jump off from in saying what they want to.

  Here, for example, Elizabeth rejects the draft, but it still gives her momentum to move to her clearest and strongest statements about multiracial diversity, the horror of racism, and so forth.

4. With all of this in mind, the "sudden" turnaround at the end of the mediation seems neither sudden nor unbelievable, but rather a natural outgrowth of the way the conversation has progressed.

- The mediator's final check-in with Julie offers her the choice of how to respond to Elizabeth, to decide what if anything she wants to say; and she takes the opening.

- In response to Elizabeth's "Please . . . hear me!" and "It's not going to erase the *horror*, the *hurt*," Julie says, "I *do* hear Elizabeth"—and then she actually *reflects* to Elizabeth the very heart of what she has been asked to hear: "There's four hundred *years* of discrimination and . . . one gesture doesn't fix everything. And I *appreciate* that. Of *course* it doesn't."

  Thus, in this segment, Elizabeth accepted the "challenge" to explain herself to Julie, and Julie has now shown clearly that *she understands*.

- Then, in the final exchange, Julie says, "I just wish . . . you were willing to be open to [working together] . . . instead of

. . . questioning my motives and *dismissing* it," and Elizabeth responds, "I don't want to *hurt anyone*. And as much as I may disagree with you, I don't want to leave you *hurt!*"

Here, it is Julie who asks for understanding. And Elizabeth is ready to offer it, because the parties' shifts have changed their interaction *from alienating and demonizing to connecting and humanizing*—and Elizabeth wants to hold that new, positive ground.

The conclusion of the conversation confirms a key premise of the transformative model: *people want to be neither victims nor victimizers*. Elizabeth is not at all a victim by the end of this conversation—and she is equally unwilling to become a victimizer by denying Julie recognition.

The disagreements between the parties remain: "We still have a purple . . . house!" But they have *transformed their interaction*, and this occurred as a result of *their* choices and *their* efforts. The course of this mediation illustrates all of the basic assumptions of the transformative model: people in conflict are seeking interactional transformation as much or more than reaching settlements of concrete issues. In addition, people are capable of the self-determined decision making and the uncoerced understanding of others that are needed for conflict transformation. The mediation also demonstrates how transformative mediators follow rather than lead the parties through the conversation, supporting and never supplanting party decision making, supporting but never forcing interparty understanding, and in general working to support the empowerment and recognition shifts that transform conflict interaction.

Myths and Misconceptions
About Transformative Mediation

The Purple House case offers a detailed map of how transformative mediation is enacted in one compelling and intensely emotional conflict. We presented the case in its entirety because, in general, we have found that the transformative framework is best understood by studying transcripts and videos of a wide range of cases in their unedited, unscripted forms. In transformative mediation trainings, the case examples presented are usually unedited and full length, rather than snapshot pictures of segments or phases of a session. This approach is taken because we have found that close familiarity with what "real-time" conflict interaction is like is essential to an understanding and mastery of this approach to practice. An appreciation of what the transformation of conflict interaction actually looks and sounds like, comment by comment, is for most people the best way to understand the link between purpose and practice within this approach. It provides mediators with a clear picture of what it means to take and sustain a "microfocus"—the ability to follow and support parties as they articulate and develop their own way through difficult, emotional, and sometimes "unsolvable" disputes. The transformation of conflict always occurs at the level of specific comments and sequences of comments as a session unfolds. Understanding what mediators do moment to moment creates a solid foundation on which to practice. It also provides the best way to avoid some of the common pitfalls and misunderstandings about the transformative framework in general, and about the practices that flow from it.

Ten years ago, there were few detailed case studies or videotaped examples of transformative practice available. Although the theoretical framework and ideological roots of practice were articulated and exemplified, vivid pictures of practice were far less accessible. This has changed in recent years with the increasing sophistication of training and research materials, but the early gap between theory and practice left sufficient room for a number of significant misunderstandings and myths to circulate about the nature, purpose, and uses of transformative mediation. These misunderstandings are themselves understandable, given the continuing development of this framework and its implementation; but they are also troubling because some are now widespread within the mediation field, and they have, in some instances, undermined useful discussions of the strengths and limitations of this approach to practice. These misunderstandings about the framework can be heard in informal conversations among mediators, in conference panels where the approach to practice is being discussed, and in published articles that summarize or critique the framework.

Dispelling Myths and Misconceptions

Our goal in this chapter is to address these myths and misunderstandings so that the transformative framework and its forms of practice are accurately understood. It is not our intention to respond to disagreements that some may have with this approach to practice as a whole. Rather, we want to clarify the model so that any discussion of it is built on an accurate understanding of what it is and what it is not. We therefore summarize in the following discussion several important misinterpretations of the model and discuss why each is inaccurate or a misrepresentation of the nature or purpose of the transformative approach to mediation practice.

"Transformative mediation facilitates communication, but parties' disputes tend not to get resolved."

The goal of a mediator in the transformative orientation is to support the possible transformation of the parties' conflict interaction by fostering empowerment and recognition. The mediator intervenes to support party deliberation and decision making, and interparty understanding, rather than to shape any particular settlement, impose common ground, or encourage unsupported closure of issues. However, by supporting empowerment and recognition shifts when those opportunities arise in the parties' own conversation, the mediator assists the parties in clarifying and deciding *for themselves* what they consider a successful resolution. The parties might decide, through their decision-making process, that a successful resolution is an agreement or compromise, but they might also define successful resolution as the decision to end the mediation without a settlement, to take the case to other forums, to drop the case, or to be satisfied with a better understanding of the events and circumstances that led to the conflict. In short, they may figure out a way to "live with no" even if they cannot "get to yes."

By focusing firmly on the parties' own deliberation, decision making, and perspective taking, transformative mediators encourage genuine, voluntary, fully informed settlements to emerge as and when the parties deem them appropriate. But they do not prescribe the parameters of agreement or define settlement as the only possible successful outcome for a mediation session. Reaching agreement is one decision the parties *may* make if they choose to do so.

There has been insightful research on the outcomes of transformative mediation in the largest organizational setting where this model of practice has been implemented—the U.S. Postal Service REDRESS program. Bingham has measured *closure rates* for the cases that have entered mediation in this workplace mediation program. Closure rates include all cases that are withdrawn, dropped, or settled as a result of mediation. Closure thus reflects the number of cases that do not continue beyond the mediation process to a formal hearing stage. Bingham (2003) found consistently high rates of closure within the postal service REDRESS program. Of the twenty thousand cases that were mediated in the first two years of the program, for example, 80 percent of the cases closed (Hallberlin, 2001). This finding has been generally interpreted to mean that parties have dealt with their conflict satisfactorily and therefore did not feel that they needed to bring the case to an additional forum. The high rates of closure found in this program suggest that transformative mediation provides parties with a process that addresses key concerns, whether or not the cases "settle" in a more traditional sense.

In addition, case studies of mediations from the REDRESS program suggest that parties' conflicts frequently unfold in directions that have little to do with the presenting issues that brought the case to mediation in the first place (Antes, Folger, and Della Noce, 2001). If mediators focus on reaching settlements that address the presenting issues and direct the parties' conflict interaction to make this occur, the issues that parties wanted to address might never surface. Settlement of the presenting issue becomes an irrelevant objective. Transformative mediation's emphasis on following and supporting the parties' voices helps ensure that any outcomes of the mediation are the ones that the parties want to pursue. The Purple House mediation is a good example of how the model works to achieve this.

So within the transformative framework, conflicts do indeed "get resolved"—but they get resolved by the parties rather than by the mediator, and they get resolved in a wide variety of ways. The mediator assists the parties by maintaining a focus on the process through which the *parties* define and achieve resolution, and by maintaining a broad conception of what "resolution" can be.

"Transformative mediation is only appropriate or useful in conflicts where the parties have an ongoing relationship that continues after the mediation."

Because of the transformative framework's emphasis on shifts in the parties' conflict interaction, some have assumed that transformative mediation is appropriate only in cases where the parties have or want to continue a relationship. Questions have been raised about why the transformation of the parties' interaction should be the focus of the mediator's work if the parties are not likely to have further interactions after the mediation is over.

The transformative approach assumes that all interactions between people carry relationship significance, for however long their interactions last. Every human interaction maintains or alters a "relationship"—a process of interacting and relating—that can be conducted in a negative and destructive fashion or in a positive and constructive fashion. Therefore, in any situation where the quality of the interaction matters to the parties and where the quality of the interaction will have an impact on other possible outcomes (including whether agreement is reached and what the quality of the agreement, if reached, will be), interventions that help shift the interaction from negative to positive are of fundamental value. The interaction between an insurance adjuster and a claimant or between a customer and a business owner is as vulnerable to destructive or productive influences as that of two neighbors or a divorcing couple. Productive transformation of conflict interaction allows parties to gain clarity about decisions and choices (empowerment) in light of the experience of the other (recognition) in whatever setting it occurs. And the quality of the conflict interaction that unfolds during any mediation session has a direct impact on the outcomes of mediation sessions, even if parties are never engaged with one another again.

In a personal injury case, the parties attending the mediation were the injured party, an African American woman in her sixties, her attorney, and the adjuster for the injurer's insurance company. The insurance company conceded liability but questioned the extent of the woman's injury, the need and legitimacy of her medical care, and therefore the overall amount of damages that should be paid. The mediator allowed the parties to present their views to each other, and a discussion ensued between the attorney and the adjuster. The attorney tried to explain how the injury, which affected the muscles and ligaments of the woman's knee and thigh but involved no broken bones, had limited her mobility and restricted her activity. The adjuster kept repeating that this was "a soft-tissue leg injury to a sixty-plus female, not worth more than" a given amount, according to actuarial tables, and that the medical bills for such an injury couldn't have been as great as she claimed. Then the mediator saw that the woman herself wanted to speak and invited her to do so. She spoke slowly but clearly, recounting in detail and with obviously genuine emotion what her life had been like before the injury and what it was like now. Before, despite her age, she'd been an active churchgoer, volunteer, activist, and full participant in a whole world of social activity. Now, still unstable and in pain despite considerable therapy of different kinds, she was simply unable to get around, even with a car. She was basically housebound, isolated, lonely—the entire character of her life had changed, and she was devastated.

Her narrative was obviously genuine and powerfully affecting. When she was done, she stated simply, "I'm not really going to be able to go back to the way things were, no matter how much money you give me. That's not the point." She looked straight at the adjuster and concluded, "The point is that I'm a real person—not a 'sixty-plus female with a soft-tissue injury'—and not a liar. That's all, I'm done. Do what you want." She sat back after speaking with a sense of calm and dignity, and the adjuster was quiet for several long minutes, in which the mediator said nothing. Then the adjuster got up and said, "I want to make a call." When he came back, he reported that he had asked for and gotten approval to give her the policy limit. He told the woman he was sorry for the way he'd "categorized" her and confessed that negotiating these claims sometimes led him to forget that he was dealing with human beings, not "cases." She acknowledged that his job must be a difficult one and thanked him for what he'd done, especially for hearing her plea to be seen for who she was.

In addition to the inherent nature of relationship in any conflict interaction, the transformative framework also values the potential upstream impacts of the mediation process—the impact the session has on how people respond to conflict with others as a result of experiencing productive transformation of any conflict. When parties experience the transformation of conflict interaction in a difficult dispute of any kind, this experience—and the insights about conflict it provides—can be carried with them out of the mediation room and can influence their approaches to dealing with conflict in future situations. Studies are under way to confirm preliminary evidence that upstream impacts are a real and valued result of parties' experiences in transformative mediation (Bingham, 2003).

"In transformative practice, the mediator is largely inactive during the session."

Mediators from the transformative orientation are not *directive*. However, they are *proactive*. As the mediator's behaviors clearly indicate in the Purple House case, transformative mediators are actively engaged with the parties in conversation. They listen intently for cues that offer opportunities to work with empowerment and recognition, highlight those opportunities for the parties, and constantly invite and encourage the parties to engage in a constructive dialogue, to consider new information and alternative points of view, to gain clarity, to deliberate or "think out loud," and to make decisions for themselves. Mediators frequently check in to see where the parties would like to head next. They offer careful summaries of what parties have said, they ask whether anything that has been said by another party is "news," or—if they sense that one party is uncomfortable with the unfolding interaction—they may ask if that party wants to address whatever seems to be bothering them. All of these various behaviors are active moves that mediators make as they follow the parties along their path through empowerment and recognition shifts.

Even when the mediator is quiet for periods of time as the parties talk to one another, it does not mean that the mediator is inactive. Transformative mediators are comfortable with the parties talking to each other for extended periods of time, and they try not to get in the way when it happens. While parties speak to each other, the mediator checks for each person's reactions, tracks whether empowerment or recognition shifts are occurring, and considers appropriate and useful ways to summarize what the parties have been discussing.

The primary task for transformative mediators is to "follow the parties": to maintain a microfocus on their moment-to-moment conversation, in order to identify and highlight opportunities for empowerment and recognition. They tend not to rely on stock phrases such as, "How do you feel about that?" This is not to say, however, that "How do you feel about that?" would never be an appropriate response to something a party has just said. It might be asked to invite clarification, foster reflection, or otherwise work with the opportunities for empowerment or recognition that the party presented. However, such phrases are not the only, or even the primary, interventions of the mediator. There are times when such a question could be an inappropriate, intrusive, or even directive response, particularly if the parties are not themselves talking at the level of feelings. It will depend on what the parties have just said, and what opportunity was presented. Offering the opportunity for further clarification of feelings or attitudes is just one of many possible responses a mediator might make in working with the parties. Mediators working within the transformative framework are skilled at reading the unfolding context, a context that is continuously created as the parties interact. Without such sensitivity to where the parties are at a given moment, mediators cannot support where the parties want to head with their conflict. Recent research has documented the kinds of specific interventions that are characteristic of transformative practice (Della Noce, 2002; Della Noce, Antes, and Saul, 2004).

The following interventions are typical of a transformative mediation:

Using reflections that follow the content and emotional tone of a party's own comments

Offering reflections in a tentative manner that invites party correction

Allowing significant segments of uninterrupted party-to-party talk (intentional silence)

Following party-to-party discussions with inclusive summaries that:

- include important topics raised by both or all of the parties.
- capture the emotional tone of what was said.
- highlight points of disagreement as well as agreement.
- include the intangible as well as the tangible.

Supporting conflict talk and "following the heat" by:

- following the content and emotional tone of party conflict talk.
- keying in to terms that parties use that seem to carry "heat."
- marking points of disagreement (not just agreement or common ground).
- allowing multiple themes to develop (not just themes that seem tangible or solvable).

Highlighting process choice points by:

- including process choice points in summaries and reflections.
- offering decision points to the parties (checking in).
- offering any mediator suggestions only tentatively to emphasize opportunity for party choice [adapted from Della Noce, Antes, and Saul, 2004].

"There is no structure or order to a mediation session that follows a transformative process."

The mediator does not impose a highly structured process on the parties when working from the transformative orientation. Imposing process structure has an influence on the parties' conflict that often goes unacknowledged, and such influence is something the transformative mediator works to avoid (Folger, 2001). However, this does not mean that a transformative process lacks order and structure or that there is no framework for how mediators approach their role in the process. In general, order and structure emerge from the conversations of the mediator and the parties. The transformative approach assumes that the mediator does not have to impose a structure on the parties; parties are capable of structuring and order-ing their conversations as they need to (Della Noce, 2001; Antes and others, 1999).

The mediator helps the parties determine how they want to structure their interaction by focusing on empowerment and recog-nition throughout the mediation. For example, the mediator checks in with the parties about the goals of mediation in the opening con-versation and invites them to begin to participate in structuring the process by discussing whether they want or need conversational guidelines and what those guidelines might be. The mediator flags *process decisions* for the parties, such as what topics they want to dis-cuss and whether they want to transition from one topic to another. As the parties make these decisions, the process naturally takes shape. The Purple House mediation offers a good example of what this approach looks like, and how it works to allow the parties themselves to structure the unfolding of the process.

The case study also shows how this party-driven view of the process and structure of mediation enables parties to move in one direction for a while, then backtrack and retrace their steps, recon-sider where they see themselves heading, and then move forward again in a slightly different (or the same) direction. It allows par-ties to step to the edge of a decision-making cliff, then back off with greater clarity about the decisions they really want to make. This more cyclical view of the process is consistent with the way pro-ductive conflict interaction typically evolves and discourages medi-ator directiveness and process control. (See Figure 6.1.)

"Transformative mediation is a form of therapy and is therefore beyond the bounds of legitimate mediation practice."

In transformative practice, mediators attempt to align their behav-ior with the nature of conflict interaction. This approach acknowl-edges that talking about the past, expressing emotions, showing confusion, and being self-absorbed and defensive are part and parcel of what destructive conflict is often like. To be successful in working

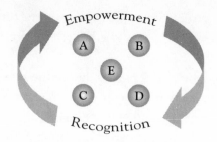

Outer ring:
Mediator's focus
Attending to empowerment and recognition

Inner ring:
Spheres of activity naturally shaped and reshaped
through the conversational interactions in the session

A: *Creating the context (How do I want to do this?)*
B: *Exploring the situation (What is this about?)*
C: *Deliberating (What does this mean?)*
D: *Exploring possibilities (What is possible?)*
E: *Decision making (What do I do?)*

Figure 6.1. A Model for Mediation as a Transformative Process.
  Source: Adapted from Della Noce (2001, p. 80).

with conflict interaction, mediators have to develop a level of comfort and tolerance for these features and need to remain focused on
working with opportunities for empowerment and recognition shifts,
during whatever forms of conflict interaction arise during a mediation
session. For some, transformative mediation's focus on the true nature
of conflict interaction has been interpreted as a step toward becoming
a therapeutic intervention. It is important to clarify whether this is
indeed the case. Both empowerment and recognition, as goals of the
transformative mediator, can be distinguished from the objectives of
different forms of therapy.

Some therapy has as its objective the working out of a client's
unresolved feelings about parents or early childhood or the work-

ing out of conflicted feelings about some current situation. Many therapists, in pursuing these objectives of resolving conflicted feelings, are highly directive and relatively unconcerned with a client's giving recognition to family members or others, except insofar as it helps their own emotional state. In effect, this type of therapy is a form of problem solving, concerned with addressing emotional problems (Haley, 1987; Roberts, 1992). It is not concerned with supporting client empowerment or recognition, and the distinction of objectives is fairly clear.

Other types of therapy, however, focus more on the process of learning how to handle the problems that the client faces, whether from the past or in the present, as a strengthening process for the individual (Haynes, 1992). There is a similarity between the objective of this type of therapy and empowerment, and the term empowerment is sometimes used in the literature of therapy in a similar sense. The distinction to be drawn here is that in transformative mediation, supporting empowerment is never a sole objective; it is always linked to the possibility of recognition shifts as well. In therapy, empowerment is often an objective unto itself—the client's attainment of a state of adjustment, well-being, autonomy, and so forth.

Finally, in some forms of therapy, usually with couples or family members in close relationships, the objective seems to encompass not only empowerment within the individuals themselves but also recognition between them (see, for example, Boszormenyi-Nagy and Krasner, 1986). The objectives envisioned by this kind of therapy are similar to those of transformative mediation. We do not see this connection between mediation and some forms of therapy as problematic. If the goals of empowerment and recognition as defined make sense and are of real value, and if an approach to doing mediation exists that can attain them, then we should not be concerned if mediation encompasses some of the same objectives as some forms of therapy. This is especially so in a culture where therapy is generally practiced only with parties in intimate relationships, whereas

conflict and interactional crisis affect people far beyond this context. Many astute mediators in the field have seen these implications but have hesitated to suggest that they were there. The
mediation field has tended to be hypersensitive about preserving
strict divisions among mediative and therapeutic processes—draw-
ing lines that have at times been ignored in practice and have at
times held mediation back from realizing transformative objectives
(Forlenza, 1991). If mediation is to be helpful in transforming conflict interaction, then its overlap with some therapeutic processes
needs to be acknowledged and accepted.

*"A mediator can combine theoretical frameworks or shift strate-
gically between frameworks."*

Mediators sometimes assume that it is possible to combine transformative practice with elements and objectives of other models of
practice that are more focused on problem solving and reaching
agreement. At issue is whether it is possible for mediators to "do
both" at the same time, or to shift strategically from one framework
to another in the course of a mediation. Our experience is that combining models is not possible, because of the incompatible objectives of different models and the conflicting practices that flow from
these diverse objectives.

Transformative mediation makes clear assumptions about the
nature of conflict, the capabilities of parties, the appropriateness of
emotional expressiveness, and other key features of conflict that are
inconsistent with other forms of practice. Any approach to mediation that aims at controlling conflict or producing settlements is
seeking a very different objective and is based in very different assumptions about human nature and conflict interaction—as discussed at length in Chapter Seven. When models of mediation rest
on very different underlying values and premises, their objectives
cannot be sought simultaneously, and shifting between them leads
to confusing and inconsistent practices. It is impossible, for example,
for a mediator to simultaneously support autonomous party decision

making and substitute the mediator's judgment for that of the parties. Similarly, it is not possible to advise parties to remain future oriented in their discussions, so as to keep them moving toward agreement, and at the same time allow parties to discuss the past in ways that reveal opportunities for empowerment and recognition. The result of this incompatibility is that mediator practices that are characteristic of the transformative model are viewed as inappropriate, inconsistent, or even dangerous by those who practice within a more settlement-oriented framework. Similarly, characteristic practices of settlement-oriented mediation (such as imposing preset ground rules or containing emotional expressiveness) are counter to the objectives of transformative practice.

Two mediators from two different states who were quite skilled in the transformative approach, and who trained other mediators in the transformative approach for the USPS, were evaluated for competency in unrelated programs in their respective states on the basis of supposedly "neutral" and "generic" checklists of "skills." Both were found "incompetent" in their mediation skills. An examination of the checklists themselves showed that the skills that "counted" were neither neutral nor generic, but were based exclusively on the problem-solving framework. In other words, all the checklist demonstrated was that the transformative mediators were not conducting competent problem-solving practice. This was no surprise, because competence in transformative practice cannot be evaluated according to a problem-solving skills checklist: the theoretical premises, mediators' goals, and therefore mediator practices, are very different in each framework. . . . some of the very interventions that are considered "good practice" in one framework are considered "bad practice" in the other [Della Noce, Bush, and Folger, 2002, pp. 59–60].

One theoretical framework is inevitably favored over another by each mediator or mediation program, depending on the goals and values of the mediator and the program in which the mediator works. Some mediators indicate that during an unfolding session they adopt a transformative focus on empowerment and recognition initially but move from this approach when the parties get "stuck" or reach impasse. They then feel the need to change orientations and work from more of a settlement orientation. This role-switching approach ultimately leads the actual mediation practice out of the realm of the transformative framework. It is very much like decision-making groups that say they run their meetings by a consensus process but switch to majority voting when consensus cannot be reached. Keeping open the option of switching process commitments fundamentally changes the orientation of the group to its process. People know that they will vote, so why give the effort and creativity it takes to reach consensus? In the same sense, mediators who leave open the option of switching orientations reveal their hesitancy about the goals of the transformative approach itself. Parties are left to make their own decisions, but only as long as significant obstacles do not arise. When they do, the focus of the mediator shifts toward settlement production.

The idea of combining settlement-oriented and transformative practice is not unlike another process-combination idea that was quite popular in the 1970s and 1980s and has since lost its luster. The "med-arb" process combined elements of the mediation and arbitration processes. The "med-arbiter" started out using the mediation process, trying to bring about a voluntary agreement; however, if the parties could not reach agreement, the med-arbiter "switched hats," conducted an arbitration hearing, and rendered a binding award. However, the constituent parts of med-arb were basically inconsistent: the informality and confidentiality of the mediation phase compromised the neutrality that the med-arbiter would need if the case proceeded to the arbitration phase. At the same time, the threat of the med-arbiter's possible judgment in the arbitration phase inhibited parties' open expression in the mediation phase. Med-arb was a process at war with itself. We believe that the same would be true of a combined settlement-transformative version of mediation.

A final problem involves the need for accountability of mediators for the quality of their practice. Accepting the notion of a combination model will inevitably make it possible to justify any mediator practice and conversely make it impossible to sanction any specific practice. Whatever the practice, it can almost always be argued that it fits one model or the other and therefore is legitimate. The result would be an "anything goes" practice environment that offers no way to hold mediators themselves accountable (Stulberg, 1997). Some would argue that this has long been the case and that the field's slow and painful efforts to improve and regularize the quality of practice would be undermined by the combination model approach.

Although the preceding discussion should clarify our view that combining models cannot be sustained coherently as a permanent approach to practice, we want to acknowledge equally clearly that for many mediators, combining practices is the natural first step in initiating an *evolution in practice* toward a different model. Indeed this is an evolution that we ourselves went through and that we have seen many others go through over the last decade. This evolution starts with awareness and expression of concerns about one's current practices, followed by the adoption of new techniques and methods that attempt to address those problems. Then, because many of the adopted changes are incongruous with key elements of the mediator's former model and theoretical framework, the changes lead to eventual adoption of an alternative model or framework that better captures the mediator's underlying sense of purpose and objectives. For us, this evolution ended with the development and adoption of the transformative framework, because it provided the theoretical and ideological foundations for a type of practice that moved away from the problems we saw with many institutionalized forms of mediation practice. For others who are in a similar transition that starts with questioning current practice, it may also mean the adoption of the transformative framework or alternatively the adoption of an as-yet-undefined framework of practice. However, even though we see the phase of combining practices as a natural and valid step toward a new model, we do not see it as a viable form of practice per se.

"Transformative mediation imposes a set of values on the parties whereas other forms of practice do not."

In presenting the nature and purpose of transformative mediation, we have been very explicit about its underlying foundations—the values and ideology on which it is based. Discussing the transformative approach to practice in these explicitly ideological terms has led some to assume that this approach to practice is the only one that is value based and that transformative mediation imposes its process values on parties whereas other forms of practice do not. This is an inaccurate and misleading view. It is important to recognize that *all* forms of mediation practice are based in a set of core values and premises—ways of thinking about what productive conflict is, what human beings are capable of, and what third parties should do as they intervene. Transformative mediation is based on a set of relational values, whereas other models of practice are based on values stemming from interest-based negotiation approaches to conflict. These values are clearly different. They are rooted in individualistic, transactional, and economic premises that tend to pervade thinking about conflict in western societies (Gray, 1994; Putnam, 1994; Kolb and Putnam, 1997).

Because some forms of practice are built on this predominant view of conflict, it is easy to think that these widely accepted approaches to practice are value free, that they are not built on any particular set of assumptions or values. But this is clearly not the case. To choose any approach to mediation is to choose a set of values; and to enact those values in practice is, in a sense, to "impose" those values on the parties through the process that the mediator engages them in. As mediators, we inevitably assume that the values we are choosing (and the approach to practice that enacts them) are the right, appropriate, or most useful ones. The issue is not whether one form of practice imposes its values on parties and another does not, but rather whether each approach to practice acknowledges and clarifies the values that are enacted when practice is conducted—and whether practitioners are transparent about those values with clients. In Chapter Seven, we offer a more extensive exploration of the values underlying different approaches to practice and the implications that flow from the acknowledgment of value-based practice, for working with clients and for the field as a whole.

"A transformative mediator's focus in conducting practice is on changing the individual parties."

Some have assumed that in the transformative framework the mediator's goal is to achieve some sort of personal or psychological change in the parties themselves. This is another misconception. In transformative practice, the mediator's focus is on *transformation of the parties' conflict interaction* by tracking and supporting empowerment and recognition shifts as they occur. The mediator's attention and interventions remain focused here throughout the mediation. This means that mediators sustain a microfocus on the message-by-message unfolding interaction that occurs between or among the parties. In this sense, the model is essentially a communication-based rather than a psychological approach to practice.

But this is not to say that there aren't potentially useful psychological impacts on parties who participate in transformative mediation. One possible effect of experiencing conflict transformation firsthand is that parties themselves may be changed in various ways. They may experience how it is possible to be true to oneself while developing greater understanding of, respect for, or connection to people with whom they differ in important ways. When this happens, personal change can be a valuable result of experiencing the effects of such shifts in difficult conflict interaction. But the mediator's focus is never on changing the parties. None of the training methods or practice recommendations in the transformative approach promote or foster such a focus. This focus would, in fact, be counter to the fundamental principle of empowerment on which this approach to practice is based (Folger and Bush, 1996).

"Transformative mediation is ultimately driven by spiritual motives or objectives."

Similar to the previous misconception, but even more disturbing to some people, is the idea that the transformative model is a spiritually motivated enterprise. Since the publication of the first edition of *The Promise of Mediation*, we have been very explicit about the ideological assumptions underlying transformative practice. This attention to core values and worldview has been helpful in clarifying the underlying purpose behind practice and in distinguishing between differences in mediator styles and more fundamental differences in core premises and objectives of practice. The discussion about the various ideologies that support different forms of practice has, however, created a sense for some people that transformative mediation is driven—either overtly or covertly—by spiritual or religious objectives.

This is an inaccurate characterization of this approach to practice. It casts transformative mediation in a light that can create a confining and distancing perception about who can practice transformative mediation or where it can be institutionalized. Although the premises underlying this model of practice are consistent with some beliefs and worldviews of religious individuals or larger communities of faith, these premises do not specifically derive from religious or spiritual values. Nor is the goal of transformative practice to create faith-based communities around these underlying premises. The goal is to encourage a form of mediation practice that supports the core human capacity for both personal strength and interpersonal connection. This capacity is recognized as a real and central part of human nature by people of many diverse backgrounds, all living and functioning in the secular world, some with and some without explicit commitments to a religious community or belief system. The motivation behind the transformative model is a commitment to this view of human nature—and to building social processes that enact it—not to any particular tradition that may share this view.

"The development of transformative mediation is unnecessarily dividing the mediation field."

The development and articulation of the transformative model over the past decade has meant that the field has begun to come to terms with the different models of practice that are viable. It has also brought an increasing acknowledgment that these differences are not just differences in style, or practice technique. They are not differences in how to draw on different methods to reach the same ends, but differences about the fundamental purposes of practicing mediation, and the practices those purposes require. They reveal deeper differences in ideology that affect definitions of what ethical practice is, what policies are needed to support practice in different settings, and what training is needed to reach different objectives. These differences also create diverse expectations for what success is, and for what outcomes and impacts can be expected from the mediation process.

The increasing acceptance of transformative mediation has brought these differences—and the consequent choices they present—to the fore. The field at large, as well as individual practitioners and program administrators, is now faced with clearer choices about why we practice the way we do. For some, the articulation of these differences, and the discussion it has engendered, has meant that the field has been divided. For others, it has meant that there is now more diversity of practice in the field as well as firmer and more well-articulated grounds on which to decide between approaches to practice.

We believe that the mediation field is still in the process of learning to live with these core differences. It is figuring out how to coexist professionally when different choices exist and different ideologies undergird these choices (Folger, 2002). These differences, and the question of how to live with them within the field, are the subject of Chapter Seven.

Understanding and Accepting Differences in Mediation Practice

It is important to dispel these misunderstandings and misconceptions of transformative mediation. They stand in the way of understanding the purpose that drives transformative practice, and they create confusion about similarities and differences across models of mediation. In an important sense, sustaining an accurate understanding of transformative mediation requires an acceptance of the differences that exist in the way mediators choose to practice. Blurring the differences that exist among the various approaches, or exaggerating them for the sake of argument, does little to foster accurate and productive assessment of any of the diverse approaches to mediation. As the field has become more comfortable with the existence of very different forms of practice, the misconceptions and myths about transformative practice are becoming less salient. This is a healthy sign in the evolution of a relatively young field. In the next chapter, we step beyond clarification of the model and discuss the reasons why, at a deeper ideological level, transformative mediation has become increasingly appealing to many practitioners.

7

Paths Toward the Future
Living with Differences in Values and Practice

In the previous chapters, we laid out the theory and practice of the transformative model of mediation in considerable depth. We described how the model is based on a theory of conflict as inter-actional crisis, and we explained its view of the mediation process as one of conflict transformation and the mediator's role as sup-porting the empowerment and recognition shifts that change party interaction from destructive to constructive. We then presented an extended case study to illustrate many of the specific practices of the model in a concrete and challenging situation, and we discussed and clarified a number of common misconceptions about the model. Overall this volume represents a significant advance in breadth, depth, and clarity over our original articulation of the model in the first edition. This advance was made possible through the hard work of many people over the past decade—colleagues whose work helped generate new insights on theory, training, practice and assessment methodology, and implementation strategy. We are grateful for their contributions to this work, and we look forward to continuing col-laboration in the decade to come.

In addition to presenting a refined articulation of the transforma-tive model, we described how transformative mediation has attracted steadily increasing interest and support over this past decade. We pointed to the field's increasing recognition of problems with pre-vailing, settlement-oriented mediation practices; and we illustrated the kinds of suggestions being made for changes in practice—many of which involve shifts toward core elements of the transformative model. Finally, we presented some concrete examples of how the model is being adopted by mediators and mediation programs operating in diverse arenas and how its core principles are being extended into new areas of conflict intervention beyond mediation as such. Based on these developments, we can be confident that the transformative model has gained a firm foothold in the mediation field.

However, one important set of questions remains unaddressed, the answers to which are quite important to any discussion about what the future may hold, for the transformative model and for the field as a whole. Those questions are as follows: *Why* has this model attracted the interest and support it has received in recent years? What is its "value-added," for both practitioners and users of mediation? What has appealed to them and induced practitioners to develop, master, and implement it?

At one level, these questions have already been answered in Chapter Three, in our discussion of the growing dissatisfactions and criticisms among some people about mainstream practice, and our discussion of the growing commitments many are making to the transformative model. However, those discussions only *identify* the values that some people find distressingly absent from conventional practice and richly present in transformative practice—such as self-determination, communication, and connection. What those discussions do not fully explain is *why* these values matter so much to some people—even though they don't matter much at all to others. Answering this question is the focus here, because we believe that the answers will help us chart the way forward.

In short, we now ask this: What is the driving force that makes the values of the transformative model so meaningful to those who are drawn to it? In general, the answer can be summed up in one word: *ideology*—meaning a fundamental set of beliefs about the nature of the social world. More specifically, we believe that the shift toward acceptance of the transformative model reflects an ideologically based movement in one or both of two directions—movement *away* from an essentially negative vision of human conflict, and movement *toward* a different, essentially positive vision.

Movement Away: The Ideology of Social Separation and Conflict Control

What is it that is driving people like Welsh, Press, Alfini, Mayer, and others to question the methods of mainstream mediation, especially as practiced in the courts and other major institutional users of the process? The explicit answer given earlier is that these practices "dilute" and frustrate the originally intended aims of the mediation process, especially the goals of self-determination and mutual engagement, and instead focus much too heavily on the single-minded goal of settlement.

However, other experts believe that the kinds of mediator practices in question—directing discussions to interests and problem solving, limiting party communication and emotional expression, evaluating party claims (or needs), making recommendations, pressuring parties to accept them—are actually successful in securing settlements, ending conflicts, and thereby avoiding the need for formal procedures that involve private and public aggravation and expense. If this is true—and most believe it is, despite the questions raised by some—then why should these practices *not* be embraced?

Settlement-Oriented Practices

In fact, it is clear that many *do* embrace settlement-oriented practices, including not only institutional clients like courts but also practicing mediators and mediation scholars. Consider some examples, drawn from a wide spectrum of mediation practice:

• According to one major mediation text, "For a mediator to assist parties in reaching an agreeable solution, he or she must . . . minimize or neutralize the effects of negative emotions," and the two primary strategies for doing so involve "venting emotions" and "suppressing emotions" (Moore, 2003, pp. 168, 173–174, 181). Another well-known text suggests that the mediator ask questions that imply to the parties that expression of their feelings is "irrelevant and counterproductive" and that the mediator is "interested in ideas for solutions to [their] problems" (Saposnek, 1983, p. 177).

- There is a strong trend in practice, according to one study, toward "abandoning or greatly minimizing the joint session, preferring instead to move quickly to caucus and keep the parties separate for the remainder of the mediation." The author gives two reasons for the trend: "Mediators indicate that they fear that emotional . . . or inflammatory remarks will be made during joint session and that these remarks will make constructive conversation and settlement much more difficult to achieve." In addition, they "prefer the control that the use of caucus provides over the transmission and framing of information," which also makes settlement easier to achieve (Welsh, 2001b, pp. 810–811).

- A recent study of performance tests used to measure mediator competency or award certification found that almost all existing tests favor mediator behaviors such as "controlling . . . the process and making process decisions consistent with progress toward resolution"; "encouraging interest-based problem solving"; "emphasizing common ground and deemphasizing disagreement"; and "discouraging and limiting expression of negative [or] intense emotions." All of these behaviors are favored because they are seen as effective in securing sound settlements, which the tests regard as the goal of the process (Bush, 2004, pp. 979–980).

- An article reported that in a case that was already in court, the parties decided on their own to try mediation—and an agreement was reached. However, there was strong evidence that the mediator had pressured one party into it, and that party wanted to retract the agreement. The judge refused to allow this. Even though he acknowledged that mediator "bullying" was improper, his greater concern was to limit what he saw as the party's "frontal attack on the mediation process itself." That concern was paramount, because the "mediation process has been responsible for the resolution of countless cases in this district, thereby avoiding the necessity for expensive adversary proceedings, including . . . trials" (Welsh, 2001a, p. 14).

- A mediator specializing in commercial disputes, speaking at a statewide mediation conference, noted that when parties reach impasse it often frustrates their lawyers. In fact, lawyers are often eager to have the mediator do whatever is needed to break such impasses, and they actually *expect* the mediator to do so. In light of this, the mediator said, he sometimes teams up with a recalcitrant party's lawyer, staging a conversation about the negative consequences of not settling—a conversation the party is allowed to "overhear." The point is to "loosen" the party's "unreasonable" position, in effect pushing him into changing his demands in an effort to secure a settlement.

- In conducting research on court-connected mediation for a statewide mediation office, the researchers were told about a mediator who was very highly regarded by the judges. That mediator "never allowed the parties in the same room . . . , and told the parties that she knew the judge personally and what he would do if the case went in front of him." The judges nevertheless referred many cases to her because of her high settlement rates. In fact, in the same study, one judge said that he had kept what he called "batting averages" for the available list of mediators over several years—that is, settlement rates—and he would not use a mediator with a batting average under 90 percent. There is no point, he said, in referring cases to mediators who "just sit there and be neutral" (Folger, 2002, pp. 3–4).

- One scholar stated that "a little bit of evaluation or some steering of one or both parties toward a reasonable position is required, both to prevent injustice and to facilitate settlement." Indeed he asserted that "the most highly sought mediators are those who . . . use some measure of evaluation . . . to [facilitate] settlement" (Stempel, 1997, pp. 969, 973).

These examples of settlement-oriented practices and attitudes about them could be supplemented by many others (Kolb and Kressel, 1994; Grillo, 1991; Alfini, 1991; Burns, 1998). Taken together, such examples reflect the reality that, for many, the achievement of a settlement that avoids further proceedings and ends the conflict on reasonable terms is a benefit that trumps all others. Achieving settlement is not a "necessary evil," but a positive good, of greater value than self-determination, engagement, or other benefits that might have to be limited to accomplish it.

Yet for many others in the field, the kinds of practices just cited are deeply disturbing, and the view that such practices are justified by the settlements they generate is indefensible. In fact, it is precisely this "skewed" prioritization of benefits—placing settlement above all other values—that is pushing some people *away* from mediation as institutionalized in the courts and similar venues. It is important to examine more closely what it is that so disturbs people here—because this is one of the major forces behind the shift toward interest in the transformative approach. What *is* the value implicit in the preference for settlement over self-determination, engagement, and other benefits of mediation? What vision of the world does that value rest on? In our view, it is that underlying value and vision that people disturbed by settlement-based practices are really moving *away from*.

Underlying Ideology

Despite the common expression heard in the mediation field that "conflict is not a bad thing in itself," many people implicitly view conflict interaction as an *essentially negative phenomenon*. That is, although conflicts may ultimately have *productive outcomes* that involve mutual gains—just like mutually beneficial transactions in the marketplace—this productive outcome is always threatened, as are other interests such as public order and efficiency, by the *process of conflict* itself: the *interaction* of the parties. This is true because party interaction is inevitably volatile and unpredictable: unless carefully controlled, it may become chaotic and explosive, or it may lead toward outcomes that are not in the best interests of all parties. Therefore, as evident in the settlement-oriented practices just illustrated, it is considered inherently desirable to manage and control conflict—both in a way that forestalls continuation, spread, or escalation of the conflict and also in a way that ensures a fair and reasonable outcome.

But consider what is implicit in this conflict-interaction-is-negative premise. First, the premise assumes that unless conflict is adequately controlled, it will probably have harmful effects—escalating hostility and potential violence, impasse and continuation of the problem, or resolution on unfair or unwise terms. This assumption rests on another one: that human beings lack the capacity both to effectively govern their own affairs and to adequately consider others. This *deficit view* of human capacity is the basis of and is supported by studies on *barriers to conflict resolution*, inherent flaws in human cognition that undermine the abilities both to make sound decisions and to perceive others empathetically (Mnookin and Ross, 1995; Neale and Bazerman, 1991). In this view, without firm direction and control from some outsider, conflict interaction probably will end in escalation, impasse, or bad agreements, rather than in a productive outcome (Kolb and Kressel, 1994).

Second, the view that conflict interaction is negative implies that life would be better if there were no conflict at all! Of course this is impossible: social interaction inevitably leads to conflict, and social interaction is necessary because no one is self-sufficient. Still, if social interaction were unnecessary, if each individual could meet all his desires and needs without having to relate to others, then there would be no conflict to begin with, and no potentially harmful conflict interaction. Indeed this is where the negative-conflict-interaction premise points: social interaction *itself* is at some level a negative, because it inevitably leads to dangerous conflict interaction. Social interaction is nevertheless a "necessary evil"—we must interact with each other to fulfill our desires. Therefore we must have means of containing the destructive force of the conflict interaction that inevitably ensues. And this is the most important purpose of all dispute resolution processes, including mediation. In short, implicit in the negative view of conflict interaction is a negative view of social interaction itself. And implicit in both is a negative view of the capacities of the human beings who are the participants in all of this.

A more formal statement of this ideology can be offered, based on what is often called the *individualist worldview:* the human world is composed of radically separate individuals, each driven by his unique desires, each interested in others only as instruments for the fulfillment of his desires (Sandel, 1982; Murphy, 1981; Rawls, 1971). In this individualist world, if a person could fulfill his desires without having to interact with others at all, this would be entirely satisfactory, even ideal. That is, interaction with others is important only if it is needed for the fulfillment of one's desires. Of course, this usually means that social interaction is necessary, even though it is not ideal. Unfortunately, however, interaction often leads to conflict, which then becomes an obstacle to fulfillment for all involved—because in the ensuing conflict interaction the participants, lacking full capacity for either agency or empathy, will probably reach stalemate, make a bad agreement, or escalate the conflict destructively. The imperative then is to control the conflict interaction so that damage is minimized, and life and the pursuit of fulfillment can move forward. Therefore the control and management of conflict, by whatever means necessary, is seen as valuable and desirable.

In the context of the conflict resolution field, this view can be called the *ideology of social separation and conflict control*. It is connected, in the broader world of political and social thought, to what is often called the *ideology of individualism*. The social world is really only an aggregation of separate individuals, useful at times for each other but essentially separate from each other—and often dangerous to themselves and each other, because they are not fully capable of either agency or empathy. Social institutions are therefore needed to facilitate joint pursuits, but they are even more important to protect against oppression and self-inflicted harm (Della Noce, 1999; Bush, 1986; Sandel, 1982). Individualist ideology therefore views conflict as something to be controlled judiciously—so it does not spread or persist, so it does not lead to oppression, and so it does not squander satisfaction through impasses and poor deals. At the same time, individualist ideology views social interaction itself as something to be tolerated but watched carefully, something likely to produce problems—something ultimately to be feared as a negative force. And paradoxically, it views human beings themselves as lacking in the very capacities needed to engage in both social interaction and conflict without harming themselves and each other.

The Connection Between Practices and Ideology

Consider an excerpt from one well-known study of mediators, which describes the settlement-based approach to mediation practice in the following terms:

> [For some mediators] getting agreements that work is the overriding goal. . . . Settlement-oriented mediators want to find a substantive outcome that will result in a "deal." . . . First, the mediator interrogates the parties for some period of time until he or she develops a sense of how to deal with the issues presented or solve the particular problem. . . . As the mediators readily acknowledge, they are often ahead of the parties on these issues. They know what should happen, but the challenge is to make it occur. Thus, discussions often bog down as the parties get stuck and repeat their claims or are not yet ready to

move to any new way of seeing their issues. . . . [Settle-
ment-oriented mediators] tend to be directive in their
style. They orient their activities toward concrete problem solving and frequently make suggestions on matters
of substance. Most are comfortable with the idea that they
are expert in the particular substantive domain in which
the dispute occurs, and they use this expertise as the
touchstone of their efforts at persuasion and influence.
These settlement-oriented mediators are quite willing to
acknowledge that they make judgments about what is a
good and bad agreement and try to influence the parties
in the direction of the good. . . . They thrust themselves
forcefully into the conflict and are strongly inclined to
believe that without their substantive and procedural
know-how, the parties would flounder and settlement
would be elusive [Kolb and Kressel, 1994, pp. 470–474].

Key elements of the ideology described in this section are evident in this scholarly description of settlement-based practice—
including the clear assumption of party self-centeredness and
incapacity, as well as the strong concern, even fear, for the various
harms that may follow if control is not exercised to produce a good
agreement. Other descriptions of settlement-based mediation reflect
the same implicit ideological base (Stulberg, 1981; Moore, 2003;
Haynes and Haynes, 1989). We therefore suggest that the beliefs
about conflict, social interaction, and human nature described in
this section constitute the premises that—if accepted—support and
almost necessitate the adoption of the directive, controlling practices that prevail in the field today, which have been documented
in many studies of mediators' behavior (Welsh, 2001a, 2001b;
Burns, 1998; Shailor, 1994; Donohue, 1991; Greatbatch and Dingwall, 1989; Folger and Bernard, 1985). We note also that the preceding excerpt is drawn from a study of mediators working in many
contexts, not only court-connected mediation programs. Examples

of settlement practices like those cited earlier support the view that the emphasis on settlement stems largely from the demands of institutional consumers of mediation, like the courts. But the practices that have been emphasized to meet the demands of institutional users have almost certainly spread and affected mediation practice as a whole.

Whatever the context in which these practices are employed, we believe that it makes sense to see a connection between settlement-oriented mediation practices and the larger ideology of social separation and conflict control, as exemplified in the preceding excerpt. It is this underlying ideology, we believe, that ultimately explains why many are becoming so disturbed by the practices of mainstream, settlement-oriented mediation. Their aversion is not simply to these practices themselves, or even to the way in which they dilute self-determination and limit communication or engagement. Rather, their impulse to move away is rooted in a much deeper aversion to an underlying ideological message that is so fundamentally *pessimistic* on all levels: conflict must be controlled because social interaction itself is a negative force, and this is so because human beings are incapable of engaging in either social interaction or conflict without destructive consequences. This view of the human social world, and of human beings, is simply too unattractive for many to accept—and too inconsistent with people's deep sense of what the human world really represents, at least in potential.

It is noteworthy that many of those now questioning settlement-oriented practices frame their concerns in terms of the field's having moved away from its original premises and vision (Welsh, 2001a; Mayer, 2004). The implication is that there are not only different practices possible but also a different underlying vision on which to rest them. That alternative vision is what those who are moving away from the ideology described in the preceding discussion are reaching for. And that vision is what underlies the transformative model of mediation.

Movement Toward: The Ideology of Social Connection and Conflict Transformation

While some have shifted toward transformative practices as part of a movement *away* from a negative view of the social world, others have been making the same shift—in a more pronounced and intentional fashion—as part of a movement *toward* what they see as a richer and more positive view of that world. Just as aversion to settlement-oriented practices is rooted in a deeper discomfort with the ideological foundation that supports (and even demands) them, attraction to transformative practices is rooted in a deeper resonance with an ideological foundation of a very different character.

Transformative Practices

In Chapter Three, we reported some of the powerful comments given to us by mediators and program directors, describing their views of the benefits of implementing the transformative model, such as these:

- "Our practice of being present in the moment or 'following' the parties translates into a respectful way of being with people. Based on my observations, exit interviews, and debriefing processes with mediators, our clients notice that our way of mediating responds to conflict in a different and a positive way: they feel respected and they appreciate our patience with them. . . . [Transformative practices] imply 'no judgment' of others' ways and are respectful of others' humanity, capabilities, processes and decisions" (Wahlrab, 2004).

- "[We] see the benefits [of transformative practice] for clients. Experienced mediators often report that it is great to see people figure out the problems for themselves, having an 'aha' moment, and offering 'sincere apologies' without the resistance we felt before" (Paranica, 2004).

- "We discovered, too, how important the focus on party interaction was in terms of allowing conversations related to race and class unfold. . . . While this naturally means the conversation is unpredictable and may be uncomfortable, it also means that, usually for the first time, parties are supported in their efforts to talk about deeply held feelings, assumptions, and beliefs that may have played a part in the difficulties they have had relating to one another. Furthermore, because of our adherence to transformative principles, our mediators do not use the mediation process as a way of advancing their own notions of justice and equality" (Gonsalves and Hudson, 2003).

• "After embracing the transformative orientation [even in cases involving domestic violence], we found ourselves asking fewer questions during intake, being more open-ended and present with parties, moving from 'active' to 'deep' listening. We also trusted the parties more, believing in their capacity to both raise important issues and/or determine for themselves if mediation was appropriate for their situation. We no longer screened out cases, regardless of circumstances, as we no longer felt expert; we were trusting the parties to be the experts on their own lives. . . . and to make informed decisions about their participation in mediation" (Miller and Wellock, 2004).

It is certainly possible to explain the attraction that the transformative model has for people like these by saying that they see and value its benefits to the parties they serve: helping them to regain their sense of strength of self and understanding for the other party and ultimately to change their interaction to a constructive rather than a destructive one. However, the question here is similar to that raised earlier regarding those expressing aversion to settlement-based practices: Why do these benefits seem so important to some people, whereas others dismiss them as having only peripheral value—if indeed any value at all? What is the underlying vision and set of beliefs that give these benefits their significance and thus make the practices that generate them worth learning and following? Answering these questions will help explain the second force behind the shifts in the field toward transformative practices: a movement toward a larger, positive vision of social interaction that underlies those practices.

Underlying Ideology

An increasing number of people in the field are coming to realize that conflict interaction itself is an essentially *positive* phenomenon, on many different levels. First of all, the process of conflict itself, the interaction of the parties, may be unpredictable but it is *not* inherently explosive, exploitative, or inefficient. On the contrary, if patiently supported rather than tightly controlled, conflict interaction will likely lead not to escalation or impasse, but to greater calm and better communication; it will lead not to injustice or oppression, but to party decisions that consider and respond to each other's needs based on genuine choice and understanding—as in the Purple House case. That is, it will produce outcomes that are just and reasonable *in the parties' own eyes* and therefore will bring real satisfaction and closure, and stand up over time. Moreover, and even more important, it is in the unfolding conflict interaction itself that—given proper support—parties will be able to reclaim the sense of strength and connection that the occurrence of conflict undermined and that they deeply value. Finally, when the interaction between them is humanized, the outcome—whatever it may be—will have a different meaning and quality than it would otherwise have, because they will see the situation and each other in the light of their common humanity, regardless of their differences.

Consider the premises implicit in this view that conflict interaction is positive. First, the belief that conflict interaction, properly supported, will probably have beneficial effects on many levels rests on a premise already presented in Chapter Two: human beings have inherent capacities for both agency and empathy—the capacity to make sound decisions about their own affairs and the capacity to consider and understand the situations and perspectives of others. In other words, there is an *inherent supply* of the capacity for strength and connection in human beings, rather than an inherent deficit, so that outside control is not needed in order for conflict interaction to move in a productive rather than a destructive direction. On the contrary, although outside *support* may be helpful, control is usually counter-productive, because it reduces the parties' opportunity and ability to activate these inherent capacities.

Second, the view that conflict interaction is positive carries the implication that social interaction in general, far from being a necessary evil, is a fundamental good. This premise is connected with the view mentioned earlier in this volume, that human beings are inherently social beings. That is, while having separate self-consciousness and agency as individuals, we also have an inherent consciousness of our connection to each other, as part of humanity as a whole and as part of smaller human communities, all the way down to the two-person "community" involved in every interpersonal interaction. As a result of this dual, personal and social consciousness, we as human beings are by nature averse to both social submergence and social isolation. Rather, we need and seek measures of individual autonomy *and* social connection, freedom *and* responsibility, and a healthy balance and integration of the two. As noted in Chapter Two, there is considerable evidence to support this view of human nature—but even beyond the evidence, it is a view that resonates powerfully with many people as an accurate reflection of their sense of themselves and their fellow human beings.

Given this view of human nature, it is clear that social interaction is not just a means to an end, a way of satisfying desires for things we cannot attain on our own—a tool that we would cheerfully discard if there were a simpler, safer way of satisfying those desires. Rather, social interaction is a process of discovering and becoming fully "who we really are," forging an identity that is not fixed or predetermined at life's beginning. It is through this interaction, in effect, that we "constitute" ourselves, give meaning to our lives, and thereby create the basis for deciding what goals we actually want to attain, separately and together—a constitutive process that continues throughout life. In other words, we are works in progress, and as social constructionist thinkers have long argued, social interaction is the process by which the progress is made (Berger and Luckmann, 1966; Gergen, 1999). It is also the process by which we transcend the unwanted isolation of the seemingly separate self and realize our participation in a common humanity larger than ourselves. In all of these ways, social interaction—far from being threatening—is profoundly nourishing of our human identity.

This view of human nature and social interaction has taken hold in many fields today. It is often called the *relational worldview* (McNamee and Gergen, 1999), although other labels are used as well. For example, in the field of developmental psychology, Carol Gilligan's influential work on women's moral development (1982, 1988) identifies the tension between a "morality of rights [that emphasizes] separation" and a "morality of responsibility [that emphasizes] connection" (1982, p. 19); and she suggests that the two modes of moral thinking can be integrated, that "responsiveness to self and responsiveness to others are connected rather than opposed" (p. 61). In political philosophy, Michael Sandel's critique of individualism (1982) stresses the need to integrate our consciousness of separate individuality and social connection and argues that this can occur only through social interaction in communities that are not "instrumental" but "constitutive"—interaction that allows and asks the individual to "participate in the constitution of its identity" (p. 144). Sandel's work has inspired a school of *communitarian* political and social thought that has attracted numerous scholars in the fields of law, sociology, and political science, among others (Etzioni, 1998). In feminist theory, thinkers have drawn from both of these influences, arguing that there is a "dialectical need for connectedness within freedom and for diversity within solidarity" and that the human self is only created by processes of interacting with others (Ferguson, 1984, p. 196). Legal sociologist Joel Handler (1988) calls this "communitarian feminism" and observes that "the feminist conception of social interaction enhances autonomy, empowerment, and community simultaneously [and] can foster both individuality and connectedness" (p. 1041).

Indeed Handler describes a common view of human nature and society that has emerged from work in fields as diverse as law, political science, feminist theory, sociology, ethics, and communication. The central themes of this view, which he calls *dialogism*, are the need and the possibility for integrating the human experience of separateness and connection, and the centrality of social interaction in doing so—interaction that involves "dialogue, conversation, questioning" (p. 1070), and "the intimacy of human relations in personal, face-to-face encounters" (p. 1059). Key to the dialogic view, Handler points out, is the premise that human beings "want to [and are] able to enter into a conversation" (p. 1093)—that is, they have both the desire and the capacity for agency and empathy. Besides the thinkers already mentioned, Handler cites, as sharing this dialogic view, Bernstein (1983), Habermas (1984), and others. Important recent work in the field of professional ethics presents a similar view to Handler's dialogism, building on more traditional sources in classical philosophy (Koehn, 1998). Finally, Della Noce (1999, 2002) identifies other important strains of work in the fields of communication and social theory that also incorporate many elements of the relational worldview. In sum, a consistent set of ideas about human identity and social interaction, which we have called the relational worldview, has emerged in recent decades and has found support in a very wide range of fields and disciplines.

The relational conceptions of human nature and social interaction lead to a strikingly positive view of conflict interaction. The essence of this view is that conflict interaction—precisely because it occurs at moments of great challenge to the human sense of agency and connection—offers an unusually potent opportunity to strengthen and deepen both. Conflict interaction can actually *enhance* social interaction, as well as the human experience of both autonomy and connection in balanced relation. This view is expressed eloquently by yet another thinker interested in the relational or dialogic worldview, who has linked transformative mediation to important streams of work on lawyers' ethics and moral philosophy. Legal ethicist Robert Burns (2001) suggests that conflict interaction can be—depending on how it unfolds—a form of what he calls *moral conversation* or *moral discourse*, meaning a form of interaction that is both noninstrumental and nonmanipulative, in which each party treats the other not as a means to an end, but as an ultimate end. He explains, citing philosopher Hanna Pitkin:

> The center of gravity of authentically moral discourse is the conversation between an agent and one who is actually or potentially adversely affected by his actions. . . . Moral conversation provides a way of "healing tears in the fabric of relationship and maintaining the self in opposition to itself or others. . . . [I]t provides a door through which someone, alienated or in danger of alienation from another through his action, can return. . . . The point of moral argument is not agreement on a conclusion but successful [not strategic] clarification of two people's positions. Its function is to make the position of the various protagonists clear—to themselves and to the others. Moral discourse is about what was done, how it is to be understood and assessed, what position each is taking toward it and thereby toward the other, and hence what each is like and what their future relations will be like. The hope, of course, is for reconciliation, but the test of validity in moral discourse will not be reconciliation but truthful revelation of self. . . . Moral discourse is useful, is necessary, because the truths it can reveal are by no means obvious. Our responsibilities, the extensions of our cares and commitments, and the implications of our conduct, are not obvious. . . . The self is

not obvious to the self" [Burns, 2001, pp. 709–710, citing Pitkin, 1972, pp. 151–154].

The connection that Burns makes between conflict interaction and moral conversation is echoed by some of the relational thinkers cited previously. For example, Gilligan (1982) mentions that "awareness of the connection between people gives rise to . . . belief in communication as the mode of conflict resolution" (p. 30). But Burns goes further and shows very clearly how the relational vision finds a positive potential within conflict interaction: the process of conflict interaction is, in the relational worldview, a "door through which someone . . . can return" (p. 709), through which the parties can return to themselves and each other, deepening the quality of their interaction and their awareness of both themselves and each other. Indeed, precisely because of the sense of unclarity and disconnection that it creates, conflict presents the opportunity for a much more potent form of social interaction than is found in normal human affairs, a moral conversation. It allows the parties a uniquely powerful occasion—in the terms of relational ideology—for a "dialogue" that can "constitute" their separate identities and their shared meanings, for "the intimacy of human relations in personal, face-to-face encounter" (Handler, 1988, p. 1059). And, as implied in both Burns's account and the preceding discussion, it is part and parcel of the relational view that human beings have not only the *desire* for both autonomy and connection but also the *capacity* for both. That is, although circumstances may provoke human responses of weakness and dependency, or responses of selfishness and isolation, all human beings retain an inherent desire and capacity to transcend the circumstantial responses and to act with both self-determined agency and other-regarding empathy (Della Noce, 1999).

In the context of the conflict resolution field, the overall view just described can be called the *ideology of social connection and conflict transformation*. That is, viewed within relational ideology, not only is conflict interaction *not* a destructive force to be feared and controlled, but it is a *positive force* to be embraced and harnessed for its potential to "open the door"—through conflict transformation— to all of the kinds of benefits just described: genuinely meaningful outcomes and hence real closure and—equally or more important— restoration of the parties' sense of both strength and connection. If this positive potential of conflict interaction is realized, the result is to enhance social interaction in general, just as a broken limb is stronger after the break has healed. Furthermore, social interaction itself is not a process to be tolerated and feared, but a process to be welcomed and fostered as a profoundly positive force in human life, because it is the core process for constituting human identity and shared meaning. Finally, human beings themselves have the inherent desire and capacity to engage in social interaction—and conflict interaction—constructively, not only without destroying each other but with the ability to turn conflict itself into an opportunity to deepen and enhance interaction, personal strength, and interpersonal understanding.

The Connection Between Practices and Ideology

It is significant that Burns connects his positive account of conflict interaction with transformative mediation specifically, in which he sees the concrete possibility of conflict transformation through moral conversation, a possibility he also sees in a form of *client-centered legal counseling* advocated by Thomas Shaffer (1994) and others. Burns, in effect, sees transformative mediation as embodying the relational ideology of social connection and conflict transformation. In this connection, consider the following excerpt from a recent study that identified the common patterns found in the practice of competent transformative mediators. Consider especially the implicit premises that underlie the kinds of practices described:

> "Constructive conversation" is an important *root metaphor* for mediators working in the transformative

framework. . . . When mediators feel pulled toward narrowing, directive or solution-focused behaviors that would place their agenda above the agenda of parties, the conversation metaphor reminds them of the purpose of mediation and that the focus should be on the parties' interaction and their choices about whether and how to have the conversation [Della Noce, Antes, and Saul, 2004, pp. 1023–1024].

In the transformative framework, mediators orient the parties to their own agency—that is, their own potential ability to exert power or achieve certain goals in the mediation session. It means using language that signals the parties' ability to act and to decide, if they so choose, as well as language that signals the parties' central role in the mediation. This is in contrast to language that signals that the mediator has the central role in the process. In general, a mediator is . . . "getting out of their way" as opposed to "getting in their way" [Della Noce, Antes, and Saul, 2004, p. 1026].

Supporting the parties' "conflict talk" is an essential strategy for a transformative mediator. . . . The mediator must be comfortable in the presence of conflict talk, and orient toward supporting rather than containing it. . . . The mediator follows the unfolding conversation, listening for places of difference, contention, or heat, where choices can be highlighted or possibilities for building greater interpersonal understanding emerge [Della Noce, Antes, and Saul, 2004, pp. 1030–1031].

For the transformative mediator, the emphasis on party empowerment requires that the mediator highlight *all possible decision points* and offer them to the parties.

Moreover, the mediator makes no distinction between so-called "process" and "content" decisions. Mediation is viewed as an ongoing process of decisionmaking by the parties [Della Noce, Antes, and Saul, 2004, p. 1033].

It should be clear that key elements of the ideology of social connection and conflict transformation are evident in this description of common transformative practices—including the clear assumption of party capacity, as well as the confidence that when conflict interaction is properly supported, it will not escalate destructively but rather shift in a constructive direction. The accounts of transformative mediation theory and practice presented in Chapters Two, Four, and Five reflect the same ideological base, as do descriptions elsewhere (Beal and Saul, 2001; Della Noce, 1999; Folger and Bush, 1996; Pope, 1996; Bush, 1989–1990).

Our essential point is this: it is the beliefs described here—about social interaction, human nature, and conflict interaction—that support, justify, and even demand the practices of the transformative model. In other words, just as we argued that there is a connection between individualist ideology and settlement-based practices, we maintain that there is a connection between relational ideology and transformative practices. Moreover we believe that it is the underlying ideology that ultimately explains why many are becoming drawn toward transformative practice, in varying degrees. The attraction is not simply to the specific practices themselves nor even to the way in which they generate specific benefits—enhanced clarity, strength, understanding, connection, genuine closure. The impulse to move toward transformative practice is rooted in a much deeper resonance with the underlying ideological message, a message that is strikingly optimistic and positive on many levels: conflict interaction can be tapped for its positive potential to enhance social interaction, which is itself an essential positive force in constituting human identity and shared meaning. And this potential for conflict transformation is real and attainable because human beings themselves have inherent, deep reserves of capacity and motivation for self-reliant agency and other-directed empathy.

This rich view of the social world, and human beings, resonates powerfully with many in and beyond the mediation field, and this is the second force behind the movement toward the transformative model. When conflict interaction is seen from within this worldview, then there is a tremendous attraction toward practices of intervention, in mediation and otherwise, that will bring out the positive potential that lies within it. We therefore believe that the shifts in the field toward transformative practice are explained by and reflect two profound ideological impulses—a movement away from the ideology of social separation and conflict control, and a movement toward the ideology of social connection and conflict transformation.

The Paths Forward: Living with Difference in the Mediation Field

Given this view of the larger forces behind the shifts in the field toward transformative practice, what then are the prospects for the future of the mediation field as an overall enterprise? This book, and especially this chapter, has shown that there are real and deep differences in the mediation field today, as to both practice approaches and underlying ideologies. It is increasingly recognized that mediation practice differs not just by individual stylistic variations but by models of practice—including the transformative model—that are quite distinct from one another. More and more, practitioners are declaring their primary allegiance to one of these models rather than the others. So at the level of practice, the mediation field is pluralistic rather than homogeneous, and this is well acknowledged.

In addition, underlying the differences in practice models are differences in fundamental beliefs about human nature, social interaction, and conflict—differences in ideology. Although these differences are not always acknowledged, they are surfacing more and more. For example, in presenting the views of those who support different approaches to practice, the literature often points to the tension between values like self-determination and communication on the one hand and values like efficiency and fairness on the other (Welsh, 2001a; Mayer, 2004). As discussed earlier in the chapter, this tension is really an expression of the two different ideologies underlying the differences in practice models. Indeed one purpose of this chapter has been to clarify these values-based roots of practice differences.

Clarification of difference, at both the practice and values levels, is a useful step in moving the field forward in a way that treats diversity as an advantage rather than an obstacle. Clarification can lead to more deliberate choices about the approach to practice that we want to take, as well as to greater understanding of the different approach chosen by someone else. Clarification can build bridges rather than burn them; and this has been our intent in exploring differences in practices and ideology, both in this book and in our other work (Folger and Bush, 1994; Della Noce, Bush, and Folger, 2002). That exploration leads to the conclusion that the differences found in the field today represent a diversity that will persist for a long time to come—because that diversity provides an important resource for realizing the full private and public benefits of mediation, in a society that is itself diverse at many levels.

Living with Diversity for a Long Time to Come

There are many parties in conflict for whom conflict transformation is of primary importance and whose needs will best be met by a transformative process—as exemplified in the Purple House case. Moreover the public values of civility, responsibility, and community—values best served by transformative interventions—are of ever increasing importance in our society. At the same time, there are many other parties who say that what they want most is to achieve an end to their dispute as cheaply and quickly as possible.

And courts and other private and public institutions cannot help but place great value on the resources saved by disposing of cases in a way that avoids formal proceedings. In sum, there is a real diversity of user demand—private and public—in the field, and that is likely to continue for a long time.

The likely persistence of diversity in user demand is linked to another, deeper diversity. Some believe, as we do, that our society is slowly but steadily moving toward a relational social order in which the need for conflict control will diminish—although it is clear that this movement will be slow and gradual and that the individualist worldview will meanwhile hold sway, especially in large institutions and systems. Some, by contrast, hold strongly to the individualist worldview and doubt that the possibility of conflict transformation will ever become widespread. But it is hard to deny that the relational worldview is being enacted in certain social contexts, and the possibility of a relational social order cannot be completely dismissed. In other words, there is no single ideology firmly in place; rather, there is a diversity of beliefs about society and conflict, both in the larger society and in the mediation field, which will probably persist well into the new century.

Given this diversity of both user demand and societal beliefs, it is clear that the diversity of practices in the field represents a critical resource. In this context of diverse demand and beliefs, it would be unrealistic to dismiss the value of conflict processes that serve private parties and societal decision makers who feel the necessity of controlling conflict and its harmful consequences. It would be equally unwise to dismiss the value of processes that serve private parties seeking conflict transformation and promote the public values that flow from it. In short, the different paths of practice discussed in this chapter are both serving important functions, for private parties in conflict, and for societal goals. Indeed this is clearly why different and distinct approaches to practice have been able to establish themselves and attract practitioners and users. The social demand is real for each of the different approaches.

To put the matter more concretely, settlement-based practice and transformative practice are both likely to continue as distinct models for the foreseeable future. Given the well-established institutional uses of mediation by major public and private users, settlement-based practice is not going to stop attracting practitioners and clients any time soon. However, as we have demonstrated, the "market" for transformative mediation is established and growing, and therefore practitioners of this model are likely to grow in number and as a share of the field. The challenge for the field is to develop ways of living with the diversity in practices and beliefs that the private and public users of mediation are demanding and that practitioners have been responding to. Meeting this challenge, as members of a service-oriented field, means pursuing excellence by both remaining true to core values and making room for others to develop according to their own understanding of practice.

Choosing with Clarity and Being Transparent

One approach to living with the diversity of demand, an approach that seems attractive to many, is actually to retreat back into the premise of homogeneity, slightly altered. That is, some argue that effective mediation practice is really a combination of all of the different models, with the practices of each being deployed as needed in response to the desires of the parties and the needs of the situation (Test Design Project, 1995; Williams, 1997; Hoffman, 1999). According to this view, we should continue to view mediation as a single, homogeneous process, in which the elements and skills of all of the models are combined.

We discussed in Chapter Six why we do not believe that the different models of practice can be integrated or combined, especially when it is understood that the primary models are really two in number—settlement-oriented and transformative. The practices and premises of these two models of practice are so different that it is difficult to imagine how any practitioner could combine them in a coherent and principled way. This point will certainly be argued strenuously by many—indeed it already has been—but we cannot debate the matter further in this book. We hope our clarification of the issues involved will facilitate discussion of the subject in the future.

Rather than combination of practices, our view is that living with the diversity of demand means that mediators should take advantage of the increased awareness and information about different models and make clear choices about the kind of service they want to provide to clients, and hence the model of practice they want to employ. Of course, many mediators may find it useful and even necessary to try out different practices in order to find which approach ultimately makes sense to them. And, as discussed in Chapter Six, mediators who are making a transition from one model to another will probably go through a period of combining practices. In the long run, however, mediators will serve their clients best by choosing a path of practice consistent with their own preferences and beliefs, and once they've chosen it, following that path conscientiously.

One key aspect of serving clients in this way is transparency about the model of practice being used. Clients are entitled to be informed, in language they can understand, about the kinds of practices employed by the professional who is serving them. When they are given this information, they are better able to decide whether the approach taken by a particular mediator will work to meet the needs they hold paramount—whether for settlement, conflict transformation, or otherwise. Without this information, clients are likely to be disserved, and damage can be done to the reputation of not only the individual mediator but also the field as a whole (Press, 1998). Equally important, the clarity required of the mediator to make his or her practice transparent is likely to improve the quality of practice in and of itself.

Supporting the Diversity of Practice

In terms of steps that can be taken by policymakers and groups, rather than individual practitioners, to meet the diversity in demand discussed in this chapter, the key principle to be followed should be support for diversity and pluralism in practice, rather than sameness and homogeneity. Clarity about difference—especially in the realm of policy—can support better practice in the field as a whole, ultimately providing better service to the public (Della Noce, Bush, and Folger, 2002). Practically, this means that the field should, in all possible ways, allow and support both of the diverse paths practice is taking—but support each *separately*, so as to better foster the development of professional excellence.

At the first level, given the different goals that are the bases of the two main approaches to mediation, it makes sense that policies reflect this difference. Policies regulating practice should no longer be generic or homogeneous, because practice itself is not generic or homogeneous. For example, standards of practice and ethics should be different for settlement-based and transformative practitioners (Bush, 2002). Indeed, the failure to adopt this pluralistic approach has already caused serious problems for practitioners and clients, because the attempt to regulate all mediation by a single set of standards inevitably subjects practitioners to conflicting ethical obligations (Bush, 1992, 2002). The time has come to draft ethical standards separately: one set for practitioners whose role is to generate fair and reasonable settlements and one set for practitioners whose role is to support conflict transformation.

Other examples of policies that need to be "pluralized" by adoption of parallel but different regimes, for similar reasons, include the following: requirements for the content of training programs, and for certification of trainers; performance tests and evaluation forms; and required qualifications for practice, including especially substantive knowledge requirements (Della Noce, Bush, and Folger, 2002; Bush, 2004). When practitioners, trainers, and others in the field are judged by standards appropriate to the model in which they practice, practice diversity and quality are supported, and clients are better served. Moreover when policies are created with diversity of practice in mind, practitioners need not be fearful of exclusion or unfairness. Each can find his or her own place in the field, without being subjected to standards that don't fit the nature of his or her practice.

At a different level, and probably more controversial, it may be beneficial for the field at this juncture to encourage the formation of different and parallel organizations, rather than trying to merge everyone into a homogenizing organization that does not allow difference to surface in full force. By this, we do not mean what has been the practice in the past—different organizations for mediators working in particular substantive domains, such as family, community, or environmental conflict. We mean different organizations—cutting across those domains—for practitioners following each of the different models (Folger, 2002). Practitioners with their own distinct view of practice—and its underlying premises—need to have forums of their own, in which they can explore issues, develop ideas, and nurture good practice. When they have such "space to themselves" to explore issues and develop on their own terms, then exchange with others who hold a very different view of practice will become easier, friendlier, and more productive. In truth, this follows a fundamental transformative principle: *empowerment precedes recognition*. But it also follows a principle of common sense from everyday life: we all need room to gather and formulate our thoughts before we can express and exchange them productively with others. Concern for each other within the field—as well as concern for the field as a whole—suggests, even demands, the creation of separate space in which to build the basis for dialogue and common enterprise. The public we serve can only benefit from such attention to our own ongoing professional development.

Walking Different Paths Toward the Future

This last suggestion, about organizational pluralism, leads to a larger analogy that is helpful in imagining how the development of the mediation field might unfold most constructively from this point. Some decades ago, the therapy profession faced a situation similar to the one we see in our field today. Two separate and distinct approaches to therapy had developed, *psychodynamic talk therapy* and *systems therapy*. The two approaches were based on different premises and used different practices. The first viewed clients' problems as deeply rooted in past experiences and employed probing of the individual's past to unearth, analyze, and disentangle them. The second viewed clients' problems as stemming from present systemic patterns and sought to develop specific behavioral strategies to change dysfunctional patterns. Because the premises and practices were so different, there was no coherent way to combine the approaches. Nevertheless the practitioners of these two distinct approaches to therapy learned to live with their differences. And the differences proved to be stimulating for the field as a whole and beneficial to clients seeking different kinds of help.

Our field too has reached a moment when it includes practitioners working from very different premises and employing very distinct practices. Our main focus in this book has been to elaborate the premises and practices of one of those approaches—transformative mediation. However, we acknowledge the different premises and practices of the other, and we take the view that both of these approaches have value in the world we currently live in; both can be beneficial to clients seeking different kinds of help. Given this state of diversity in approaches to practice, the conclusion we reach is that we can learn from other professions and realize that the mediation field today can walk two different paths toward the future and still retain its sense of common enterprise and public service.

There is room, for the foreseeable future, for all the value that both paths can bring, even though we will almost certainly continue to differ on many points. However, like practitioners in other professions, like Elizabeth and Julie in the Purple House case, like human beings all over the world with deep and important differences, we can develop the strength of our own path and do our best to understand those on the other—and find the common humanity that it is the promise of mediation to reveal.

References

Abel, R. "The Contradictions of Informal Justice." In R. Abel (ed.), *The Politics of Informal Justice*. New York: Academic Press, 1982.

Advanced Practitioner Membership Work Group. "Report and Recommendations for Advanced Practitioner Member (AMP) Status." Association for Conflict Resolution, June 2003. [www.acrnet.org/about/taskforces/APWorkgroup.htm].

Ahrens, E. "When We Listen, People Talk." [www.mediate.com/articles/ahrens8.cfm]. 2002.

Alfini, J. J. "Trashing, Bashing, and Hashing It Out: Is This the End of 'Good Mediation'?" *Florida State University Law Review*, 1991, *19*(1), 47–75.

Alfini, J. J., and McCabe, C. G. "Mediating in the Shadow of the Courts: A Survey of the Emerging Case Law." *Arkansas Law Review*, 2001, *54*(2), 171–206.

Alfini, J. J., and others. *Mediation Theory and Practice*. Newark, N.J.: Matthew Bender/LEXIS, 2001.

Antes, J. R., Folger, J. P., and Della Noce, D. J. "Transforming Conflict Interactions in the Workplace: Documented Effects of the U.S. Postal Service REDRESS Program." *Hofstra Labor & Employment Law Journal*, 2001, *18*(2), 429–467.

Antes, J. R., and others. "Is a Stage Model of Mediation Necessary?" *Mediation Quarterly*, 1999, *16*(3), 287–301.

Barker, E. "Tips for Dealing with Emotion in Mediation." [www.mediate.com/articles/ebarker2.cfm]. 2003.

Beal, S., and Saul, J. A. "Examining Assumptions: Training Mediators for Transformative Practice." In J. P. Folger and R.A.B. Bush (eds.),

Designing Mediation: Approaches to Training and Practice Within a Transformative Framework. New York: Institute for the Study of Conflict Transformation, 2001.

Beck, A. T. *Prisoners of Hate: The Cognitive Basis of Anger, Hostility, and Violence.* New York: Perennial/HarperCollins, 1999.

Bellah, R. N., and others. *The Good Society.* New York: Knopf, 1991.

Berger, P. L., and Luckman, T. *The Social Construction of Reality.* New York: Doubleday, 1966.

Bernard, S., Folger, J. P., Weingarten, H., and Zumeta, Z. "The Neutral Mediator: Value Dilemmas in Divorce Mediation." *Mediation Quarterly,* 1984, *4,* 61–74.

Bernstein, R. *Beyond Objectivism and Relativism: Science, Hermeneutics and Praxis.* Philadelphia: University of Pennsylvania Press, 1983.

Bettencourt, B. A., and Sheldon, K. "Social Roles as Mechanisms for Psychological Need Satisfaction Within Social Groups." *Journal of Personality and Social Psychology,* 2001, *81*(6), 1131–1143.

Bingham, L. B. "Mediating Employment Disputes: Perceptions of Redress at the United States Postal Service." *Review of Public Personnel Administration,* 1997, *20*(Spring), 20–30.

Bingham, L. B. *Mediation at Work: Transforming Workplace Conflict at the United States Postal Service.* Washington, D.C.: IBM Center for the Business of Government, 2003.

Bingham, L. B., and Nabatchi, T. "Transformative Mediation in the U.S. Postal Service REDRESS Program: Observations of ADR Specialists." *Hofstra Labor & Employment Law Journal,* 2001, *18*(2), 399–427.

Boszormenyi-Nagy, I., and Krasner, B. R. *Between Give and Take: A Clinical Guide to Contextual Therapy.* New York: Brunner/Mazel, 1986.

Bouman, A. "Liberating Literacy: Writing on the Margins of American Society." *Educator,* 1991, *5*(2), 48–51.

Bryan, P. E. "Killing Us Softly: Divorce Mediation and the Politics of Power." *Buffalo Law Review,* 1992, *40*(2), 441–523.

Burger, W. "Isn't There a Better Way?" *American Bar Association Journal,* 1982, *68,* 274–277.

Burns, R. P. "Some Ethical Issues Surrounding Mediation." *Fordham Law Review,* 2001, *70,* 691–717.

Burns, S. "The Name of the Game Is Movement: Concession Seeking in Judicial Mediation of Large Money Damages Cases." *Mediation Quarterly,* 1998, *15*(4), 359–367.

Bush, R.A.B. "Dispute Resolution Alternatives and Achieving the Goals of
Civil Justice: Jurisdictional Principles for Process Choice." *Wisconsin Law
Review*, 1984, *4*, 893–1034.

Bush, R.A.B. "Between Two Worlds: The Shift from Individual to Group
Responsibility in the Law of Causation of Injury." *University of California
Los Angeles Law Review*, 1986, *33*(6), 1473–1563.

Bush, R.A.B. "Efficiency and Protection, or Empowerment and Recognition?
The Mediator's Role and Ethical Standards in Mediation." *Florida Law
Review*, 1989, *41*(2), 253–286.

Bush, R.A.B. "Mediation and Adjudication, Dispute Resolution and Ideology:
An Imaginary Conversation." *Journal of Contemporary Legal Issues*,
1989–1990, *3*, 1–35.

Bush, R.A.B. *The Dilemmas of Mediation Practice: A Study of Ethical Dilemmas and
Policy Implications*. Washington, D.C.: National Institute for Dispute
Resolution, 1992.

Bush, R.A.B. "'What Do We Need a Mediator For?': Mediation's 'Value-Added'
for Negotiators." *Ohio State Journal on Dispute Resolution*, 1996, *12*(1),
1–36.

Bush, R.A.B. "Handling Workplace Conflict: Why Transformative
Mediation?" *Hofstra Labor & Employment Law Journal*, 2001, *18*(2),
367–373.

Bush, R.A.B. "Substituting Mediation for Arbitration: The Growing Market for
Evaluative Mediation, and What It Means for the Alternative Dispute
Resolution Field." *Pepperdine Dispute Resolution Law Journal*, 2002, *3*(1),
111–131.

Bush, R.A.B. "One Size Does Not Fit All: A Pluralistic Approach to Mediator
Performance Testing and Quality Assurance." *Ohio State Journal on
Dispute Resolution*, 2004, *19*(3), 965–1004.

Bush, R.A.B., and Pope, S. G. "Changing the Quality of Conflict Interaction:
The Principles and Practice of Transformative Mediation." *Pepperdine
Dispute Resolution Law Journal*, 2002, *3*(1), 67–96.

Bush, R.A.B., and Pope, S. G. "Transformative Mediation: Changing the
Quality of Family Conflict Interaction." In J. Folberg and others (eds.),
Divorce and Family Mediation. New York: Guilford Press, 2004.

Charbonneau, P. "How Practical Is Theory?" In J. P. Folger and R.A.B. Bush
(eds.), *Designing Mediation: Approaches to Training and Practice Within a
Transformative Framework*. New York: Institute for the Study of Conflict
Transformation, 2001.

Chasin, R., and others. "From Diatribe to Dialogue on Divisive Public Issues: Approaches Drawn from Family Therapy." *Mediation Quarterly,* 1996, *13*(4), 323–344.

D'Alo, G. E. "Accountability in Special Education Mediation: Many a Slip 'Twixt Vision and Practice?" *Harvard Negotiation Law Review,* 2003, 8, 201–250.

Davis, A. "The Logic Behind the Magic of Mediation." *Negotiation Journal,* 1989, *5*(1), 17–24.

Delgado, R., and others. "Fairness and Formality: Minimizing the Risk of Prejudice in Alternative Dispute Resolution." *Wisconsin Law Review,* 1985, *6,* 1359–1404.

Della Noce, D. J. "Seeing Theory in Practice: An Analysis of Empathy in Mediation." *Negotiation Journal,* 1999, *15*(3), 271–301.

Della Noce, D. J. "Mediation as a Transformative Process: Insights on Structure and Movement." In J. P. Folger and R.A.B. Bush (eds.), *Designing Mediation: Approaches to Training and Practice Within a Transformative Framework.* New York: Institute for the Study of Conflict Transformation, 2001.

Della Noce, D. J. "Ideologically Based Patterns in the Discourse of Mediators: A Comparison of Problem Solving and Transformative Practice." Ann Arbor, Michigan: UMI Dissertation Services, 2002.

Della Noce, D. J., Antes, J. R., and Saul, J. A. "Identifying Practice Competence in Transformative Mediators: An Interactive Rating Scale Assessment Model." *Ohio State Journal on Dispute Resolution,* 2004, *19*(3), 1005–1058.

Della Noce, D. J., Bush, R.A.B., and Folger, J. P. "Clarifying the Theoretical Underpinnings of Mediation: Implications for Practice and Policy." *Pepperdine Dispute Resolution Law Journal,* 2002, *3*(1), 39–65.

Della Noce, D. J., Folger, J. P., and Antes, J. R. "Assimilative, Autonomous, or Synergistic Visions: How Mediation Programs in Florida Address the Dilemma of Court Connection." *Pepperdine Dispute Resolution Law Journal,* 2002, *3*(1), 11–38.

Domenici, K., and Littlejohn, S. W. *Mediation: Empowerment in Conflict Management.* Prospect Heights, Ill.: Waveland Press, 2001.

Donohue, W. *Communication, Marital Dispute and Divorce Mediation.* Hillsdale, N.J.: Erlbaum, 1991.

Dukes, F. "Public Conflict Resolution: A Transformative Approach." *Negotiation Journal,* 1993, *9*(1), 45–57.

Etzioni, A. *The New Golden Rule.* New York: Basic Books, 1996.

Etzioni, A. (ed.). *The Essential Communitarian Reader.* Lanham, Md.: Rowman & Littlefield, 1998.

Ferguson, K. E. *The Feminist Case Against Bureaucracy*. Philadelphia: Temple University Press, 1984.

Fineman, M. "Dominant Discourse, Professional Language and Legal Change in Child Custody Decisionmaking." *Harvard Law Review,* 1988, *101*(4), 727–774.

Fisher, R., and Brown, S. *Getting Together*. New York: Viking Penguin, 1989.

Fisher, R., and Ury, W. *Getting to Yes: Negotiating Agreement Without Giving In*. Boston: Houghton Mifflin, 1981.

Fiss, O. M. "Against Settlement." *Yale Law Journal,* 1984, *93,* 1073–1090.

Fleischer, J. M. "Directing and Administering a Mediation Program: The Transformative Approach." *Mediation Quarterly,* 1996, *13*(4), 295–304.

Folberg, J., and Taylor, A. *Mediation: A Comprehensive Guide to Resolving Conflicts Without Litigation*. San Francisco: Jossey-Bass, 1984.

Folberg, J., and others (eds.). *Divorce and Family Mediation: Models, Techniques and Applications*. New York: Guilford Press, 2004.

Folger, J. P. "Who Owns What in Mediation? Seeing the Link Between Process and Content." In J. P. Folger and R.A.B. Bush (eds.), *Designing Mediation: Approaches to Training and Practice Within a Transformative Framework*. New York: Institute for the Study of Conflict Transformation, 2001.

Folger, J. P. "Mediation Goes Mainstream: Taking the Conference Theme Challenge." *Pepperdine Dispute Resolution Law Journal,* 2002, *3*(1), 1–9.

Folger, J. P., and Bernard, S. "Divorce Mediation: When Mediators Challenge the Divorcing Parties." *Mediation Quarterly,* 1985, *10,* 5–23.

Folger, J. P., and Bush, R.A.B. "Ideology, Orientations to Conflict and Mediation Discourse." In J. P. Folger and T. S. Jones (eds.), *New Directions in Mediation: Communication Research and Perspectives*. Thousand Oaks, Calif.: Sage, 1994.

Folger, J. P., and Bush, R.A.B. "Transformative Mediation and Third-Party Intervention: Ten Hallmarks of a Transformative Approach to Practice." *Mediation Quarterly,* 1996, *13*(4), 263–278.

Folger, J. P., and Bush, R.A.B. (eds.). *Designing Mediation: Approaches to Training and Practice Within a Transformative Framework*. New York: Institute for the Study of Conflict Transformation, 2001a.

Folger, J. P., and Bush, R.A.B., "Developing Transformative Training: A View from the Inside." In J. P. Folger and R.A.B. Bush (eds.), *Designing Mediation: Approaches to Training and Practice Within a Transformative Framework*. New York: Institute for the Study of Conflict Transformation, 2001b.

Folger, J. P., and Poole, M. S. *Working Through Conflict: A Communication Perspective*. Glenview, Ill.: Scott, Foresman, 1984.

Folger, J. P., and others. *Working Through Conflict: Strategies for Relationships, Groups and Organizations*. (4th ed.) Reading, Mass.: Addison-Wesley, 2001.

Forlenza, S. G. "Mediation and Psychotherapy: Parallel Processes." In K. G. Duffy, J. W. Grosch, and P. Olczak (eds.), *Community Mediation: A Handbook for Practitioners and Researchers*. New York: Guilford Press, 1991.

Galanter, M. "A Settlement Judge, Not a Trial Judge: Judicial Mediation in the United States." *Journal of Law and Society*, 1985, *12*, 1–18.

Gergen, K. J. *An Invitation to Social Construction*. London: Sage, 1999.

Gilligan, C. *In a Different Voice: Psychological Theory and Women's Development*. Cambridge, Mass.: Harvard University Press, 1982.

Gilligan, C. "Adolescent Development Reconsidered." In C. Gilligan, J. V. Ward, and J. McLean Taylor (eds.), *Mapping the Moral Domain*. Cambridge, Mass.: Harvard University Press, 1988.

Glendon, M. A. *Rights Talk: The Impoverishment of Political Discourse*. New York: Free Press, 1991.

Golann, D. *Mediating Legal Disputes: Effective Strategies for Lawyers and Mediators*. New York: Little, Brown, 1996.

Goleman, D. *Emotional Intelligence: Why It Can Matter More Than IQ*. London: Bloomsbury, 1995.

Gonsalves, P., and Hudson, D. T. "Supporting Difficult Conversations: Articulation and Application of the Transformative Framework at Greenwich Mediation." Greenwich, England: Greenwich Mediation Center. [www.greenwichmediation.org.uk]. 2003.

Gray, B. "The Gender-Based Foundations of Negotiation Theory." In R. J. Lewicki and others (eds.), *Research on Negotiation in Organizations*. Vol. 4. Greenwich, Conn.: JAI Press, 1994.

Greatbatch, D., and Dingwall, R. "Selective Facilitation: Some Preliminary Observations on a Strategy Used by Divorce Mediators." *Law and Society Review*, 1989, *23*, 613–641.

Greatbatch, D., and Dingwall, R. "The Interactive Construction of Interventions by Divorce Mediators." In J. P. Folger and T. S. Jones (eds.), *New Directions in Mediation: Communication Research and Perspectives*. Thousand Oaks, Calif.: Sage, 1994.

Grillo, T. "The Mediation Alternative: Process Dangers for Women." *Yale Law Journal*, 1991, *100*, 1545–1610.

Guthrie, C. "The Lawyer's Philosophical Map and the Disputant's Perceptual Map: Impediments to Facilitative Mediation and Lawyering." *Harvard Negotiation Law Review*, 2001, *6*, 145–188.

Habermas, J. *The Theory of Communicative Action*. Vols. 1 and 2. (T. McCarthy, trans.) Boston: Beacon Press, 1984.

Haley, J. *Problem-Solving Therapy*. San Francisco: Jossey-Bass, 1987.

Hallberlin, C. J. "Transforming Workplace Culture Through Mediation: Lessons Learned from Swimming Upstream." *Hofstra Labor & Employment Law Journal*, 2001, *18*(2), 375–383.

Handler, J. F. "Dependent People, the State, and the Modern/Postmodern Search for the Dialogic Community." *University of California Los Angeles Law Review*, 1988, *35*(6), 999–1113.

Harrington, C. B. *Shadow Justice: The Ideology and Institutionalization of Alternatives to Court*. Westport, Conn.: Greenwood Press, 1985.

Harrington, C. B., and Merry, S. E. "Ideological Production: The Making of Community Mediation." *Law and Society Review*, 1988, *22*(4), 709–735.

Haynes, J. M. "Mediation and Therapy: An Alternative View." *Mediation Quarterly*, 1992, *10*(1), 21–33.

Haynes, J. M., and Haynes, G. L. *Mediating Divorce: Casebook of Strategies for Successful Family Negotiations*. San Francisco: Jossey-Bass, 1989.

Hensler, D. R. "In Search of 'Good' Mediation: Rhetoric, Practice, and Empiricism." In J. Sanders and V. L. Hamilton (eds.), *Handbook of Justice Research in Law*. Norwell, Mass.: Kluwer, 2001.

Hensler, D. R. "Suppose It's Not True: Challenging Mediation Ideology." *Journal of Dispute Resolution*, 2002, *1*, 81–99.

Herrman, M. S. "On Balance: Promoting Integrity Under Conflicted Mandates." *Mediation Quarterly*, 1993, *11*(2), 123–138.

Hoffman, D. A. "Confessions of a Problem-Solving Mediator." *Society for Professionals in Dispute Resolution News*, 1999, *23*(3), 1–4.

Intrater, K. A., and Gann, T. G. "The Lawyer's Role in Institutionalizing ADR." *Hofstra Labor and Employment Law Journal*, 2001, *18*(2), 469–477.

Jorgensen, E. O. "Relational Transformation in Mediation: Following Constitutive and Relational Rules." *Mediation Quarterly*, 2000, *17*(3), 295–312.

Jorgensen, E. O., and others. "Microfocus in Mediation: The What and How of Transformative Opportunities." In J. P. Folger and R.A.B. Bush (eds.), *Designing Mediation: Approaches to Training and Practice Within a Transformative Framework*. New York: Institute for the Study of Conflict Transformation, 2001.

Koehn, D. *Rethinking Feminist Ethics: Care, Trust and Empathy*. London: Routledge, 1998.

Kohn, A. *The Brighter Side of Human Nature: Altruism and Empathy in Everyday Life*. New York: Basic Books, 1990.

Kolb, D. M., and Kressel, K. "Conclusion: The Realities of Making Talk Work." In D. M. Kolb and Associates, *When Talk Works: Profiles of Mediators*. San Francisco: Jossey-Bass, 1994.

Kolb, D. M., and Putnam, L. L. "Through the Looking Glass: Negotiation Refracted through the Lens of Gender." In S. Gleason (ed.), *Workplace Dispute Resolution: Directions for the Twenty-First Century*. East Lansing: Michigan State University Press, 1997.

Kolb, D. M., and Associates. *When Talk Works: Profiles of Mediators*. San Francisco: Jossey-Bass, 1994.

Lappé, F. M., and DuBois, P. *The Quickening of America: Rebuilding Our Nation, Remaking Our Lives*. San Francisco: Jossey-Bass, 1994.

Lind, A. E., and Tyler, T. T. *The Social Psychology of Procedural Justice*. New York: Plenum, 1988.

MacIntyre, A. *After Virtue: A Study in Moral Theory*. Notre Dame, Ind.: University of Notre Dame Press, 1981.

Mayer, B. S. *Beyond Neutrality: Confronting the Crisis in Conflict Resolution*. San Francisco: Jossey-Bass, 2004.

McCorkle, S., and Mills, J. "Rowboat in a Hurricane: Metaphors of Interpersonal Conflict." *Communication Reports*, 1992, *5*, 57–78.

McEwen, C. A., and Maiman, R. J. "Mediation in a Small Claims Court: Achieving Compliance Through Consent." *Law and Society Review*, 1984, *18*(1), 11–49.

McNamee, S., and Gergen, K. J. (eds.). *Relational Responsibility: Resources for Sustainable Dialogue*. Thousand Oaks, Calif.: Sage, 1999.

Menkel-Meadow, C. "Toward Another View of Legal Negotiation: The Structure of Problem-Solving." *University of California Los Angeles Law Review*, 1984, *31*, 754–842.

Menkel-Meadow, C. "Pursuing Settlement in an Adversary Culture: A Tale of Innovation Co-Opted or 'the Law of ADR.'" *Florida State University Law Review*, 1991, *19*(1), 1–46.

Menkel-Meadow, C. "The Many Ways of Mediation: The Transformation of Traditions, Ideologies, Paradigms, and Practices." *Negotiation Journal*, 1995, *11*, 217–242.

Miller, J. B., and Wellock, S. J. "Comments on Transformative Mediation at the Dutchess County (New York) Mediation Center." Submitted to the authors, Feb. 2004.

Mnookin, R. H., and Ross, L. "Introduction." In K. Arrow and others (eds.), *Barriers to Conflict Resolution*. New York: Norton, 1995.

Moen, J. K., and others. "Identifying Opportunities for Empowerment and Recognition in Mediation." In J. P. Folger and R.A.B. Bush (eds.),

Designing Mediation: Approaches to Training and Practice Within a Transformative Framework. New York: Institute for the Study of Conflict Transformation, 2001.

Moore, C. M. "Why Do We Mediate?" In J. P. Folger and T. S. Jones (eds.), *New Directions in Mediation: Communication Research and Perspectives.* Thousand Oaks, Calif.: Sage, 1994.

Moore, C. M. *The Mediation Process: Practical Strategies for Resolving Conflict.* (3rd ed.). San Francisco: Jossey-Bass, 2003.

Murphy, C. G. "Liberalism and Political Society." *American Journal of Jurisprudence,* 1981, 26, 121–158.

Nader, L. "Disputing Without the Force of Law." *Yale Law Journal,* 1979, 88, 1019–1021.

National Public Radio. "Profile: Listeners' Comments on How Their Lives Have Changed Since September Eleventh." *Morning Edition Archives,* November 9, 2001.

Neale, M. A., and Bazerman, M. H. *Cognition and Rationality in Negotiation.* New York: Free Press, 1991.

Neilson, L. C., and English, P. "The Role of Interest-Based Facilitation in Designing Accreditation Standards: The Canadian Experience." *Mediation Quarterly,* 2001, 18(3), 221–248.

Northrup, T. A. "The Dynamic of Identity in Personal and Social Conflict." In L. Kriesberg and others (eds.), *Intractable Conflicts and Their Transformation.* Syracuse, N.Y.: Syracuse University Press, 1989.

Osborne, D., and Gaebler, T. *Reinventing Government.* Reading, Mass.: Addison-Wesley, 1992.

Paranica, K. "Comments on Transformative Mediation at the Grand Forks (North Dakota) Mediation Center." Submitted to the authors, Jan. 2004.

Pitkin, H. *Wittgenstein and Justice: The Significance of Ludwig Wittgenstein for Social and Political Thought.* Berkeley: University of California Press, 1972.

Pope, S. G. "Inviting Fortuitous Events in Mediation: The Role of Empowerment and Recognition." *Mediation Quarterly,* 1996, 13(4), 287–294.

Pope, S. G. "Beginning the Mediation: Party Participation Promotes Empowerment and Recognition." In J. P. Folger and R.A.B. Bush (eds.), *Designing Mediation: Approaches to Training and Practice Within a Transformative Framework.* New York: Institute for the Study of Conflict Transformation, 2001.

Press, S. "Commentary." *Mediation Quarterly,* 1998, 15(4), 368–371.

Press, S. "Memorandum to the Association for Conflict Resolution Board of Directors." June 17, 2003. (On file with the authors.)

Putnam, L. L. "Challenging the Assumptions of Traditional Approaches to Negotiation." *Negotiation Journal*, 1994, *10*(3), 337–346.

Putnam, R. D. *Bowling Alone: The Collapse and Revival of American Community.* New York: Touchstone, 2000.

Rawls, J. *A Theory of Justice*. Cambridge, Mass.: Harvard University Press, 1971.

Riskin, L. "Mediation and Lawyers." *Ohio State Law Journal*, 1982, *43*, 29–60.

Riskin, L. "Toward New Standards for the Neutral Lawyer in Mediation." *Arizona Law Review*, 1984, *26*, 329–362.

Riskin, L. "Understanding Mediators' Orientations, Strategies, and Techniques: A Grid for the Perplexed." *Harvard Negotiation Law Review*, 1996, *1*, 7–51.

Roberts, M. "Systems or Selves? Some Ethical Issues in Family Mediation." *Mediation Quarterly*, 1992, *10*(1), 3–19.

Rosen, R., and Berger, L. *The Healthy Company: Eight Strategies to Develop People, Productivity, and Profits*. Los Angeles: Tarcher, 1992.

Rubin, J. Z., and others. *Social Conflict: Escalation, Stalemate, and Settlement.* (2nd ed.). New York: McGraw-Hill, 1994.

Sandel, M. *Liberalism and the Limits of Justice*. Cambridge: Cambridge University Press, 1982.

Saposnek, D. *Mediating Child Custody Disputes*. San Francisco: Jossey-Bass, 1983.

Saul, J. A. "Comments on Transformative Mediation at the Community Dispute Resolution Center, Ithaca, New York." Submitted to the authors, Feb. 2004.

Scheff, T. *Microsociology: Discourse, Emotion, and Social Structure*. Chicago: University of Chicago Press, 1990.

Schwartz, S. L. "The Mediated Settlement: Is It Always About the Money? Rarely!" [www.mediate.com/articles/schwartz2.cfm]. 2003.

Senft, L. P. "Comments on Transformative Mediation at the Baltimore (Maryland) Mediation Center." Submitted to the authors, Feb. 2004.

Senft, L. P., and Savage, C. A. "Alternative Dispute Resolution in the Courts: Progress, Problems, and Possibilities." *Penn State Law Review*, 2003, *108*(1), 327–348.

Shaffer, T. L., and Cochran, R. F., Jr. *Lawyers, Clients, and Moral Responsibility.* St. Paul, Minn.: West, 1994.

Shailor, J. *Empowerment in Dispute Mediation: A Critical Analysis of Communication*. New York: Praeger, 1994.

Shonholtz, R. "Neighborhood Justice Systems: Work, Structure and Guiding Principles." *Mediation Quarterly*, 1984, *5*, 3–16.

Shonholtz, R. "The Citizens' Role in Justice: Building a Primary Justice and Prevention System at the Neighborhood Level." *The Annals of the American Academy of Political and Social Science*, 1987, *494*, 42–52.

Silbey, S. S., and Merry, S. "Mediator Settlement Strategies." *Law and Policy*, 1986, *8*, 7–32.

Singer, L. R. *Settling Disputes: Conflict Resolution in Business, Families, and the Legal System*. Boulder, Colo.: Westview Press, 1990.

Spiegel, D. *Living Beyond Limits: A Scientific Mind-Body Approach to Facing Life-Threatening Illness*. New York: Random House, 1993.

Stempel, J. W. "Beyond Formalism and False Dichotomies: The Need for Institutionalizing a Flexible Concept of the Mediator's Role." *Florida State University Law Review*, 1997, *24*, 949–984.

Stulberg, J. B. "The Theory and Practice of Mediation: A Reply to Professor Susskind." *Vermont Law Review*, 1981, 6, 85–117.

Stulberg, J. B. *Taking Charge: Managing Conflict*. New York: Free Press, 1987.

Stulberg, J. B. "Facilitative Versus Evaluative Mediator Orientations: Piercing the 'Grid' Lock." *Florida State University Law Review*, 1997, *24*(4), 985–1005.

Susskind, L. E., and Cruikshank, J. *Breaking the Impasse: Consensual Approaches to Resolving Public Disputes*. New York: Basic Books, 1987.

Susskind, L. E., and Field, P. *Dealing with an Angry Public: The Mutual Gains Approach to Resolving Disputes*. New York: Simon & Schuster, 1996.

Task Force on Mediator Certification. "Report and Recommendations to the Association for Conflict Resolution Board of Directors." Association for Conflict Resolution, Mar. 2004. [www.acrnet.org/about/taskforces/certification.htm].

Test Design Project. *Performance-Based Assessment: A Methodology, for Use in Selecting, Training and Evaluating Mediators*. Washington, D.C.: National Institute for Dispute Resolution, 1995.

Tomasic, R. "Mediation as an Alternative to Adjudication: Rhetoric and Reality in the Neighborhood Justice Movement." In R. Tomasic and M. M. Feeley (eds.), *Neighborhood Justice: Assessment of an Emerging Idea*. White Plains, N.Y.: Longman, 1982.

Wahlrab, T. Comments on Transformative Mediation at the Dayton (Ohio) Mediation Center." Submitted to the authors, Jan. 2004.

Wahrhaftig, P. "An Overview of Community-Oriented Citizen Dispute Resolution Programs in the United States." In R. Abel (ed.), *The Politics of Informal Justice. Vol. 1: The American Experience*. New York: Academic Press, 1982.

Welsh, N. A. "The Thinning Vision of Self-Determination in Court-Connected Mediation: The Inevitable Price of Institutionalization?" *Harvard Negotiation Law Review*, 2001a, 6, 1–96.

Welsh, N. A. "Making Deals in Court-Connected Mediation: What's Justice Got to Do With It?" *Washington University Law Quarterly*, 2001b, 79(3), 787–861.

Williams, M. "Can't I Get No Satisfaction? Thoughts on *The Promise of Mediation*." *Mediation Quarterly*, 1997, 15, 143–154.

About the Authors

· ·

Robert A. Baruch Bush and *Joseph P. Folger* are the acknowledged originators of the transformative model of mediation and its best known exponents. Their collaboration began with the first edition of this book, which won the Annual Book Award from the International Association for Conflict Management in 1995. After articulating the transformative theory of mediation for the first time in that volume, they directed several major projects—funded by the Hewlett and Surdna Foundations—aimed at the development of key resources for transformative practice, including training materials, practice guides, and policy tools. Bush and Folger are cofounders and fellows of the Institute for the Study of Conflict Transformation, a nonprofit think tank devoted to supporting the transformative model of conflict intervention. They work together on an ongoing basis with an expanding circle of colleagues in the United States and abroad to continue and strengthen the development of transformative practice.

Robert A. Baruch Bush is the Rains Distinguished Professor of Alternative Dispute Resolution (ADR) Law at Hofstra University School of Law, where he teaches courses on mediation, ADR, and other subjects. He has practiced, taught, and written about mediation for nearly thirty years, since organizing a community mediation program in 1976, under the auspices of the American Arbitration Association, in San Francisco, California. Bush is the author or coauthor of over two dozen books, articles, and chapters on mediation and ADR, several of which have won awards for scholarship. His work is widely cited by other scholars, and it is excerpted in many major mediation and ADR texts. He has served as consultant for various public agencies, including court and school systems in New York, California, and Florida, as well as for the Hewlett Foundation's Theory Center program. Bush has lectured on transformative mediation and has developed and conducted mediation skills training at programs and conferences throughout the United States and in many countries abroad. His mediation is featured on a videotape entitled "The Purple House Conversations," a transcript of which forms the basis for Chapters Four and Five of this volume.

Joseph P. Folger is professor of Adult and Organizational Development at Temple University, where he teaches courses in third-party intervention, mediation, communication and conflict, small-group process, and team facilitation. He began his work as a practitioner at the Center for Conflict Resolution in Madison, Wisconsin, and has served on the boards of the Ann Arbor Mediation Center and the Center for Mediation in Higher Education. He is a former program chair for the National Conference on Peacemaking and Conflict Resolution and has helped launch several mediation programs. Folger is also a senior consultant with Communication Research Associates, where he specializes in executive coaching and team development. Folger has published extensively in the mediation and communication fields and is coauthor of the award-winning text *Working Through Conflict: Strategies for Relationships, Groups and Organizations*, now in its fifth edition. Folger has lectured extensively on the transformative framework of practice in the United States and abroad and has conducted trainings in the model in diverse program settings.

Index